THE
LEXICAL
APPROACH

The State of ELT and a Way Forward

MICHAEL LEWIS

THOMSON

★

HEINLE

Australia Canada Mexico Singapore Spain United Kingdom United States

The Lexical Approach
The State of ELT and a Way Forward
Michael Lewis

Publisher/Global ELT: *Christopher Wenger*
Executive Marketing Manager, Global ELT/ESL: *Amy Mabley*

Printed in the UK.
    4 5 6 7 8 9 10   06 05 04 03 02

For more information contact Heinle, 25 Thomson Place, Boston, MA 02210 USA,
or you can visit our Internet site at http://www.heinle.com

ISBN: 0 906717 99 X

Acknowledgements

I am grateful to many people who have discussed ideas in this book with me, particularly those who contribut 'Words of Wisdom' opposite. Peter Wilberg first impressed on me the importance of collocation; Henry Widd struck a cord with 'random lexicalisation' and my colleague Jimmie Hill has proved, as usual, an invaluable s board. Equally, many with no contact with language teaching have exercised more influence than they know by aging me to think about language, people, values and what it is in life that matters.

The Author

Michael Lewis taught English in Sweden at all levels from primary school to adult. In 1981 he co-founded LTP. He ha lectured on language and methodology in most European countries, Japan, the States and Central America. He is th author of *The English Verb* and a number of student texts and co-author of *Business English* (with Peter Wilberg) an *Practical Techniques for Language Teaching* (with Jimmie Hill). His main current interests lie in the areas of gramma vocabulary and the development of a lexical approach and appropriate teacher-friendly classroom materials.

Cover design by Anna Macleod
Printed in England by Commercial Colour Press, London E7.

Words of Wisdom

Many people — professional colleagues, friends, and writers have wittingly or unwittingly influenced me. I have always gathered particular sentences or phrases which seem to me to express an idea more precisely or succinctly than I have thought it, or heard it expressed before. The few which follow have profoundly influenced my thinking on matters touched on in this book. I hope their creators recognise them, and do not wish to disown insights which seemed to me at the time, and still seem, profound.

The human mind cannot help but make meaning.
Sister Margaret Walshe, Crawley, 1988.

We improve our ideas through a lengthy trail of broken images and abandoned illusions.
Don Cupitt, Writing about the history of ideas.

The teacher's primary responsibility is response-ability.
Peter Wilberg, Editorial Meeting 1988.

You cannot learn what you do not understand.
Professor Henri Adamchiewski, IATEFL 1992

Grammar is what has always made English a school subject.
Jimmie Hill, Private Conversation 1984

When students travel, they don't carry grammar books, they carry dictionaries.
Professor Stephen Krashen, British Council Conference, Milan 1987

Most examples in textbooks and grammar books are randomly lexicalised.
Professor Henry Widdowson, TESOL Convention, San Francisco 1990

If you want to forget something, put it in a list.
Earl Stevick, Writing about memory.

Our purpose is to help students make maximal sense from minimal resources.
Otto Weiss, IATEFL 1989.

Contents

Principles and implications of the Lexical Approach

The Lexical Approach develops many of the fundamental principles advanced by proponents of Communicative Approaches. The most important difference is the increased understanding of the nature of lexis in naturally occurring language, and its potential contribution to language pedagogy.

Key principles

Language consists of grammaticalised lexis, not lexicalised grammar.

The grammar/vocabulary dichotomy is invalid; much language consists of multi-word 'chunks'.

A central element of language teaching is raising students' awareness of, and developing their ability to 'chunk' language successfully.

Although structural patterns are acknowledged as useful, lexical and metaphorical patterning are accorded appropriate status.

Collocation is integrated as an organising principle within syllabuses.

Evidence from computational linguistics and discourse analysis influence syllabus content and sequence.

Language is recognised as a personal resource, not an abstract idealisation.

Successful language is a wider concept than accurate language.

The central metaphor of language is holistic—an organism; not atomistic—a machine.

The primacy of speech over writing is recognised; writing is acknowledged as a secondary encodement, with a radically different grammar from that of the spoken language.

It is the co-textual rather than situational elements of context which are of primary importance for language teaching.

Socio-linguistic competence—communicative power—precedes and is the basis, not the product, of grammatical competence.

Grammar as structure is subordinate to lexis.

Grammatical error is recognised as intrinsic to the learning process.

Grammar as a receptive skill, involving the perception of similarity and difference, is prioritised.

Sub-sentential and supra-sentential grammatical ideas are given greater emphasis, at the expense of earlier concentration on sentence grammar and the verb phrase.

Task and process, rather than exercise and product, are emphasised.

Receptive skills, particularly listening, are given enhanced status.

The Present-Practise-Produce paradigm is rejected, in favour of a paradigm based on the Observe-Hypothesise-Experiment cycle.

Contemporary language teaching methods and material tend to be similar for students at different levels of competence; within the Lexical Approach the materials and methods appropriate to beginner or elementary students are radically different from those employed for upper-intermediate or advanced students. Significant re-ordering of the learning programme is implicit in the Lexical Approach.

Introduction

Two themes run through this book — firstly, an assessment of the nature and role of lexis and the implications of taking lexical items rather than words and structures as the units of language. The lexical nature of language and the implications for language pedagogy are assessed. The second theme is a survey of contemporary language teaching practice. In particular I assess many features of standard materials and orthodox methodology and find them severely wanting, often in direct conflict with what we know of the nature of both language and learning.

The book draws on many elements of research in applied linguistics, in particular corpus lexicography, discourse analysis and modern work in English grammar. The book is, however, primarily a work of methodology not applied linguistics. It is precisely for this reason that the two themes are inextricably linked throughout the book. The argument in favour of increased attention to lexis within language teaching is essentially an applied linguistics matter, but it is language teachers who must implement any change. Unless they can be persuaded that a great deal which is now standard practice is suspect, or even nonsense, no change, however theoretically supported, will be accepted.

The first chapter approaches the contemporary situation through the terminology familiar to most teachers. This terminology, frequently used loosely and with inadequate theoretical support, provides the basis for many of the more absurd practices common in contemporary language teaching. Much of this terminology is dismissed as half-baked and, in later chapters, discarded. Some readers may be irritated that I assume they hold certain conventional views when in fact they do not. To them I apologise, but in defence would point out that while writing the book I have presented many of its themes in conferences, seminars, and workshops. The views I assume to be 'standard' are those which teachers attending such seminars have put forward, often forcefully. Teachers who attend in-service training are, almost without exception, better informed, and consequently more 'progressive', than the great majority of teachers who, regrettably, remain fixed in the practices to which they were introduced during their initial teacher training. Even the best informed and most progressive teacher must at times operate with colleagues or students whose attitudes to language and learning are more conservative. I am, therefore, concerned to see where both the sense and nonsense of contemporary language teaching have come from, so that the reader may genuinely evaluate the proposals of the Lexical Approach in relation to this contemporary framework.

The text has, I hope, positive proposals for teacher development. Although many ideas are 'rejected' or 'comprehensively discarded' such judgements are never glibly made. They are always, I hope, informed by a clear theoretical perspective. Language teaching sometimes claims to be a profession. If it is, its practitioners cannot simply rely on recipes and techniques; they need an explicit theoretical basis for their classroom procedures. In my view, too few language teachers exhibit the kind of intellectual curiosity and readiness to change which is normally associated with professional status. Linguistics and methodology are both comparatively new disciplines and major developments have occurred in recent years. It is disappointing that so few teachers are anxious to inform themselves about such changes, and incorporate the insights into their teaching; it is more disappointing that many teachers are actively hostile to anything which, for example, challenges the central role of grammatical explanation, grammatical practice and correction, all ideas which the Lexical Approach demotes or discards.

The distinguished philosopher Karl Popper has demonstrated that there is a fundamental asymmetry between proof and disproof. It is in the nature of empirical knowledge that we cannot 'prove' anything; our knowledge is developed by a process based on disproving, ridding ourselves of error. Writing on a topic much wider than language teaching he says: *'Minimise unhappiness' is not just a negative formulation of the Utilitarian maxim 'Maximise Happiness'. There is a logical asymmetry here: We do not know how to make people happy, but we do know ways of lessening their unhappiness.* There is immediate relevance for applied linguistics and language learning — we do not know how language works, or how learning proceeds. We do, however, know a great deal about what language is not, and how it does not work; a great deal about procedures which do not help learning. The nature of empirical research frequently leads us to challenge or dismiss the status quo; we are, inevitably, unable to 'prove' our own position, only to assert that it represents movement in the right direction. So it is with the Lexical Approach. This approach is based on a perception of language and learning as essentially holistic, or organic. As such, much standard syllabus sequencing and the Present-Practice-Produce paradigm can be shown to be inadequate. Whether we will ever know enough about language and learning to provide fully convincing alternatives is doubtful, but we certainly do not at the moment. What we do have, however, is knowledge about language and learning which allows us to judge certain content and methodology to be **better** than we have had in the past. This does not, of course, rule out the possibility of our current improvements being, in their turn, developed and revised.

The Lexical Approach invites readers to dismiss, or at least radically de-emphasise materials and procedures which violate either the nature of language or the nature of learning. It has positive suggestions to make about the nature and role of lexis, different attitudes to text, and strategies for 'chunking' language (dividing it into its component 'bits', which are not the traditional vocabulary and structure which teachers and students assume).

In Chapter 4 I discuss the concept of 'negotiated meaning'; what you take from a book may be very different from what the author puts into it. We cannot ask 'what the text means', for each reader brings to it different knowledge, experience, attitudes and needs. My hope, above all, is that the text will encourage you to think that language is important, and that language teaching is useful and valuable. A foreign language can be a valuable personal asset, liberating financially, culturally and emotionally. Helping people acquire such an asset is a worthwhile occupation. The fact that you have opened this book at all suggests that you would like to perform your task as well as possible, and wonder whether you could do it better than you are at the moment. I hope that, having finished this book, you will feel that it has contributed to your understanding, so that you in turn may be better at helping others to acquire increased ability in a foreign language, something which might generally improve their own lives, and the lives of those with whom they come in contact.

Chapter 1

Background

PART 1 — Terminology

Language is, of course, the central subject matter for language teachers. It is somewhat surprising, therefore, that many language teachers have a dislike, or even contempt for the precise terminology of their subject, sometimes dismissed as 'jargon'. On many occasions, however, precise thought is made easier by the use of well-defined terms. It is necessary, therefore, before we begin to develop any innovative ideas to clear the ground by establishing a terminology which provides a framework for everything which follows.

Syllabus and Method

A syllabus defines the **content** of a teaching programme. However it is specified, it is concerned with **what** is to be learned. Traditionally, language teaching syllabuses were grammar-based. Later, so called notional/functional syllabuses were devised and many contemporary textbooks claim to employ a 'multi-syllabus'. A primary focus of this book it to consider the role of lexis within the syllabus. The term **syllabus** is used in contradistinction to **method**, which is about **how** the teaching is to be conducted. Nowadays, most methodologists are happier to talk about how learning is facilitated rather than how teaching is conducted, but the distinction with syllabus remains important.

It is self-evident that one can change syllabus without changing method, or change method without changing syllabus. Despite the obvious contrast, it remains true that a seminal work of the 70's, Wilkins' *Notional Syllabuses,* clearly intended by its title to be about the content of language teaching, probably exercised its primary influence by provoking changes of method. Many aspects of syllabus and method are closely inter-related, and unless, for example, methodological implications of syllabus changes are thought through, the most likely result is confusion. This book suggests several major changes in the content of what is taught. The changes in content imply quite radical changes of method. Much of the proposed new content will be difficult to use effectively unless teaching materials, and teachers' attitudes develop so that syllabus and method are in harmony.

The English word 'methods' in language teaching is about classroom strategies. The same course book can be taught using different methods. For some speakers of Romance languages, 'new methods' have suggested new textbooks, which they have adopted while retaining the same classroom procedures as before. Such a course of action is likely to produce confusion and disappointment. If the newly adopted course book contains very different contents from that previously used, it is important that teachers are willing to change their classroom procedures — again content and procedure, syllabus and method, need to be in harmony.

Approach

An 'approach' is an integrated set of theoretical and practical beliefs, embodying both syllabus and method. More than either, it involves principles which in the case of language teaching, reflect the nature of language itself and the nature of learning. If syllabus is the what of language teaching, and method the how, approach is the **why**. An approach provides principles to decide what kind of content and what sorts of procedures are appropriate. These choices should not be arbitrary, but need to be based on explicitly stated theoretical principles — philosophical principles, to do with the nature of language; psychological principles, to do with the nature of learning; and, within a broader context, socio-political educational principles, to do with the purpose of education. An approach is much more comprehensive than any syllabus. It should not be too difficult to reach consensus about structures, functions and skills. But all learning takes place in a wider context — socially as part of an education system, individually as part of a person's self-development. It is not primarily the language which is being learned, but a person who is learning.

In the early 70's, language teaching underwent something of a revolution. Previously, structural syllabuses had been dominant. These were challenged by the work of Wilkins and Van Ek (whose original work was largely concerned with the content of courses for adults in continuing education — it remains a surprise that so much of the work was used — or mis-used — to influence textbooks intended for schoolchildren). The change was essentially one of syllabus. Simultaneously, however, other work developed what later came to be called the Communicative Approach (CA). This was well-named, for it was indeed an approach — wider than syllabus or method. Among other things, it urged the use of real tasks in the classroom which necessitated communication, decreased emphasis on correction, increased student autonomy, increased emphasis on receptive skills, the use of language data not produced specifically for language teaching purposes and a whole host of other ideas. It concerned itself with materials, methods, the purpose of learning, the sociology of the classroom and many other factors. Many of the insights of CA remain accurate, and highly relevant. Unfortunately, they also remain largely un-implemented, as textbooks made changes of content and sequence — essentially matters of syllabus — and then presented the books as embodying 'the communicative approach'. This was considerably less than the truth. Although some changes of methodology resulted, many major methodological implications were not implemented. Most importantly of all, educational systems, and teacher training did not embrace many of the wider factors.

The primary purpose of this book is to argue for a change of approach. There are proposals for major changes of syllabus and method. Neither of these, however, is likely to be effective unless it is understood within the wider context of the Lexical Approach. If syllabus is about what teachers present, and method is about the techniques by which they present it, approach is about what teachers **value.** The whole of this book is, fundamentally, about questioning our present values in language teaching.

Structures

This word, once central to all language teaching, is now somewhat out of fashion. It is most often used to talk about structural syllabuses. Until 20 years ago such syllabuses were unchallenged. Language teaching was based on the assumption that students first needed to master particular sentence frames — structures. The assumption was that once they had mastered these, they could subsequently learn how to 'fill the gaps' in structurally correct sentences, by expanding their vocabulary and simply inserting new words into slots within the sentences. The structures which were, and to a large extent still are, perceived as central to language teaching were precisely, and exclusively those of well-formed English sentences. 'Grammar' was equated with sentence grammar, mastery of different sentence patterns, themselves based on variations within the verb form. To many teachers, a structural syllabus is synonymous with mastering the tense system of the English verb. This is surprising, for to most linguists the English verb has only two tenses — Present Simple and Past Simple. Chalker[1], for example, in the introduction to her *Current English Grammar* writes as follows:

> The now orthodox abandonment of the idea of an English 'Future tense' will not, I hope, worry any readers. ... Once one accepts that the English tense system is binary, and that *will* and *shall* are just two of the modals, the whole verbal system and its meaning appears much neater and more understandable.

Despite such developments and improvements in the analysis of English, the theoretical insights have hardly influenced textbooks or classroom teaching at all. Structure is still equated with grammar, and grammar is still equated with sentence grammar. The Lexical Approach implies a decreased role for sentence grammar, at least until post-intermediate levels. In contrast, it involves an increased role for word grammar (collocation and cognates) and text grammar (supra-sentential features). In the last 20 years linguists have analysed an enormous amount of authentic English text and, as a result, have described a very wide range of patterns to be found within the text. These patterns may be sub-sentential, sentential, or supra-sentential. Patterns from each of these categories have varying degrees of generative power — they allow the learner to produce novel language, to estimate that a particular piece of language will be possible, without having met it before. This was the role that structures were traditionally supposed to play. Nowadays, it is clear that confining our concept of generative patterns to particular sentence structures is unnecessarily restrictive.

Functions

This term was introduced into language teaching only about 20 years ago. It was coined by Wilkins and can be very simply defined: a function is the **social purpose of an utterance**. If we ask the question *Why did the speaker say that,* the answer will come in the form of a function — (s)he was making a request, offering to help, refusing an invitation etc. Most language teachers are very familiar with such labels, which frequently represent units in the textbook. Wilkins' own explanation of function can be found in *Notional Syllabuses* (page 22):

> The third type of meaning conveyed by an utterance is a matter of the function of the sentence (utterance) as a whole in the larger context in which it occurs. The sentence does more than communicate information. When it is uttered, it performs a role both in relation to other utterances that have been produced, and as a part of the inter-active processes involving the participants. An account of the internal grammatical relations and therefore of the ideational meaning does not tell us much about the use to which the sentence is being put by the speaker. ... Although questions of use have not always been considered part of semantics, they are of great relevance to the language teacher who is preparing pupils for the process of communication.

Functions represented a major change in syllabus design. They are, in the technical sense, pragmatic in character, being concerned with the social purpose of the utterance. They are now so much part of language teaching that it is difficult to recall quite what a radical shift was represented. Previously, strict structural sequencing tended to prevail. Nowadays, it is a commonplace that sentences such as *Would you like a cup of tea?* can be introduced early in a learning programme, without structural analysis. This was not so before the influence of pragmatics was felt.

The change has considerable relevance to our present discussions, for I shall argue later that other kinds of language, in particular, institutionalised sentences and lexical phrases, can be introduced in the early stages of learning **without** analysis, to a much greater extent than has hitherto been the practice. This idea is central to the Lexical Approach.

Functions are relatively easy to understand and describe and they were enthusiastically taken up by textbook writers. The other component of the syllabus-type proposed by Wilkins was more abstract and it is to this that we now turn.

Notions

Surprisingly, in *Notional Syllabuses*, Wilkins does not define notions, and they have always remained rather elusive. He wrote (page 24):

> It is possible to think in terms of a functional syllabus and a conceptual syllabus, although only a syllabus that covered both functional (and modal) and conceptual categories would be a fully notional syllabus.

This is the only point in the whole book at which he refers to 'conceptual categories', and normally he uses the term 'notion' to cover that half of his notional syllabus which is not functions. In the circumstances, it is hardly surprising that this element in his thinking was little taken up by textbook writers, and remains unfamiliar to most teachers.

He did, however, divide notions into **specific notions** and **general notions**. The utterance *Could you pass the ... please* exhibits the function of Asking for something. The 'something' for which I ask, is a specific notion: *salt, book*. It is immediately apparent that under this analysis functions are little more than a different way of arranging sentences, and specific notions little more than a new name for vocabulary. Such an analysis facilitates minor re-ordering within the syllabus, which indeed happened, but little more than that.

More importantly, general notions were, according to Wilkins, semantico-grammatical categories. Among those listed in *Notional Syllabuses* are Time, Duration, Time Relations, Frequency, Quantity, Sympathy, Flattery, Divided and Undivided Reference. Few of these will be recognised by teachers as headings within their present textbooks!

It is interesting to note that Wilkins was proposing, in his own terms, not **semantic** categories, but **grammatico-semantic** categories. In brief, he was suggesting re-grouping structures under categories of meaning. As with the remainder of his work, it was essentially a matter of re-arrangement within syllabus.

With hindsight it is possible to see that this was insufficiently radical — dissatisfied with the traditional sequence of structures, he sought a sequence more appropriate for adults, frequently on relatively short, intensive language courses in continuing education. The concept (introduced by Pit Corder) of 'high surrender value' was a powerful influence. The idea was that the most useful things should occur early in a course. Wilkins[2] says quite explicitly: *The problems faced in determining the grammatical content of general courses are more those of staging and sequencing.* Despite asserting that he is primarily concerned with meaning, he makes explicitly clear the fact that he regards vocabulary or lexis as subordinate:

> No attempt is made within this framework to account for the lexical content of learning. This is probably approached in terms of subject matter and situation. (page 21):

> The lexical content of learning, therefore, can be largely derived from an analysis of the topics likely to occur in the language use of a given group. (page 76)

The Lexical Approach suggests a much more central, even defining, role for lexis. Although general notions have so far had little influence on the content of language teaching, they remain useful categories, providing we see them as semantic cateogories, rather than restricting them to the grammatico-semantic categories as advocated by Wilkins. Structural syllabuses include the category *The Comparative*; within a meaning-centered syllabus it may be appropriate to introduce the category *Comparison*, grouping together different items which compare, more or less overtly:

He hasn't got the background his brother has.
A disappointingly small crowd was waiting at the airport.
The educated class has always been relatively mobile.

These examples are not untypical — we see immediately that if we call *Comparison* a notion, the linguistic realisations of that notion are at least as frequently lexical as they are grammmatical. Recent research suggests that using lexical items as pattern generators is more helpful than restricting that role to grammatical forms.

Behaviourism

Behaviourism was a general learning theory, applicable to all forms of learning. It is particularly associated with Skinner. Behaviourism sees learning in terms of habit formation. The habits are formed by imitation, and reinforced by repetition. This gives rise to two classroom strategies of considerable importance:

— Successful performance encourages future successful performance.
— Incorrect performance ('errors') should be avoided.

These two ideas were explicit within behaviourist learning theory, and exercised considerable influence on language teaching up to the end of the 1960's. The residual influence today is more covert and insidious. The ideas led to the idea of programmed learning, and to a lock-step view of syllabus and progress. Monfries, in the introduction to her then popular *Oral Drills in Sentence Patterns*, is adamant that students should not be allowed to proceed to a new drill until they have mastered the one upon which they are currently working. This kind of building brick approach was once axiomatic. In the same way, errors, for example in speech, were considered dangerous. An oft repeated error was, according to behaviourist learning theory, increasingly likely to become an ingrained habit. Ellis[3] observes:

> Errors, according to behaviourist theory, were the result of non-learning rather than wrong learning. In either case there was almost total agreement that errors should be avoided.

Researchers in second language acquisition would no longer accept the relevance of behaviourist learning theory to large areas of language learning. Nowadays, the students' grasp of the grammatical system at any time is seen as partial and provisional, and will develop through hypothesis formation and experiment. Within such a model, error is not only not to be avoided, but is an essential part of the learning process. The Lexical Approach totally rejects the Present-Practise-Produce paradigm advocated within a behaviourist learning model; it is replaced by the Observe-Hypothesise-Experiment cyclical paradigm.

It might seem curious to mention behaviourism at this early stage. Again and again in what follows, however, it will be seen that received methodology remains strongly influenced by the discredited tenets of behaviourism. When their rationale is discredited, the practices themselves need to be reviewed, and in some cases simply rejected.

Models and Targets

This distinction is, for many teachers, a comparatively new one. At first sight, it can appear hair-splitting, but it is a complex, and contentious issue. At this stage, it is necessary only to define the terms. **Model** language is language included in the textbook or otherwise introduced into the classroom, as language worthy of study. It may consist of 'real' language, produced for purposes other than language teaching but introduced into the classroom as part of the learning materials, or it may be material specially written for language teaching purposes (which is, or is not appropriate is one of the contentious issues). Model language, in its broadest sense, is language presented to the student as examples of how English is, or can be, used. **Target** language is the objective of the teaching programme — language which, it is assumed, the student will ultimately be able to use. (Where 'use' may mean actively produce or receptively understand).

Until recently few teachers would have made the distinction at all, and even today it is probably true that most teachers and students assume that target and model coincide. To highlight some of the difficulties, consider the following statements. Do you find yourself decisively agreeing or disagreeing, or are you more inclined to reply *Yes, but ...* ?

1. Learners of English should try to speak English like native speakers.

2. Australians have Australian accents, Scots have Scottish accents, so surely Germans should have German accents when they speak English.

3. The language presented to students in textbooks and on tape should be natural — exactly what native speakers really write or say, hesitations, mistakes and all.

4. If we expect students to speak English, the model we offer them in class should also be spoken English — which means many hours of tape and video rather than textbooks.

5. Most non-native speakers of English really need a kind of neutral, 'international' English, not the highly culture-bound English of a native-speaking Scot, American, or Englishman.

The statements offered above are to highlight some of the difficulties in this area. They certainly do not represent my own views on this highly complex topic. The selection, overt or covert, of both model language and target language represents a major theoretical problem, from both a linguistic and a socio-cultural point of view.

PART 2 — Basic Dichotomies and Polarities

We turn now to a set of terms which aid clarity of thought by establishing two contrasting ideas. In some cases these represent two opposite extremes — polarities — in others they simply divide into two parts — dichotomies. The kind of binary thinking encouraged by this type of terminology is almost always a simplification, which highlights some feature of the subject matter, but only at the expense of de-emphasising, or positively suppressing, other aspects. I shall argue that many of the terms introduced, and commented on briefly here, have had a seriously inhibiting effect on the development of thinking about the syllabus and methods appropriate to language teaching.

1. Spoken language and written language

The terms have their obvious meaning, but several quotations from Halliday are of great importance:

> Written language is not spoken language written down. Writing and speaking are not just alternative ways of doing the same thing; rather they are ways of doing different things.[4]

> People were still unconscious of the nature of spontaneous conversation, and have remained so to this day.[5]

> In a literate culture, we tend not to take the spoken language seriously.[6]

are many implications in these few quotations. The fact that textbooks
ain the principal teaching materials in the age of tape and video recorders
partly because of the prestige of the written language. Much of the
language presented as model or target in language teaching remains the
relatively formal sentence-based language of written text. No grammar of
spoken English yet exists, although many language teaching programmes
claim to emphasise spoken English. Many of the dialogues in textbooks are
much closer stylistically to written, rather than spoken, English. The
importance of the distinction will be discussed extensively later.

2. Vocabulary and Grammar

Rather surprisingly, these two terms are probably among the most
misunderstood in language teaching. They, too, are the subject of extensive
discussion below. It is precisely the binary kind of oppositional thought
encouraged by this terminology which has inhibited the development and role
of lexis in syllabus design. At this stage, we adopt the ordinary definitions of
these words, as used every day by teachers and students. 'Grammar' is
normally equated with structures, sentence patterns, different verb forms ('the
tenses'), prepositions and those other supposedly generative bits of the
language which are practised in grammar exercises. Roughly speaking,
grammar is seen as a set of sentence frames with slots, into which appropriate
'vocabulary', or words can be fitted.

Most students equate 'vocabulary' with words. Teachers complain that
students translate word by word, but at the same time ask *Are there any
words you don't understand.* Many 'bits' of language (lexical items) do not
consist of a single word (*by the way, the day after tomorrow, coffee table, I'll
see you later.*) but precisely because the grammar/vocabulary dichotomy
seems so straightforward, there is a tendency to simplify what is, in fact, one
of the most complex and revealing aspects of language analysis.

3. Receptive and Productive Skills

Language may be sub-divided in many different ways. One of the most
obvious, and helpful is into four skills: listening and speaking, reading and
writing. For many years a singularly inappropriate terminology was used,
describing listening and reading as passive skills, in contrast to the active
skills of speaking and writing. As anyone who has ever listened to a foreign
language for an extended period knows, listening is far from a passive skill.
Careful, accurate and involved listening can be exhausting. Present day
terminology is more helpful, dividing the skills into **receptive** and **productive.**

Initial L1 learning is exclusively based on listening. L2 learning is, in some
ways, different from L1, but equally it is in some ways similar. All language
which we produce is ultimately based on language which we have previously
met — based on memory, acquisition of the underlying system, or perhaps
pure mimicry. Spoken language is, in a very real sense more basic than
written language. All of these considerations lead us to suspect that a well-
balanced learning programme will, in the early stages, place great emphasis
on receptive skills, in particular, listening.

Unfortunately, received orthodoxy may be very different. Many courses at the present time require students to produce language — often whole sentences — from the earliest stages. Two principal reasons for this may be advanced:

a. The residual influence of behaviourism, which held that correct production was a step towards further correct production. This view is now largely discredited.

b. The advent of functional syllabuses introduced into coursebooks language of high utility in the early stages. The implication, or explicit requirement, is that students should practise in class this 'useful' language. This conclusion is based on a confusion. Wilkins' initial work was directed towards adults on short courses. The implication was that the learner would **only** do a short course, and **needed** to be able to produce certain language very quickly. It was an unjustified leap of faith to assume that this was the best way for all students — in particular school students on long-term courses — to acquire mastery of the language. Clearly, students should be **encouraged** to use the foreign language from the beginning of their course. There is considerable evidence that **requiring** them to do so — effectively forcing them into producing highly defective speech — can be demotivating and counter-productive. Teachers must recognise that well-directed listening is a cognitively involving activity which is a legitimate part of a learning programme. The false precepts of behaviourism and the unfortunate implications of the mistaken term 'passive skills' need to be comprehensively discarded.

The early stages of language learning are characterised by the student's struggle to make any sort of sense of the new language. We know that it is the reception of lexis which will form the most important activity in the earliest stages. Expressed more crudely, the first thing students need to do is to learn to understand quite a lot of words. This seems self-evident, but it was not many years ago that the vocabulary content of courses was deliberately restricted until students had developed a certain mastery of basic structures. Despite the self-evident value of vocabulary in making sense of the language to which you are exposed, it remains something of a Cinderella.

Receptive skills, however, involve more than vocabulary. As I argued extensively elsewhere (*The English Verb, LTP 1986*) certain grammatical items contribute to meaning. Many contrastive pairs of sentences — *Will/Are you going to ask him?, It happened at/in Cambridge. I/you must/can't have left it somewhere/anywhere here.* — convey different meanings, through grammatical rather than lexical choices. Learners need to understand these differences as well as, and I would suggest before, necessarily being able to produce them themselves. This involves the recognition of **grammar as a receptive skill,** and exercises need to be devised which encourage the **perception** of difference of meaning. This is an area which is hardly touched on at all in contemporary language teaching, which too often equates grammar with the students' ability to produce correct sentences.

Every teacher is familiar with students who are relatively fluent, but highly inaccurate. Such students have grasped the fundamental purpose of language

— communication — but an inability to observe the language around them, or even their own production, seems to inhibit them from progressing towards more standard 'correct' language. Krashen, whose work is referred to extensively below, talks about students as good or bad monitors. Teachers often encourage students to check or edit their own work, consciously trying to compare their own product with a supposed ideal; it is fashionable to talk about language awareness. Monitoring, editing, and awareness all direct our attention in the same way — towards the student's ability to **observe** language closely. These observation-based activities contain a large receptive element. Receptive skills are not simply important in elementary classes, they remain important for all language learners, inside and outside the classroom.

One word of warning is appropriate — correct production by a student is not evidence that the student has mastered the language in question, only evidence that the student has produced the correct language on that particular occasion. Students producing particular language correctly today quite definitely does not guarantee that they will be able to produce the same material correctly tomorrow. Learning, and acquisition of the systems of English cannot be linearly sequenced in this way, however inconvenient this may be for textbook writers and teachers. Once teachers recognise this, and see their own purpose as primarily to aid the student's long-term acquisition of the system of English, it is easier to value, and concentrate on receptive work in the classrooom. Too often teachers feel guilty because the students are not saying enough, or are not saying enough **yet**. It is by no means obvious that they should be. A revolution may not be required, but teachers could usefully give higher priority to receptive skills.

In passing, we may note one important methodological change. Many initial teacher training courses present the slogan *Reduce teacher talking time (TTT), increase student talking time (STT)*. This is an over-simplification. Uncontrolled teacher talk resulting from nerves, or the urge to fill silence is usually unhelpful, and to this extent TTT should be reduced. On the other hand, there is clear evidence from work done by Krashen, Prabhu (who based a whole programme in India on students responding to controlled teacher input), Asher's work on Total Physical Response (TPR) and others, that students' general language abilities develop most rapidly in the early stages if the approach is largely based on controlled listening. O'Neil[7] has argued:

> I think of all the informal, brief 'spoken paragraphs' which teachers can use as models for their students' own production as essential to language teaching, and I am constantly astounded when I see teachers refusing to do this because they associate it with being 'teacher centred'.

Orthodox methodology suggests that one of the teacher's primary tasks is to control the students' language output. If receptive skills are to be given their full value it is clear that equal emphasis should be given to the teacher's ability to control his or her **own** language. Over-simplification of the idea of teacher talking time has resulted in many teachers rejecting, or under-valuing a technique which can be of great value to their students.

4. Competence and Performance

This is the most theoretical distinction with which we will be concerned. It is particularly connected with the name of Chomsky. In his definition linguistic **competence** is the tacit knowledge of language structure, which is unconscious and not subject to introspectional report. It is an abstract idealisation, defined by him as 'the perfect knowledge of the ideal speaker-listener in a homogeneous speech community'. It contrasts with linguistic **performance**, which is concerned with the processes of encoding and decoding. We can observe performance but we have no way of observing, or indeed knowing anything about, competence. Chomsky's theory emphasised ideal objects in abstraction from language in actual use and from many of the socio-cultural features which condition language use. Hyams has referred to competence as 'a garden of Eden' view of language. He says: *The controlling image is of an abstract, isolated individual, almost an unmotivated cognitive mechanism, not, except incidentally, a person in a social world.* At the time the distinction was made syllabuses were almost exclusively structural. Learning a language was synonymous with mastering the structures of the language, that is, achieving competence. The tacit assumption was that once you had mastered the system, you could generate any sentence you wished. It was axiomatic that native speakers possessed 'native speaker competence'. Chomsky's thinking was entirely theoretical, and his abstract model exercised considerable influence.

Nowadays, for most linguists and methodologists, it is largely discredited. Many objections can be made. Widdowson has pointed out that the concept of 'native speaker competence' is not well-defined. Which native speakers? There are, in the real world, no idealised speaker-listeners and no homogeneous speech communities.

In order to defend the competence/performance dichotomy, it was necessary to ignore huge amounts of language actually produced by native speakers. If the evidence supported the theory, it was used; if the evidence contradicted the theory, the evidence was dismissed as 'degenerate'. Competence, by definition, could not be empirically investigated. Its existence was merely asserted. Performance, as Widdowson[8] pointed out, rapidly became a term for:

everything which cannot be conveniently accounted for in the proposed model of description. ... A residual category containing everything which is not accounted for under competence. (subsuming) everything about language which is imperfect or irregular, systematic features being accounted for within competence.

Widdowson went on to point out that knowing a language is not only a matter of knowing how to form correct sentences, but how to use these sentences in acts of communication. Chomsky's model totally ignored this. It was, to some extent, an extension of de Saussure's idealisation represented by the *langue/parole* distinction. Widdowson pointed out that this distinction all too often: ...*leaves out of account those very aspects of language with which the language teacher must primarily be concerned.* Wilga Rivers has remarked:

It is all very well for theorists like Chomsky to say that in performance terms language is a chaos and that it is not worth studying. The teacher replies: Yes it is this chaos into which our students must plunge.

By setting up the dichotomy so clearly, the attention of other applied linguits was turned to factors ignored within the competence model. Emphasis shifted to performance, and to language as it is actually used. Non-idealised factors were acknowledged, and observations of real data became increasingly important. Such fields as pragmatics and discourse analysis are based on the importance of performance. This change of emphasis made ideas such as functions and the communicative value of language in real use theoretically respectable.

Nowadays, we can make statistical statements about performance data — we can talk about how language is **usually** used, supporting such statements by reference to empirical data. This change of emphasis is of much more than theoretical interest; it has important practical consequences, in helping us to identify more appropriate content for syllabuses. It also permits the organisation of data in innovative ways, which turn out to have important implications for the perception of pattern within language. This area is developed more fully in the chapters on lexis.

One negative effect of the misuse of Chomsky's distinction is the unnecessary prominence given to the concept of the 'educated native speaker'. Many non-native teachers of English who use English fluently and effectively in a wide range of situations still have an unfortunate tendency to compare themselves to the hypothetical, but non-existent 'educated native speaker'. This can lead to a wholly unnecessary inferiority complex. On the whole, the native speaker meets more naturally produced English than the non-native; if the native speaker is 'educated' it may be possible to introspect perceptively into this data. On the other hand, effective use of English, and *a fortiori* effective teaching of English, depend much more on a whole range of other factors — personality, confidence, creativity, education and social sensitivity. Non-native speakers need to focus on the combination of factors which make them effective members of the international speech community which uses English, rather than worrying about the unimportant factor of whether they are, or are not, native speakers.

5. Usage and Use

This distinction, first made by Widdowson, focuses attention on language used to perform communicative acts, rather than simply to exemplify possible well-formed sentences in the language. He coined the term **usage** for language which conformed to the codified paradigms of the language. Usage is independent of context, and allows us to say that a sentence is a **possible** English sentence. It gives us no information at all about its actual occurrence, or, if it does occur, about the context in which it is appropriate.

In contrast, **use**, describes the functional and contextual appropriacy of an utterance. The contextual meaning of an utterance may differ radically from its surface meaning. The philosopher J.L. Austin's great contribution to language teaching was the development of the concept of illocutionary force. Essentially, this is the idea that we need to ask what the speaker's intention was in producing a particular sentence. Except in language teaching, sentences are not produced as exemplifications of the language, but in order to achieve purposes. *I don't know what you mean*, said in a particular way and in a particular context may be a statement of bafflement, with (implied) request for clarification. In this case, the use reflects the surface meaning of the words. Equally, the same sentence said in a different way and in a different context may be an expression of disbelief or even outrage. In this case, the pragmatic meaning — the purpose that the speaker intends — is not reflected in the surface structure. What are frequently called indirect speech acts occur in all languages, but their precise linguistic realisations are language-specific. Consider the differences between:

Can you come tomorrow?
Could you come tomorrow?

Can you wait until tomorrow?
Can't you wait until tomorrow?

No amount of purely structural analysis will reveal the contextual meaning which these sentences, and the contrast between them, can create.

The relationship between use and usage is complex. It may be that a knowledge of usage is a prerequisite for competent use; it is certainly not the case that the ability to use is based on knowledge of usage **alone**.

Over-emphasis on mastery of what we imagine to be the basic structures of the language has frequently resulted in language teaching greatly over-emphasising usage. Many sentences occurred in textbooks, and were used in grammar practices which were well-formed English sentences, but which it was difficult to imagine anyone actually using. Teachers tend to accept, and even praise, well-formed sentences which are possible, but implausible or unnatural. While that may be forgivable, it is less so that teachers and textbook writers use such sentences themselves. The problem arises partly because of an over-valuing of written language, and language at sentence-level. Spoken language is much more deictic and phrase-based. The language which is used in the classroom all too easily falls half way between spoken and written language:

I don't like to drink coffee.
Many modern drugs can alleviate suffering.

Neither of these two sentences is 'wrong'; both are correct examples of usage. It is, however, difficult to contextualise either of them — to imagine them as examples of use.

6. Signification and Value

This distinction is also Widdowson's, and to some extent mirrors the previous one. **Signification** expresses the codified meaning of a word, such as may be found in a dictionary. A sentence such as *This is my hand* may exemplify the codified meaning of *hand*, but it is difficult to imagine such a sentence used in natural communication. Widdowson claims such sentences are meaningful as **sentences**, but meaningless as **utterances**, precisely because they do not contribute to communication.

Chapter 4 considers the nature of meaning; here, we content ourselves with a simple distinction. Perhaps the most 'obvious' sort of meaning is signification. It is what many people would call 'what the word really means', the meaning you can look up in the dictionary, the (supposed) **constant** meaning. The fact that if you make a quick pencil sketch of a ladder on an otherwise blank sheet of paper the sketch immediately evokes the word *ladder* in my mind leaves us in no doubt that there is such a thing as signified, de-contextualised meaning. Many people, teachers and students alike, assume that this is the **only** kind of meaning. Questions such as *What does this word mean?* (rather than *What does this word mean here?*), or *How do you say* möglichkeit *in English?* show a concentration on individual words, and the supposed constancy of their de-contextualised meaning which is not reflected in real language use.

Occasions of real use, particularly of the spoken language, quickly reveal a different picture. On a particular occasion, a word may be used so that its **value** in communication is similar to, or very different from, its signification:

I don't think this ladder's long enough — we'll have to call the fire brigade.
He's a real company man, keep your head down, climb the ladder, don't upset anybody and wait for your next promotion.

The children want a dog for Christmas, but I don't see how we can have a dog when we live in such a small house.
I'll get the dog who did this if it's the last thing I do.

Here, words which we think of as having particular meanings are used with extended or metaphorical meanings. Context and real world experience help us to interpret the **value** (contextualised meaning) as different from the **signification** (de-contextualised meaning).

It is worth remarking that this is particularly the case with de-lexicalised pro-forms. If my book and spectacles lie on the table out of my reach, you will know which I require if I say *Could you pass that/those, please*. It is clear that *that* has the value *book*, and *those* the value *spectacles*. If the salt and pepper are on the table, however, *Could you pass that please* is ambiguous; the value of *that* is unclear. *Do,* used as a pro-verb (a verb which may stand for a wide range of other verbs, in the same way that pronouns can stand for a wide range of other nouns) has quite different values in these contexts:

You don't seem to care what happens to the business these days.
— I do!

You know Jack Robertson, don't you?
— I do. We met last year in Frankfurt.

In the real world language is used for pragmatic purposes — to get things done. You make your meaning **as clear as it needs to be** for the other participant in the conversation to understand as clearly as is necessary to achieve your common purpose. Normally, you are not trying in any formal sense to say what you mean precisely, you are simply trying to get something done. This gives rise to a very important distinction between 'correct' and 'successful' language. The former, traditionally central to language teaching, emphasises usage, signification, and formal criteria of correctness; the latter emphasises pragmatic effectiveness. It is successful language which more adequately mirrors the true nature of language, as means rather than end.

7. Cohesion and Coherence

These terms both refer to what makes discourse or text 'hang together'. These dialogues illustrate the two terms:

Can you play tennis tomorrow?
—No, I am afraid I can't. I've got to go to the hospital tomorrow.

Can you play tennis tomorrow?
—I've broken a string in my racket and I won't have time to get it fixed.

Cohesion is the grammatical linking of one part of a text to another. In the first dialogue above, there is an explicit cohesive device: *I can't*, linking to *Can you ...* . Cohesion may not be so explicit, but it is characterised by repetitions of similar grammar or lexis across sentence boundaries, or in the case of conversation, across turn boundaries. Teachers experienced in teaching students to write will know that students frequently need to practise making their writing more cohesive. Cohesion is one of the factors which makes a text something more than a sequence of sentences. This can be explicitly taught and practised, not only in relation to written text but also to informal conversation.

The second dialogue illustrates **coherence**; the conversation 'hangs together' without direct grammatical links. In this case the links are rhetorical and situational. We recognise the link *string-racket-tennis*, and in a more general way, that you cannot play tennis with a broken racket, so expressing the impossibility of playing is, as a communicative act, a possible way of responding to the question. Cohesion is about **grammatical** linking; coherence about **pragmatic** linking, the connection between two communicative acts. The two are not totally distinct, but an awareness of both allows us to see more clearly how extended text hangs together. This is another distinction which reflects the increasing importance in language teaching of text larger than individual sentences.

8. The Classroom and the 'Real World'

A pattern begins to emerge in our dichotomies. Chomsky's competence was an idealisation, untarnished by the messiness of real language use. Performance became a rag-bag term for all the untidy aspects of language which are evident if we examine real language data. Usage and signification represent reassuringly stable, analysable and describable concepts. Use, value and both cohesion and coherence are more intangible, elusive, situation-specific and even ephemeral. All of the latter, however, have come into use as interest has increasingly been focused on naturally occurring language.

Natural language is produced for purposes, to achieve pragmatic ends. The means are now available to capture such language use in great detail if we so sh. Traditionally, the only naturally occurring language which could be captured easily was printed text. The prestige of literacy frequently led to the prestige of literature. While good literature is unquestionably naturally occurring text, it is in many ways the least natural of text-types, highly self-conscious in purpose, and correspondingly in construction. Good literature endures. Valuing the language of literature endorses the idea of permanence. Obliquely, by omission, the ephemeral spoken language is devalued. Most grammar books and dictionaries are still predominantly based on so-called good quality written text. We are reminded of Halliday's remark that even today no grammar of spoken English exists.

In recent years corpus lexicography, in which large quantities of naturally occurring text are analysed, has become a realistic possibility. The dictionaries emerging from the Cobuild project based at Birmingham University are producing interesting information about the relative frequency of different uses of language items. The raw data produced from research of this kind needs careful interpretation before being incorporated in teaching materials, but it suggests a number of radical changes in the content of language teaching materials.

Modern technology permits the recording, on tape or video, of naturally produced spoken English. There is a temptation to assume that this real world use should provide both model and target for language learning. Such a course of action would almost certainly lead to disappointment. Applied linguists, lexicographers and discourse analysts should unquestionably base their research and analysis on naturally occurring data. The result should be increasingly accurate descriptions of how English is used. Such descriptions will unquestionably challenge received opinions. New descriptions should inform the decisions of textbook writers, editors and teachers, but it is by no means obvious that naturally occurring data should provide either the model or the target for language learning.

In the past, the gulf between the classroom and the real world was often too great. The classroom was an empire of its own — with its rules and laws, power structure and criteria for success and failure. Sometimes these were widely divorced, often consciously, from the real world. Spelling tests, translating texts about topics remote from your own interests, mindlessly repeating half-understood sentences — all of these activities have been defended as good classroom practice on the grounds that they were aids to learning. No conflict was seen in the assertion that in order to acquire one skill for use outside the classroom, you practised a quite different skill within the classroom. Such attitudes now seem (at least within the Western educational tradition) dated, and educationally unsound. I certainly have no wish to defend them. At the same time, one important fact is to be borne in mind — in one sense the classroom is not the real world, and in another sense it is. Classrooms are not essentially places where you have informal conversations, conduct negotiations, develop personal relationships etc. In any humane classroom such activities are a natural part of the sociology of the classroom. They are not, however, the primary purpose. There is a great deal of difference between socialising, negotiating, building relationships and **practising** socialising, negotiating and building relationships. Failure to communicate in the real world has differing consequences depending on what you fail to communicate. Failing in a practice in a classroom has quite different consequences — varying from getting you a bad mark to making a positive contribution to your learning. The classroom is not to be equated with the real world in that you do many things in your life outside the classroom which form little or no part of classroom activity. On the other hand, when you attend a class, for the 45 or 90 minutes that you are there what happens to you **is** your real world activity. To enjoy theatre you need to engage in the willing suspension of disbelief — you need to enter the conventions of the theatre — no point in being surprised when the dead body of Macbeth gets to his feet to take his bow. In the same way the classroom has its conventions and all the participants need to be aware of the accepted conventions if they are to maximise the effectiveness and benefit to themselves of what happens. Classrooms are places where, it is claimed, you will learn more quickly and effectively than would otherwise be the case.

Old-fashioned syllabuses ignored real world language use and concentrated on largely de-contextualised presentation of structure, vocabulary and language skills. There is a tendency now to over-react, and to assume that if it isn't 'real' it is not useful or effective. A moment's reflection on the nature of language reveals that, in the case of language learning, this is untrue. It is possible to learn a language simply by listening to it spoken. Such a strategy 'works' and indeed has much to commend it. A person who relied **exclusively** on this strategy, however, would end up with a relatively impoverished vocabulary, for written text contains a much higher ratio of lexical items to total running words than does spoken text. So, however much we may believe students learn by listening, a well-organised teaching programme would undoubtedly include carefully selected written texts. These could be naturally occurring texts, but we would have to delay most of them for some time in the learning programme as students would simply not be able to handle them in the early stages of learning. We know, however, that vocabulary (or lexis) carries more of the meaning of a text than does the grammar. We have also identified the concept of signification, de-contextualised meaning. So it is possible to learn de-contextualised words, by for example matching them with pictures. This is in no sense a real world activity, **except** in the real world of the language classroom. The Lexical Approach suggests that much greater emphasis needs to be placed on students building a large vocabulary much more quickly than in any traditional syllabus. This will undoubtedly involve large numbers of (relatively) de-contextualised words. I shall argue later that this is a highly effective classroom strategy, despite its conflict with real world language use.

Too often 'the classroom' and 'the real world' are presented, or talked about as being mutually exclusive. The truth is quite different — the classroom is **part** of the real world, different only in having a different set of conventions, relationships and strategies. For much of the time, effective classrooms will involve working with natural language from the external 'real world', and using classroom procedures which will be as useful outside the classroom as in it. For part of the time, however, teachers need unashamedly to introduce language and classroom strategies which clearly reflect the nature and purpose of classrooms as places where learning can be accelerated and made more effective.

9. Product and Process

In language teaching a **product** is any language which the student creates. Characteristically the student presents this as a complete, finished whole for consideration, and usually evaluation, by the teacher.

Products are created as a result of **processes**. An essay is not produced as a totality, a single completed whole. It is produced through a process of planning, revision, organisation, re-organisation, and many other steps. Cohesion and coherence occur precisely because the language user(s) is/are aware of the ongoing development within the text. Process is a developing, dynamic concept. In this it contrasts with the static nature of product.

Although most apparent in the creation of written text, it must be emphasised that processes are at work in all language use — decoding what is said to you, encoding your own thoughts in speech, reacting to the other participants in a conversation. All natural language use, receptive or productive, is based on cognitively involving processes.

This dichotomy is helpful in indicating that most teachers are, consciously or unconsciously, product-orientated. They see their jobs in terms of correcting essays, marking exercises, commending or criticising pronunciation, and a whole variety of other product-orientated activities. Learning, on the other hand, is process-orientated. We know that it is cognitive involvement, struggling, trying, hypothesising, revising, and other activities of this kind which are the basis of learning. As we shall see later, teachers should almost always be process-, rather than product-orientated. Any 'final exam' is an exception, but in general a change of the teacher's mind-set from product to process is not only helpful, it is essential.

10. Accuracy and Fluency

These terms are principally used to describe two different kinds of exercise. The explicit purpose of **accuracy** exercises is that students should get the language 'right', usually by forming correct sentences. There was a time when for all practical purposes **all** exercises were of this type. Teaching was conducted on the basis of behaviourist theory: accuracy was perceived not only as the ultimate goal, but as the route to the goal. 'Accurate' language was highly valued, and all other language use was viewed negatively.

Fluency exercises arose as people understood that accuracy alone was not enough. It became clear that, even if knowledge of what was correct was necessary, it was not sufficient. In addition, students needed to be able to **use** the language, particularly spoken language, and fluency practice was the intended preparation for this. Typically, accuracy exercises had a unique, 'correct' answer, while fluency practice was much more open-ended. Within the supposed tri-partite paradigm of Present-Practise-Produce, the Practise phase was seen as accuracy-based, while the Produce phase offered students wider situations in which to operate, with a greater opportunity to be creative but also more opportunity to get things wrong. There was a covert paradigm too:

Present — a wholly teacher based activity.

Practise — student involvement, but teacher controlled.

Produce — student-centred.

Within a building brick, lesson-by-lesson approach, individual lessons were frequently constructed on this paradigm. For reasons of time, the phase most likely to be omitted was the last. Regrettably, this intrinsic difficulty was reinforced by the desire of teachers to give 'good lessons'. The covert paradigm is from ordered, teacher-centred behaviour to unstructured-student-centred struggle. It is hardly surprising, that even at this stage, many teachers resisted fluency exercises disliking their (relatively) unstructured nature, lack of clearly defined 'answers' and the challenge presented to their methodology. Many methodologists, trying to cope with this opposition, suggested a simple shift — correct accuracy exercises **when** the mistake is made; draw attention to general, selected errors **after** fluency practices were completed. This was a more or less explicit compromise, but it will be noted that 'wrong' language (which nowadays we might see as hypothesis testing with useful negative feedback) was still felt to call for explicit teacher correction. The compromise was too half-hearted. It is important to develop an understanding of why fluency practice is a good thing in itself, rather than reducing it to a half-hearted accuracy practice. Within the parameters we have already established, much inaccurate language can also be successful — it can achieve the pragmatic ends of the user. Within those terms, language which communicates meaning effectively, but at the expense of breeches of the code is to be valued, and used constructively within the teaching programme, rather than merely 'corrected'.

Recently researchers have sought to explain native speaker fluency. Fluent natural speech is very rapid, and it seems unlikely that it is constantly created *ab initio* from a knowledge of the underlying grammatical system. Several researchers, most notably Nattinger and DeCarrico have suggested that language is retained in 'chunks'. These may be of different kinds including multi-word items, sentence heads and fully institutionalised sentences. These prefabricated chunks or 'lexical phrases' appear to be much more numerous than has previously been suggested. Estimates that native speakers have a repertoire running to tens of thousands are standard in the literature. Nattinger and DeCarrico[9] suggest that fluency is based precisely on these lexical phrases:

> It is our ability to use lexical phrases that helps us speak with fluency. This prefabricated speech has both the advantages of more efficient retrieval and of permitting speakers (and hearers) to direct their attention to the larger structure of the discourse, rather than keeping it narrowly focussed on individual words as they are produced. All this fits very neatly with the results of computational and language acquisition research.

Lexical phrases will form an important constituent of a programme based on the Lexical Approach.

As observed earlier, all dichotomies highlight particular aspects of a contrast or a difference, but at the expense of suppressing other aspects of that same contrast or difference. Brumfit reminds us of this point in these words:

> In one sense, the contrast between accuracy and fluency is largely metaphorical. Classrooms are always concerned with both. In spite of difficulties in defining accuracy and fluency, the distinction between them has a value in centring methodological discussion... It has been suggested in this paper that language teaching needs to concentrate far more on the concept of fluency in order to restore a genuine educational perspective to its aims (Page 189).

Brumfit's precise phrasing here is of great significance. It has been part of his particular contribution to language teaching theory to constantly remind us of a broader educational perspective. Later we identify the objectives of an Educational Syllabus. Within those broader perspectives both fluency and accuracy need to be given full value. To over-value one — in language teaching usually accuracy — is to distort the long-term objectives of any learning programme.

Willis, arguing for a task-based methodology similar to the O-H-E paradigm I propose, rather than the traditional Present-Practise-Produce which he terms 'presentation methodology' argues that the appropriate paradigm is strongly influenced by the theoretical relationship of accuracy and fluency[10]:

> A presentation methodology is based on the belief that out of accuracy comes fluency. A task-based methodology is based on the belief that out of fluency comes accuracy.

Despite the obvious fact that accuracy is a late-acquired feature of all language learning, it remains regrettably true that many teachers emphasise accuracy too early, and at the expense of fluency.

11. Learning and Acquisition

This distinction, in its precise form, is based entirely on the work of the American Stephen Krashen. While he is consistent in his use of the terms, both are used more loosely by many others to describe 'how we learn languages'.

Not many years ago one of the central issues in this field was Teacher Training. The emphasis was on teachers. It was assumed that if teachers followed certain specified procedures, students would learn. Gradually, the emphasis shifted from teaching to learning. Nowadays, the whole area of how people learn languages is usually referred to as Second Language Acquisition (SLA). Terminological confusion lies at every turn. Krashen, however, emphasises the learning/acquisition dichotomy, and draws radical conclusions from the difference. In his survey of the relevant literature, Ellis[11] (*Understanding Second Language Acquisition, Oxford University Press 1985*) offers the following definitions:

> **Acquisition** can be broadly defined as the internalisation of rules and formulas which are then used to communicate in the L 2. In this sense the term 'acquisition' is synonymous with the term 'learning'. However Krashen uses these terms with different meanings. '**Acquisition**' for Krashen, consists of the spontaneous process of rule internalisation that results from natural language use, while '**learning**' consists of the development of conscious L2 knowledge through formal study.

For Krashen, learning is always conscious, the result of study, and can be planned. In contrast, acquisition is unplanned and unconscious. His most controversial claim is that conscious learning does not aid unconscious acquisition. For him, the two are totally separate. It will be seen immediately that this suggestion represents a radical challenge to all formal teaching, stating as it does, that what students take from any activity, and what benefits them, is totally independent of the activity in which they are consciously engaged. A number of points arise immediately:

a. A little like Chomsky's competence/performance distinction, we will be able to test learning, but are unable to test acquisition. In this sense the dichotomy is unscientific, since the assertion of the importance of acquisition is not susceptible to empirical testing; the hypothesis is, in effect, unfalsifiable. This has led to the hypothesis being attacked in some quarters, but as I understand it, Krashen has never asserted that the distinction was strictly scientific in this narrow sense.

b. Intuitively introspectively, there seems to be some justification for the distinction. All of us who have learned a foreign language are at least conscious that there seem to be two different ways of internalising language — we have all learned words for specific purposes, and later found them useful. On the other hand, we are all well aware of becoming aware of distinctions, either gradually or in a flash of understanding, without consciously thinking about them. At a minimum, it seems that both conscious and unconscious learning can take place. What is contentious about Krashen's claim is that the two are totally unconnected. (Latterly, in conversation if not in writing, he has modified this extreme position to being 'at least 95% unconnected'. He cites the placing of apostrophes as probably conscious, even for native speakers.) This slight concession on his part hardly weakens his fundamental assertion, which is that it is acquisition which is of real long term value to the learner.

c. Swan, in reading Krashen's work, has come to the same conclusion as I have myself — that although Krashen talks about 'language acquisition', what he invariably appears to be talking about is the progressive mastery of the **system** of the language, what is traditionally thought of as 'the grammar'. Elements of Krashen's theory — in particular his Natural Order Hypothesis and Monitor Hypothesis — both suggest that he is concerned with the increasing understanding the learner has of the fundamental semantico-grammatical categories of the language. He makes remarkably few comments about vocabulary as such, and none appear inconsistent with the idea that consciously learned words can be incorporated into a student's language repertoire, both for understanding and productive use. My own understanding leads me to agree with Krashen's perception of the way students master the grammatical categories of the language — understanding is a process, based on provisional hypotheses, experimentation, confirmation or refutation, re-hypothesising etc. Within this framework, as we shall see in Chapter 6 the dominance of structural syllabuses is not only too narrow, but fundamentally absurd. Too superficial a reading of Krashen's work, however, can lead to a dismissal of the value of conscious learning which is more all-embracing than Krashen's own writing would imply. Within a lexical approach we shall suggest certain lexical items — words, lexical phrases, and learned utterances — may provide an important link between conscious learning and unconscious acquisition.

Krashen's work has attracted a good deal of scepticism, even vilification. This is surprising, for its claims are comparatively modest, and although they challenge some of the tenets of language teaching orthodoxy, they resonate with many people's experience of language acquisition outside formal classrooms. Perhaps Krashen's greatest mistake has been to formulate his suggestions clearly, and to state his hypotheses explicitly for it is precisely this clarity which has rendered them so susceptible to attack. His claims are most fully set out in *The Natural Approach, Alemany/Pergamon 1983*. It is important to recognise that this is partly a work advancing his own theory and position, and partly a reaction against behaviourist, structure-dominated audio-lingualism which was still very influential in American linguistic and language teaching circles at the time of his writing. In the preface, the following claim is made:

> The central hypothesis of the theory is that language acquisition occurs in only one way: by understanding messages. We acquire language when we obtain comprehensible input, when we understand what we hear or read in another language.

This means that acquisition is based on what we hear and understand, not on what we say. This claim conflicts with much earlier language teaching. The most important change, for all students but particularly beginners, is to move the emphasis from speaking — language the student produces — to listening — language to which the student is exposed. This theory claims that if you understand what is said to you, the language used will contribute to your long term ability to use that same language yourself. More precisely, it claims that this is the **only** way that language is acquired, appropriated by the student for later personal use. Contrary to many presentations of his theory, however, Krashen does not dismiss learning as useless, seeing it rather as valuable, but subordinate to acquisition. He claims quite explicitly:

> One of the central tasks of the instructor is to present an optimal balance of acquisition and learning activities. (*Natural Approach*, page 58).

This comment is, however, made in the context of the following assertion:

> Acquisition activities are central. Since acquisition is central to developing communication skills, the great majority of class time is devoted to activities which provide input for acquisition.

Krashen states explicitly the role he believes conscious learning plays. The term he coins is the Monitor Hypothesis which states that conscious learning has the limited function of allowing students to monitor or edit language **after** they have produced that language. According to the hypothesis, the language students produce will come from the reservoir of unconsciously acquired language. That language having been produced, conscious learning allows students to examine their own output critically. Within this model, part of the function of teaching is to make students more aware of language in general, and their own language production in particular. The assumption is that by accurate observation of the language around them, and accurate comparison of their own production with 'correct' language the process of acquisition is accelerated. It is helpful to remember the context of the development of Krashen's theory. Chomsky's competence/performance distinction exercised considerable theoretical influence. Hyams challenged the competence/ performance distinction, and introduced the term **communicative competence**. This term implied a shift from what the learner **knew** to what the learner could **do**. A measure of the speaker's communicative competence was the range of situation in which the speaker communicated effectively. This, initially theoretical, shift resulted in increased attention being paid to use, rather than exclusive concentration on usage; attention shifted to value as well as to signification. In Britain, the development of Hyam's idea led to what came to be called the Communicative Approach (CA). The definite article is misleading, for no two writers interpreted CA in precisely the same way, and it would be more accurate to talk about *a*, rather than *the* Communicative Approach. Krashen claims that his Natural Approach is indeed a communicative approach.

In 1985, Swan attacked the 'monolith' of the communicative approach in an article in the *English Language Teaching Journal* (ELTJ). Replying to the criticism, Widdowson, one of the architects of the approach, insisted that it was neither monolithic nor dogmatic, but a departure point for teachers.

Perhaps the single most important insight was that in changing the focus to language as communication, an inevitable corollary was a concentration on the centrality of meaning. In the second of two articles referred to above (ELTJ, April 1985) Swan says:

> For many people, the central ideal in 'communicative' teaching is probably that of 'a semantic syllabus'. In a course based on a semantic syllabus, it is meanings rather than structures which are given priority, and which form the organising principle or 'skeleton' of the textbook.

Within the same paragraph, however, he goes on to equate 'semantic' with notions. While the shift from structure to notion is desirable, it seems to me that any truly meaning-centred syllabus will need to be more radical. One of its central organising principles will need to be lexis. Indeed, this assertion is probably the single most important proposal of the Lexical Approach proposed in this book.

Two clear changes of emphasis are central to Krashen's Natural Approach:

a. Greater emphasis on vocabulary in the early stages of learning.

b. Increased emphasis on the ability to communicate messages, with correspondingly decreased emphasis on structural accuracy.

Krashen[12] is explicit on the importance of vocabulary, and his comment requires no gloss:

> Vocabulary is basic to communication. If acquirers do not recognise the meaning of the key words used by those who address them they will be unable to participate in the conversation. If they wish to express some idea or ask for information they must be able to produce lexical items to convey their meaning. Indeed, if our students know the morphology and the syntax of an utterance addressed to them, but do not know the meaning of key lexical items, they will be unable to participate in the communication. For this reason, we are not impressed with approaches that deliberately restrict vocabulary acquisition and learning until the morphology and syntax are mastered.

> Vocabulary is also very important for the acquisition process. The popular belief is that one uses form and grammar to understand meaning. The truth is probably closer to the opposite: we acquire morphology and syntax because we understand the meaning of utterances.

On the subject of how students learn, and the kind of language they produce he is equally explicit:

> Communicative ability is usually acquired quite rapidly; grammatical accuracy on the other hand, increases only slowly, and after much experience using the language.[13]

> Very early speech is quite flawed, with acquirers using mostly simple words and short phrases. It contains few function words or grammatical markers.[14]

> It is doubtful if morphology is noticed (either consciously or unconsciously) since morphology in general is not necessary at first for partial comprehension and indeed acquirers in early stages usually ignore it completely.[15]

Somewhat tongue-in-cheek Krashen has remarked that he knows two things about his own theory — 15 years research tell him it is true, and reaction from language teaching colleagues tells him it is useless. He identifies two objectors which render his theory useless — teachers and students!

If he is right, a great deal of conventional teaching achieves nothing; more may perhaps be achieved by participating in relaxing, enjoyable activities than by hard work, effort and concentration. It is hardly surprising that many teachers, whose livelihoods and self-image depend on the belief that their teaching is effective, remain to be convinced of the truth and value behind some of Krashen's claims. For myself, providing we remember Swan's warning that when Krashen uses the term 'acquisition' he refers to structure and function rather than vocabulary and lexis, I am convinced. Key elements of the Natural Approach — emphasis on listening, importance of vocabulary at all levels, particularly beginners, de-emphasis on structural accuracy, and above all the centrality of the meaning of language — are central elements in the Lexical Approach which I propose.

12. Input and Intake

I return to Krashen's central assertion: *We acquire language when we obtain comprehensible input, when we understand what we hear or read in another language.*

Input is language presented to students through reading and listening. Clearly the relative value of reading and listening may differ for different groups of students depending on facts such as their age, knowledge of Roman script or learning purpose.

Radically different attitudes to input may be found in the history of language teaching. Traditionally, the amount of input was severely restricted, and rigorously sequenced. Classroom procedures such as grammar drills, intensive pronunciation practice, and intensive reading, were based on the assumption that students would master each new language item as they met it. Having mastered one piece of input, the next step could be introduced. Input was essentially atomistic, and based on two central assumptions:

a. It is possible (and desirable) to sequence language.

b. Learning is a step-by-step process, and too much input would confuse.

These assumptions are totally at variance with the way we know people acquire their first language. Babies are surrounded by, and bombarded with input of many kinds, some of it clearly useless to the child in the first months of life. Far from trying to restrict input, however, parents and, later, nursery schools tend to overwhelm the child with spoken language, frequently paraphrasing, repeating and playing with language with, at first, little or no response from the child. The question of whether second languages are acquired in the same way as mother tongue is a contentious one but it seems more reasonable to assume that the two processes are in some ways similar than to assume that they are totally different. Most modern theorists would now agree that large quantities of diverse input are highly desirable, and a real aid to second language acquisition. It is clear, however, that not all input is equally useful to the learner. Not all input will result in **intake** — the language which the student benefits from and is, in some way able to integrate, either partially or totally into his or her own repertoire. Sadly, we all know from our own experience that intake is not necessarily the same thing as input. In all subjects, not just language, we have all had the experience of reading or revising some material only to feel the next morning that we will have to re-read the same material — we have forgotten it, or for some other reason been unable to incorporate it into our knowledge or thinking in a way which allows us to re-access and re-use it. Many factors influence the relationship between input and intake — tiredness, interest level, attention, motivation, to mention only a few. Most of these factors apply to all learning but what factors influence the relationship between language input and language intake? Once again, Krashen's Natural Approach advances two hypotheses in answer to that question.

Firstly, he refers to **comprehensible** input as the basis for acquisition. Intuitively, this tallies with our general learning experience — if we read a book or listen to a lecture which we simply do not understand, it is self-evident that it is of no lasting value to us. What seems to help, again in general rather than specifically language learning, is material which **relates to** what we already know, but in some way **modifies or extends** it. We are all too familiar with the unsatisfactory nature of dialogues between people or groups who hold different religious or political world-views. Even with goodwill, they have difficulty engaging in effective dialogue because what one party proposes is, in a very real sense, incomprehensible to the other. We can learn, and incorporate into our thinking only ideas which confirm, extend or modify the position from which we start. Krashen's Input Hypothesis summarises this experience in relation to language acquisition. He suggests that we acquire (not learn) language by understanding input that is only slightly beyond our current level of acquired competence. The implication is that we use meaning — the understanding of new messages — to help us acquire language. He says[16]:

> To state the hypothesis a bit more formally, an acquirer can 'move' from a stage i (where i is the acquirer's level of competence) to a stage $i + 1$ (where $i + 1$ is the stage immediately following i along some natural order) by understanding language containing $i + 1$.

Two points must be made about this definition. Firstly, it assumes the validity of another of Krashen's hypotheses — the Natural Order Hypothesis. According to him, grammatical structures are acquired in a predictable order, independent of any order in which they may be learned. He does not insist that the order is precisely the same for all learners, but that certain structures **tend** to be acquired early, while others tend to be acquired late, independent of any attempts by textbook or teacher to alter that order. There are some difficulties with this, in particular the difficulty of knowing precisely what we might mean by saying that a learner has 'acquired' a particular linguistic item. Despite this difficulty, what the research of Krashen and others shows reflects the experience of many language teachers — the language which students seem able to use, particularly in the early stages of learning, differs, in many cases radically, from what they have been taught and, nominally, learned. The most striking example in English language teaching is the third person **-s**. In all learning programmes this item is taught early, but it is a commonplace — indeed a source of endless frustration to teachers — that it is acquired late. This is unsurprising when we consider that the third person **-s** is always semantically redundant — the information carried by that morphological feature is invariably carried elsewhere in the sentence. However 'easy' the 'rule' for the third person **-s** may be, if language is indeed meaning-centred, it is only to be expected that semantically redundant morphological items will be 'difficult' to acquire. Viewing language as meaning-based in this way poses a serious challenge to linear concepts of level and difficulty. Whatever the truth or otherwise behind the Natural Order Hypothesis, it is at least plausible that students work simultaneously on a much wider range of language, of which they have various degrees of mastery, than traditional syllabus construction and classroom procedure would lead us to believe. There is a warning for all teachers — when they focus on a particular language item in class, even if they have their students' full co-operation, whatever attempts are made to concentrate on that particular item, it cannot be to the exclusion of surrounding language. No matter how much teachers know what they are teaching, they must accept that they are much less aware of what, at the very same moment, the students are doing. Students may be processing different language, in different ways, and making different connections. A student's 'current' perception of English is a constantly changing dynamic concept, influenced by the student's intake, not the teacher's input. If the two coincide, the objectives of the teacher's lesson plan may (or may not) be achieved; if the two are different, the student may still benefit, only on this occasion the nature of the benefit may not be apparent, to either teacher or learner.

Returning to Krashen's 'more technical definition', I must point out its pseudo-scientific nature. The **i + 1** terminology suggests a spurious accuracy, as if my English today may be assessed at a level of 37/100 with the implication that, given the right intake, I will tomorrow achieve a level of 38/100. Curiously, Krashen introduces this spurious terminology precisely because he wishes to attack the kind of structural, audio-lingual syllabuses which are based on the assumption that we know precisely what we are teaching on a particular day. Despite the unhelpful terminology, however, he goes on to explain in some detail what he means by comprehensible input, an argument which leads him to what he calls the Great Paradox of Language Teaching. In his terms, 'finely-tuned' input is achieved when the textbook material, language used by the teacher, and exercise material concentrate almost exclusively on a particular structure, such as 'the present continuous used for the future'. Such teaching is based on the assumption that we know where students are, and therefore how we can lead them step-by-step through a (predominantly linear) syllabus. Many textbooks, and much classroom teaching, at least up to intermediate level, is still conducted on this basis. In contrast, Krashen advocates what he calls 'roughly-tuned input'. This is probably what many competent teachers use when not formally 'teaching', but rather just talking to their class in the target language. In such circumstances, the teacher instinctively chooses language so that it will be understood. This necessarily involves language below, at and just above the student's current receptive level. Krashen's claim is that acquisition is essentially based on comprehensible input, and it may be that teachers are doing most for their students when they behave least like teachers[17]:

> When we 'just talk' to our students, **if they understand,** we are not only giving a language lesson, we may be giving the best possible language lesson since we will be supplying input for acquisition.

He suggests that when teachers concentrate on **communication**, and the **content** of what is said rather than linguistic form, they are, paradoxically, teaching best[18]:

> According to the input hypothesis, language acquisition can only take place when a message which is being transmitted is understood, i.e, when the focus is on what is being said rather than the form of the message. This could be referred to as the 'Great Paradox of Language Teaching'.

According to Krashen, a necessary criterion for input to be of use to the student — to be potential intake — is that it should be partially, or largely comprehensible. As his phrase 'roughly tuned' suggests, however, it is not necessary that it should be totally comprehensible. When we use language outside the classroom we do not demand of others, or of ourselves total, explicit, comprehensibility. Language is essentially a means to an end, and it is sufficient that the pragmatic purpose of utterances is achieved. It is, therefore, another paradox that language teachers, and probably their students, frequently insist that what is understood is a complete and explicit understanding of the language introduced into the classroom. A major change initially demanded by Communicative Approaches, which reappears in the Lexical Approach is the assertion that classrooms need to be input-rich, with much larger **quantities** of comprehensible input material available. The corollary will be that in using those materials, they can be 'consumed' more rapidly, and with **partial** rather than total comprehension for the students. If learning is perceived as a process this change of attitude will cause no difficulties; teachers (or students) who cling to the what-you-meet-you-master, linear approach to input will not be comfortable with the changes required by this use of language input.

For input to become intake, comprehensibility is a necessary, but not sufficient criterion. At least three other factors need to be taken into account — the students' **attitude, motivation,** and the **authenticity** of the material.

It is possible to divide language teaching materials into two categories, those specifically produced for language teaching, and other language material produced for 'real-world' purposes, but introduced into the classroom. Some writers describe these two kinds of material as, respectively, artificial and authentic. The assumption is that the latter kind of material must necessarily be better. Not many years ago language teaching materials could be astonishingly artificial, arid and remote from the student's experience. Within that context, it was unquestionably a step in the right direction to introduce more 'real' material; unfortunately, the 'reality' or otherwise of material is not intrinsic to it, but is a function of the relationship between the learner and the material. It is by no means obvious that for a 13 year old living in Athens a map of the London underground is any more real than a passage from Gulliver's Travels. Lilliput and London can be equally remote and, in this important sense, the material presented to the students can be equally inauthentic. Widdowson[19] has this to say:

> I am not sure that it is meaningful to talk about authentic language as such at all. I think it is probably better to consider authenticity not as a quality of residing in instances of language, but as a quality which is bestowed upon them, created by the response of the receiver.

> Authenticity depends on a congruence of the language producer's intentions and the language receivers' interpretation. ... I might be tempted just to select passages of discourse which are thematically relevant from a whole range of sources on the assumption that I am thereby furthering the communicative purpose for which the learners need the language. But if I then exploit these passages for the traditional kind of comprehension question, structural exercise and so on, their authentic potential remains unrealised. I might just as well have selected an extract from the Highway Code or Winnie the Pooh. The fact that the data is genuine is irrelevant.

If the learner does not enter into a relationship with the input, it is unlikely that it will contribute to intake. Artificial activities such as games may produce a more authentic experience in this sense than genuine language data used for traditional language teaching activities directed at usage, signification, and mastery of the structures of the language. We see that **authenticity** is more based in the previous knowledge, real world experience, and needs of the student than in the language data itself.

The final part of Krashen's Natural Approach is in his Affective Filter Hypothesis[20]:

> This hypothesis states that attitude and all variables relating to success in second language acquisition generally relate directly to language acquisition but not necessarily to language learning. Performers with certain types of motivation, usually but not always 'integrative' (see below) and with good self-images do better in second language acquisition. Also, the best situations for language acquisition seem to be those which encourage lower anxiety levels.

Summarised, he claims that input is more likely to become intake if learners feel good, about themselves, about the target language, and about the learning environment. He further claims that, although increasing the stress on students in class may improve their short-term learning, it has negative effects on their long-term acquisition. This is a view which I wholly endorse. It has two important methodological implications, taken up later in this book — teachers should avoid an over-insistence on production in the earliest stages, being willing to wait until students feel comfortable producing English, and at all costs over-correction must be avoided. If a student finally feels comfortable enough to produce some language, and the immediate feedback suggests failure, the effect on the student's attitude is likely to be profoundly negative. We have already seen that teachers may well be helping students' long-term acquisition when they are 'only talking to them' When, in a real sense, they are behaving least like teachers.

In the same way, if teachers react to the **content** of what students say, rather than its linguistic form, they are most likely to lower the affective filter, to encourage a positive attitude, and to aid acquisition.

Researchers have suggested that motivation is predominantly of two kinds, integrative or instrumental. The former involves a positive attitude to the culture and background of the target language, and perhaps even in its extreme form an urge to 'become' a member of the speech community of the target language. On a more mundane level, particularly for school students, it involves liking English, and thinking it is fun to use it.

'Instrumental' motivation applies to those students who see the usefulness, perhaps even necessity of learning the target language, but see it **only** as a means to an end. There are more students of this type than English language teachers sometimes admit. In the modern world English is a necessity for many non-native speakers, who may be indifferent, or even hostile to British or American culture. Language teaching materials need to recognise the legitimacy of both kinds of motivation. Although a language is intimately associated with the culture(s) in which it is used by native speakers, it is by no means the case that all those who use the language proficiently, as a second language, need to understand, identify with, or even have positive feelings towards the native-speaking cultures. Mistaken insistence by teachers or materials on the equation of language and culture can, for some learners, raise the affective filter and reduce the value of input as intake.

We may summarise that input is most likely to be most effective as intake if:

-   The input is, at least partially, comprehensible (a necessary condition).
-   The student reacts to the material with interest, annoyance, amusement etc.
-   The student is 'open', feeling good about self, target language, and learning situation.
-   The student is motivated — voluntarily wishing to turn input into intake.

13. Teaching and Learning

Almost all the distinctions discussed so far relate to the nature of language, or the process of learning. There is, however, another person involved in the whole process who should not be overlooked — the teacher. Teachers are particularly important, as research suggests that the attitudes they bring to the classroom are sometimes the single most important influence in the overall success or failure of what happens in the classroom. Traditional classrooms tended to centre on a static view of language and a teacher-centred methodology. Nowadays, at least in the Anglo Saxon and European educational traditions, the emphasis has shifted to skills, learner-centred activities, and a more developmental, process-orientated view of language and learning. Needless to say, not everyone is happy with this shift of emphasis. Many people — politicians, parents, and indeed teachers themselves — distrust the shift of emphasis and see it in terms of declining standards. Of particular importance is the attitude of teachers, for it is they who must implement any proposed changes of syllabus or method. If they feel uncomfortable with, or even threatened by, changes, the changes will either not be implemented, or, perhaps worse, will be bowdlerized and any intended improvements will merely produce confusion.

Later in this book I question much language teaching orthodoxy and often propose radically different values and objectives. It is, therefore, a matter of great concern that teachers — in this case readers — feel that their opinions and roles are given due consideration. It is essential that they understand and see the value of any proposed changes. Although this theme recurs throughout the book, it seems useful as part of the ground-clearing to introduce and highlight some of the problems.

A colleague reminds me of the story of a teacher asked in the staffroom what she had done in a particular lesson. Memorably, and perceptively she replied *I did the present perfect, but I am not quite sure what they did.* Here was a wise woman, for she recognised that it was unduly optimistic to assume that what she taught, the students learned. Our lives would be simpler if teaching and learning were isomorphic, but sadly this is not the case. Furthermore, research literature tends to tell us a great deal more about teaching than it does about learning. It is relatively easy to observe teachers, and record their activities; it is much more difficult to make any observations at all about learning or, more precisely, acquisition.

The way in which teachers teach is strongly influenced by their own self-perception as individuals, and as 'teachers'. Inevitably the teacher fulfils a variety of social functions in any lesson. Readers might like to check which of the roles below they recognise as part of their own self-image.

Instructor	Editor	Language partner
Educator	Counsellor	Cheerful steamroller
Motivator	Confessor	Instant reference book
Dictator	Fount of all truth	Sympathetic interlocutor
Assessor	Social Organiser	Representative of authority
Mandarin	Student resource	Baby-sitter
Time-keeper	Genial host	Language adviser

Experienced teachers will quickly recognise that at some time or another they assume, or have thrust upon them by their students, all of these roles. Needless to say, some of them militate directly against effective language learning.

We have already acknowledged the importance for language acquisition of affective factors. Input is more likely to become intake if it is comprehensible, related to previous experience, and a low-anxiety atmosphere prevails. Alien material is threatening, and raises the affective filter, and is unlikely to be of real use to the learner. We can apply this not only to language learning, but to other learning and new ideas.

In particular, readers may resist ideas which seem alien or threatening. It is, therefore, useful to ask on what your self-confidence as a teacher is based and, correspondingly, what changes of attitude you will find relatively easy or intimidating. Which of the following do you recognise as factors which contribute to you feeling confident, competent and effective in the classrom?

1. Your theoretical overview.

2. Your knowledge of the language.

3. Your knowledge of teaching techniques.

4. The materials you produce.

5. The preparation you put into classes.

6. Your social status.

7. Your qualifications.

8. Your personality, and the classroom atmosphere you generate.

9. The knowledge you impart.

10. The enjoyment you foster.

To what extent do you choose or avoid materials or activities by conscious reference to either the teacher roles or the self-image factors listed above?

Finally, in thinking of the learning/teaching dichotomy, is your primary concern in class to create success or to avoid failure for your learners? Do you ever, consciously or unconsciously, value 'a good lesson' — teaching — above effective learning?

Summary

It is embarrassing to look back at the claims and suggestions of the communicative approach and to compare them with what actually happens in many classrooms which claim to be 'communicative'. The principal successes of the communicative approach are that it overwhelmed structural dominance, allowed pragmatics to influence the syllabus through the introduction of functions, and led to a number of important changes in methodology. The principal failure was unquestionably that notional categories were not, in general, incorporated into textbooks — despite the contents pages of many textbooks. Most importantly, however, its proponents urged important changes which have simply been ignored:

The use of real tasks which necessitate communication
Non-correction
Emphasis on fluency not accuracy
Student autonomy
The teaching of value and use not signification and usage
Greatly increased attention to receptive skills

Of course some of these ideas have had marginal effects, but for most teachers they remain peripheral. Regrettably, step-by-step vocabulary and grammar-based syllabuses, and the use of exercises rather than tasks, remain the norm.

The Lexical Approach embraces all that the communicative approach suggested. Its principal addition is a recognition of lexis as well as, or sometimes instead of, structure **as an organising principle** affecting both content and methodology.

PART 3 — The Teacher's Mind-Set

One of the most important factors which influences what happens in the classroom is the totality of ideas, knowledge and attitudes which represent the teacher's mind-set. This complex of ideas is partly explicit, based on information given to the teacher, formal learning and the like, but much of it is implicit, based on the teacher's self-image, value system and even prejudice. Changing your mind-set is much more than adding a new technique to your repertoire or taking a different view of a particular classroom activity. Mind-set is about the **totality** of your attitudes and values and is therefore both difficult, and perhaps uncomfortable to change. The remainder of this book will argue that many teachers need to change their mind-set. Some readers will share some, or perhaps even all of the ideas I wish to emphasise and encourage; I am sure very few readers would explicitly espouse all, or even most, of the values I wish to de-emphasise. Individual readers might reflect on whether their classroom practice actually mirrors the values they claim to espouse.

It is not that one element of the dichotomies listed below should be valued to the **exclusion** of the other, but that the **emphasis** should lie in a particular direction. I suggest that many, if not most teachers, could usefully adjust the values they emphasise in the following ways:

1. From Written Language to Spoken Language.

In literate society, writing is more prestigious than speech. Dictionaries and grammars are still largely based on written language. But in language learning speech precedes writing. Almost all the world's natural language output is spoken rather than written. Spoken language is different from written language, but certainly not a defective or deficient version of it.

2. From Speaking to Listening

Listening is the primary means of linguistic input. Over-emphasising speech in the early stages of foreign language learning is inhibiting and counter-productive.

3. From Product to Process

Teachers often want or need evidence of learning, so they tend to over-value student products — essays, exercises or speech. This need can obstruct learning, which is a continuous process.

4. From Short-Term to Long-Term Aims

Learning a foreign language can be a valuable, long-term personal asset for the student.It can be inhibited by over-emphasising short-term objectives — tests, pressure to speak before you are ready etc.

5. From Answers to Questions

Learning is always provisional. Without questioning our present position, learning cannot occur. Short-term, slick answers often inhibit real developmental learning. Answers block; questions create.

6. From Explanations to Exploration

Explanations are a kind of answer, often teacher-centred. Explorations are a kind of question and a kind of process — exploration is learning-based and student-centred.

7. From Knowledge to Skill

Knowledge involves answers and explanations and is necessary, but not sufficient. What matters is not what you know, but what you can do. 'Knowing' a foreign language may be interesting; the ability to use it is life-enhancing.

8. From Accuracy to Communication

Successful communication always involves at least limited accuracy. Accuracy need not involve communication at all. Communication is a wider, more useful concept; successful language is more valuable than language which is only accurate.

9. From Structure to Lexis

More meaning is carried by lexis than grammatical structure. Focus on communication necessarily implies increased emphasis on lexis, and decreased emphasis on structure.

10. From Sentence to Text

Naturally occurring language is never merely a sequence of sentences. If language teaching concentrates on sentences as the basic unit of language, it will fail the learner.

11. From (Atomistic) Parts to (Holistic) Wholes

A symphony is not just notes, a painting not just blobs of paint. Language and communication are not strings of words and sentences.

12. From Planned Certainty to Unguided Uncertainty

Meanings, 'rules' — language itself — is fuzzier than teachers or students would like. Learning is more provisional, less measurable than the teacher or school system would like. However uncomfortable it may be, rigid sequencing, lesson planning, dogmatic rule stating, and precise definition are frequently illusions, often counter-productive. An attitude of openness and curiosity, however uncomfortable, is indispensable.

13. From Teacher-Centred to Learner-Centred

'It's quicker if I explain' — quicker for whom? Well-planned, and even well executed lessons cannot guarantee good learning. Accepting uncertainty as part of your mind-set develops patience, tolerance of the learner's problems, a willingness to support them as they struggle with the learning process.

14. From Recipes to Theory

Too often teachers ask for new ideas. Procedures are evaluated with *It works*. But why? As well as possible? Bad theory is planned certainty; good theory is guided uncertainty. Recipes are no more than loose thinking defended by prejudice. Teachers need from time to time to re-evaluate their whole position in an unashamedly theoretical way.

It is perhaps necessary to re-state that I am not suggesting that in any of the above dichotomies one element is 'right' and the other 'wrong'. It is a matter of **relative** importance, of discovering, re-discovering and re-emphasising particular ideas, while downgrading other ideas on a relative, but certainly not absolute, scale.

The change of mind-set allows one to see clearly key methodological implications. The following list provides an over-view of the implications which are discussed in much more detail later.

The following received opinions, often regarded as orthodox, are in fact all untrue or at best unhelpful over-simplifications.

1. Testing will tell you a student's level.
2. The basic paradigm is Present-Practise-Produce.
3. The influence of the student's first language is to be avoided.
4. Learners should (try to) avoid mistakes.
5. 'Correcting' helps students.
6. Explaining (grammar) helps.
7. You learn to speak by speaking.
8. Vocabulary is best learned in situations.
9. 'Communicative' teaching emphasises activity, talking and pair work, while de-emphasising grammar.
10. In the end, learning a language is about mastering its grammar, which is more important than vocabulary.

In fact, within a Lexical Approach, we can identify important theoretical and methodological ideas which challenge, or in some cases reverse, received orthodoxy. All of these will be developed in detail later, but are listed here to indicate the direction of my thinking.

1. Language consists of grammaticalised lexis, not lexicalised grammar.
2. Time is an essentially lexical concept.
3. For language teaching, co-text is more important than situation.
4. Lexical patterns can be more powerfully generative than structural patterns.
5. De-lexicalised verbs are powerful generators.
6. Semantic content is inversely proportional to generative power.
7. Metaphor is lexically patterned.

8. Different pattern-generating systems require different pedagogical treatment.
9. Inadequately grammaticalised interlanguage is fully acceptable.
10. Language is inherently Here-and-Now user-centered.

From a methodological point of view the following principles may be established:

1. Early emphasis on receptive skills, especially listening, is essential.
2. De-contextualised vocabulary learning is a fully legitimate strategy.
3. The role of grammar as a receptive skill must be recognised.
4. The importance of contrast in language awareness must be recognised.
5. Teachers should employ extensive, deictic language for receptive purposes.
6. Extensive writing should be delayed as long as possible.
7. Non-linear recording formats are intrinsic to the Lexical Approach.
8. Reformulation should be the natural response to student error.
9. Teachers should always react primarily to the content of student language.
10. Pedagogical chunking (see page 121) should be a frequent classroom activity.

The above indicates clearly, I hope, that I am concerned to establish a lexical approach, not a lexical syllabus. Lexis can contribute important **elements** to syllabus design, and may involve radical re-ordering in the same way that notions and functions did. The implications of a lexical approach are, however, much wider, involving methodology, attitudes to grammar, the treatment of error and a wide range of other factors. It is precisely because I am proposing an **approach** that it is necessary to take into consideration so many factors which contribute to the teacher's mind-set. I am not concerned to promote a more central role for vocabulary, nor even a recognition of the importance of lexis. My concern is to integrate those ideas into an over-view of language and learning, themselves seen in the wider context of contemporary philosophy and education. After establishing this background, the next chapter seeks to develop the ideas which underlie language and learning.

References

1. Current English Grammar, p8.
2. Notional Syllabuses, p5.
3. Second Language Acquisition, p22.
4. Spoken and Written Language, pxv.
5. ibid, p36.
6. ibid, p97.
7. Confessions of an Embarrassed Eclectic.
8. Explorations in Applied Linguistics, p12.
9. Lexical Phrases and Language Teaching, p32.
10. The Lexical Syllabus, p128.
11. op cit p292.

12. The Natural Approach, p155.

13. ibid, p16.

14. ibid, p20.

15. ibid, p.91

16. ibid, p32.

17. ibid, p35

18. ibid, p55.

19. op cit p165/6.

20. op cit p37/8.

Chapter 2

Developing Ideas

PART 1 — Spectra

Having established a basic terminology, we turn now to looking at ways in which that terminology can inhibit, rather than illuminate clear thought. Dichotomies simplify, but at the expense of suppression. Several key ideas are much more complex than would be suggested by the discussion so far. Several of the ideas central to our discussions are gradeable and are more adequately represented as points on a scale, cline or spectrum, rather than as polarities. Other concepts are even more complex, being multi-dimensional, rather than linear in character. Linear or oppositional consideration of these ideas is achieved only at the expense of serious distortion.

1. Vocabulary and Grammar

Central to everything that follows in our search for the Lexical Approach will be the potential generative power of certain words. This novel idea in no sense denies the generative power of certain structures. It does, however, take from 'grammar' (in the narrow sense of the structures traditional to a structural syllabus) its unique role in providing a mechanism for the creation of novel utterances. The traditional view has been that grammar is creative, while words are like building bricks, fixed packages of meaning.

The truth is much closer to a spectrum. At one end, are semantically strong words, which have limited collocational range, are (relatively) rare, and where their value almost always coincides with their signification — *haemoglobin*. At the other end of the spectrum are words traditionally recognised as grammatical, rather than vocabulary items — *this, one, of*. Such words are almost always devoid of signification, deriving their meaning almost entirely from context. Characteristically, such words collocate very widely and are recognised as key elements in the 'structure' of English. The vocabulary/grammar polarity can be maintained as long as we confine ourselves to extreme examples such as *haemoglobin* or *of*. In practice, however, the vast majority of words — *walk, house, give, have* — are more centrally situated on a spectrum. Extreme examples of vocabulary are unique, precise, and totally ungenerative; at the other end of the spectrum are the lexically vacuous, grammatical words which convey little meaning in themselves, but relate very freely with other words. In short, there is a **Spectrum of Generative Power.** Later, we will see how this spectrum provides us with a way of identifying and exploiting different words in different ways for effective language teaching.

2. Rules and Exceptions

Traditionally, vocabulary consisted of separate non-generalisable, indeed arbitrary, items, each of which was to be learned separately. In contrast, grammar was seen as subject to rules which describe all, or a large generality, of particular uses. This fiction could never be fully maintained, and in presenting any grammar 'rule', books and teachers always had to list exceptions. A fundamental problem inherent in grammar rules is the conflict between accessibility and accuracy. Many 'rules' which students can understand are very restricted in their application; they are (whether the teacher realises it or not) partial truths, or temporary fictions. Accurate rules with wide applicability and a few exceptions, are usually highly abstract and difficult to understand and of correspondingly little use to the learner. I argue later that this conflict makes it difficult, if not impossible, to present students with rules at all. That, however, is a pedagogical implication. For the moment, our considerations are more theoretical — can we usefully talk about 'rules' and 'exceptions' at all? The answer if we think in absolute terms is *No*. If we think in relative terms — along a cline or spectrum — it is self-evident that some things are totally or almost totally ungeneralisable, while other features exhibit larger and more generalisable patterns. It is not an absolute matter, but a question of a **Spectrum of Generalisability.**

One of the central functions of teaching is to streamline or short-cut the learning process. It is assumed that helping the student to make generalisations lowers memory load and is useful to learning. In those circumstances, it is the task of the textbook writer and teacher to produce useful, accessible generalisations. Somewhat surprisingly, many syllabuses are less successful at this than we might reasonably expect. This is because written language, structure, and paradigms have played a disproportionate role. Most teachers, asked to give the 'rule' for the formation of the past tense in English would suggest 'adding *-ed*'. For regular verbs this is true in writing, but rather surprisingly this morpheme is **never** pronounced /ed/. The correct pronunciation rule is:

a. Most generally, pronounce the /t/ or /d/ ending in the most convenient way.

b. Use one of /t/, /d/, /id/.

We may note that the single most powerful pattern of English is almost certainly SVO. Badly-grammaticalised, this pattern will still convey meaning: *I live there (before), He know hers.* This 'super pattern' is rarely mentioned explicitly in teaching materials. In contrast, the pure exception of the third person **-s** invariably achieves a prominence, which its non-generative nature suggests it does not deserve. Note that the third person **-s** is not only restricted to the third person, but to statements not questions, and to positives not negatives. In **all** cases **except** third person positive statements, the so-called 'present simple' is fully and accurately lexicalised by using the base form of the word — *Does he know her? She doesn't see the point.* SVO and many other widely generalisable patterns do not normally feature in language teaching materials; many non-generalisable details frequently do. This strongly suggests something is amiss.

3. Not all language is equally useful in conveying meaning.

Broadly, vocabulary carries more meaning than grammar, but as we have already recognised above this is a matter of degree rather than a stark polarity.

If we confine ourselves to a narrower view of vocabulary, it is self-evident that not all words are 'equally useful'. If we are able to make any prediction as to the situation of use, we may select quite different words as being high priority from the selection we would make for a general all-purpose language course. In selecting vocabulary we certainly need to use considerations such as **frequency, range** (the different situations or text-types in which the item may occur) and **coverage** (words with relatively 'wide' meaning which can substitute for other, more specific items). Other criteria, based on pedagogical rather than linguistic criteria, may also be employed. The key point is that different language items — words, phrases and structures — assume different positions on a **Spectrum of Communicative Power.**

Proficiency in a foreign language can seem a remote, unattainable objective for an ordinary student in a language class. Sadly, materials can often emphasise the infantilisation and feeling of despair which linguistic inadequacy can so easily produce. If students — children or mature business people — are to feel encouraged and motivated, real meaning and communication must be part of classroom activity, even at low levels of linguistic ability. Nothing is more motivating than real communication. This means low-level courses must be strongly influenced by elements with high value within the Spectrum of Communicative Power. The different kinds of meaning which can be conveyed must also be considered.

The students' intellectual and emotional level is not restricted to what they are able to express in a second language. There is covert sequencing in most syllabuses; in the early stages students are taught to communicate factual information, later opinion, and only at comparatively advanced levels, attitude. This can be intensely frustrating for mature adults studying an L2. Such people are used to conveying information, opinions, attitudes and most importantly of all, self, through L1. The most intimate elements — attitude and self—are conveyed linguistically by making an appropriate rather than merely accurate choice, and by **how** something is said, rather than **what** is said. If mature adults are to feel comfortable in the comparatively early stages of L2, material and classroom activities must be directed towards register and intonation; these cannot be relegated to the later stages of learning when students have 'mastered the basics of what they want to say'. For many students, particularly those using L2 in the work place, expressing attitude can be at least as important as ability to convey basic information or opinion.

Syllabuses are directed towards language teaching, but ultimately it is not languages which are being taught, but people. People want and need to express emotion and attitude. It is a challenge to language teachers to ensure that they provide even elementary students with at least limited linguistic resources to express these important parts of life.

It will be noted that the three spectra discussed above covertly or overtly emphasise the centrality of lexis to communication, and constantly give a high value to the earlier acquisition of a large vocabulary, and the central role of students developing a large vocabulary of **verbs**. Language teachers, usually accidentally, see vocabulary largely in terms of nouns (see page 103), and the teaching of verbs has largely been confined to work on their structure. The areas of intersection of the three spectra, Generative Power, Generalisability, and Communicative Power — will largely, though not exclusively, be filled by an increased awareness of verbs as lexical rather than structural items. It also means restoring the Present Simple to the central role in English which it naturally possesses in most natural text.

4. The Spectrum of Likelihood

Teachers and students would like language to be a matter of certainty — *Is .. correct English?* Instant unpopularity is available to anyone who answers *It depends,* or *I'm not sure, it sounds a bit odd.* There is a temptation to describe language using the right/wrong polarity. This is an over-simplification which ignores the flexibility of the language, creativity of its users and the restrictive nature of evidence upon which we usually base assertions of what is, or is not possible. MacAndrew[1] makes a valuable point:

> I recorded (these three) examples because I thought they were deviant. In fact when I came to look at them more closely and checked the authorities, I found that they were not that unusual at all. It was my own inexperience or ignorance. If you come across a piece of language that seems strange, you should first check. It might well be quite acceptable, even quite likely, but merely outside the realm of your experience.

The warning is: *I have never met it* is not synonymous with *That is not possible, natural English.*

There is such a degree of unanimity about some language that we may, as shorthand, refer to it as 'correct' or 'standard' English. Similarly, some language is so unorthodox that, as shorthand, we may refer to it as 'wrong'. Once again, however, these are extreme examples, two polarities. Much language cannot be so decisively categorised, and can be seen only in terms of more or less likely, represented on a **Spectrum of Likelihood**.

It may be useful to tell students that *weather* is usually uncountable in English; it may even be useful, for some advanced students, to draw attention to the (exceptional) lexical item *in all weathers.* It is not, however, the case that *weather* cannot be used countably as this extract from the Observer of the 21st August 1988 clearly shows:

> EL HIERRO is peaceful, smiling, alive with pleasurable surprises and totally unspoilt. Very small (30 miles at its longest, 10 at its widest), it feels, to the visitor, as big as a continent because of the numerous landscapes and weathers contained within its jagged coastline.

If teachers see language in absolute right/wrong terms, such examples which are very numerous are confusing and embarrassing. If they see language in terms of a Spectrum of Likelihood, there is no difficulty.

I sincerely hope that increased awareness of language flexibility and the creativity of its native speakers would also have an important pedagogical implication — that teachers should be more tolerant of the language produced by their (usually intermediate) students. A student who volunteers *We had an awful weather* yesterday has produced successful, communicatively powerful language. If native speakers can produce countable *weathers,* it is curiously inconsistent to regard such use as 'a serious mistake' when produced by an intermediate student. Accepting a Spectrum of Likelihood can be both linguistically and pedagogically liberating.

5. Spectrum of Acceptability

The right/wrong dichotomy can usefully be replaced by a Spectrum of Likelihood, but other considerations may apply to the language classroom. Students may produce language which is incorrect, but represents a realistic, or even brave, attempt at a particular stage in their learning programme. For motivational and psychological reasons teachers would be wise to accept such language and, perhaps while reformulating, definitely to avoid formal correction. As Karl-Heinz Ribisch reminded me, however, many teachers within state school systems are required to evaluate their students' performance not only in terms of its formal correctness, but also in relation to an official syllabus, and what constitutes 'a reasonable performance' at different stages of a student's school career. What the teacher accepts at one stage, may become unacceptable at another stage, for extra-linguistic considerations, relating to the educational system. Teachers working within formal systems need to employ criteria more complex than the simple right/wrong dichotomy; they need to consider specifically linguistic criteria, and, however regrettable this may be, the formal demands of the syllabus or system. They need what we may call a **Spectrum of Acceptability**. The development of the criteria for such a Spectrum could prove highly contentious, and will certainly differ in relation to the socio-political and educational objectives of different systems. From a theoretical point of view, the Spectrum of Likelihood should be **one** of the factors which informs the Spectrum of Acceptability.

6. Spectrum of Conventionality

All language is in a sense arbitrary. There is no reason why the signifier *dog* signifies a particular kind of animal, it is simply a matter of convention. In this highly abstract sense, all language is conventional. While true, this matter scarcely affects language teachers and learners at all.

On the other hand, some language is much more a matter of convention than other language — we refer here not to social convention or what is usually called politeness, but linguistic convention. Many millions of people in the world speak one or more languages, while remaining completely unable to read or write at all. In this important sense, spoken language is natural, and immediate in a way that written language is not. Writing is characteristic of a relatively late stage in human cultural development. In all societies which possess a writing system, writing is prestigious and often intimately associated with the religious or civil authorities. Written language often serves different purposes from spoken language, in particular when precision and durability in space and time are essential. Writing is essentially less bound to the circumstances of its production. Opportunity to disambiguate is frequently absent, so, to maximise the possibility of precise de-coding more (and different) conventions need to apply to written than to spoken language.

Acquiring the ability to understand and speak your mother tongue seems to be as natural a part of normal human development as learning to walk. Reading, however, is much less naturally picked up and needs to be taught. Many, perhaps even most, people never acquire the ability to write fluently and well, even in their mother tongue. It appears that the written language is, in important senses, 'more difficult' than the spoken language. Motherese (the language used by parents and others to infants) is invariably spoken, and almost invariably intrinsically associated to the moment of language use. It is a well known feature of child development that phrases such as *tomorrow* or *in a minute* are not comprehensible to the child until a certain point in their psychological development. Spoken language, which is about Here-and-Now, is more easily understood than spoken language where the reference frame is other than Here-and-Now. It is also easier than **any** form of written language. The essentially deictic nature of spoken language makes it less conventional than the intrinsically portable written language. Despite this obvious **Spectrum of Conventionality,** which implies the relative abstraction and consequent relative difficulty of the written language, the influence of the written language in language teaching remains powerful. It seems reasonable to suggest that by emphasising highly abstract, conventionalised forms, teachers frequently make their students' learning tasks more difficult.

7. Spectrum of Categorisation

In the introduction to her splendid grammar of English (*Current English Grammar, MacMillan*) Chalker[2] says:

> Some explanations are more satisfactory than others, but not even word classes are clear-cut or self-evident, while what is grammatically possible and what is grammatically impossible often converge in an uncertain grey area.

We have already seen that what is, or is not possible is a matter of degree or likelihood rather than absolute fact. The same qualification applies when we try to group words or structures in useful categories. If we try to make the categorisation rigid and decisive, it can only be done at the expense of ignoring or distorting data. The problem is essentially one of grey areas and fuzziness. *Blind* is usually an adjective, *business* is usually a noun but both of the following are wholly natural, unexceptional uses: *Deaf people have received more consideration under the present policy than the blind. Economic activity has increased under this government, but business confidence has declined.*

It may seem that this abstract question of categorisation is a long way from the classroom, but it does have important pedagogical implications. Words in English are exceptionally mobile, able to move from word category to word category very freely; in particular, nouns can readily be used in adjectival or verbal (to do with the verb) functions. Noun-noun collocations are powerful carriers of meaning: *Pet shop, oil prices, New Year bargain prices.* Pedagogically, if students learn words as belonging to a particular category, they may well not see, and be unwilling to experiment with, the kind of flexible categorisation which maximises communicative power.

This last point returns us to the key issue — no change in terminology is, of itself, important. The purpose is to help teachers to break from the conceptual restrictions that false dichotomies impose. Our search for a Lexical Approach based on communicative power, will be aided by seeing certain important concepts as represented on clines or spectra rather than in absolute terms.

PART 2 — Non-Linear Concepts

There are some advantages in developing particular ideas so that they can be seen on a scale or spectrum, rather than a simple opposition; the concepts, however, remain essentially linear. Some terms central to our later discussion are different in kind, and any linear reduction of them distorts in unhelpful ways.

1. Level is non-linear

Faced with a new book, a teacher typically asks *What level is it?* They appear to expect an answer which relates the book to their normal working environment which itself is based on an arbitrary number of different 'levels'. The question is meaningless. The acquisition of a foreign language is far too complex a phenomenon to be expressed on a single linear scale; it is an essentially muti-dimensional idea. Particular students' English may improve in many different ways, but not all will be revealed by any test or battery of tests however complicated. Improved scores on a test show only that the student has improved in areas which have been tested. Regrettably, some widely-used tests seem to inhibit rather than encourage a long-term improvement in language ability. Any realistic view of level involves at least the following:

a. Range or Depth? Students can either become able to do **more** things, or **better** able to do a **restricted** range of things. There is something to be said for seeing several Shakespeare plays, and something to be said for a careful, extended reading of one; both could contribute to a greater understanding and appreciation of Shakespeare's work. So with language learning, imperfect mastery over a wide range may be more useful to one student, while greater accuracy in a very particular field may be more appropriate to another. Such considerations are widely recognised in the world of business English teaching for adults. The choice is (inevitably) much less conscious in thinking of state school students but even there there are two distinct, and to some extent, conflicting ways of improving.

b. Receptive language or productive language? Most students can understand more than they can say, so there is a tendency to assume their receptive level is above their productive level. Many students, however, faced with reading for academic purposes, or listening to lectures, find that the opposite is true — they can survive in normal conversation, but the level of their receptive skills is inadequate for the new purposes to which they wish to put them. Most language testing is, quite naturally, testing productive language, so it can come as a surprise to students to realise that their receptive skills are severely defective.

c. Content or skill? A student's level is partly defined by the language content of the material which he or she has mastered but language is not used divorced from purpose (except in language classes!). Recognition of the importance of skills is reflected in their inclusion as part of the multi-syllabus of many course books, but I harbour considerable doubt at the extent to which teachers consider skills rather than intrinsic language when they ask the 'level' of a piece of material.

d. What is 'advanced' language? Perhaps a class of zero beginners are truly 'all at the same level', though even this is doubtful in the modern world where some accidental exposure to English is almost inevitable. For all other classes, the idea that all the students are 'at the same level' is clearly an illusion. Almost all language learners are intermediate. Frequently this concept is sub-divided into pre-intermediate, intermediate, post-intermediate. However necessary schools may find this double-talk, in some sense it is a vacuous concept — the students know something, but not everything, and we are not quite sure what. Unquestionably true, and equally unquestionably unhelpful.

The problem with the concept of 'level' is clarified by considering what content we might consider appropriate for a student who is deemed 'advanced'. Much so-called advanced teaching is in fact specialised teaching, in terms either of language or skills. Many private language schools run similar, specialised courses for students whose language level is far from advanced, so the equation advanced = specialised does not hold. If the equation is not *advanced = specialised*, observation of language teaching texts suggests the equation is *advanced = obscure*, but fluent educated native speakers do not pepper their conversation with words such as *mendacity* and *somnambulist*. (Both taken from a recent 'advanced vocabulary' book.) Advanced grammar is no more clear. How many readers would feel comfortable saying *Were you to ask me, ...* or *Should you need any help, don't hesitate to ask*. Are those 'advanced structures' or just the kind of language used by a particular kind of person to express pomposity and pretentiousness? If so, perhaps an advanced textbook doesn't need different language, but rather different functions: *Sounding pretentious, fulminating effectively, expressing shades of irritation*. If this appears unnecessarily facetious, it is an idea with sound credentials. In *Notional Syllabuses,* Wilkins advocates:

> The labelling of the learning units at the highest and lowest levels may be largely the same and indeed at intermediate levels the same units continue hierarchically to provide increasing expressive range. The learner is thus recycled through units with similar denominations but with greater rhetorical range. (page 59).

He illustrates by reference to a list of exponents associated with the function *seeking permission*. The list ranges through sixteen numbered items, many of which contain internal optional brackets. The following appear:

1. O.K.?
    Alright?
    Any objections?
    } (All accompanied by an appropriate gesture, e.g. lifting the telephone)

3. Please let me use your telephone?

5. Will you let me use your telephone, if I pay for the call?

9. I request that I be allowed to use your telephone.

14. Would it be too much to ask if I could use your telephone?
16. I should be most grateful if you would permit me to use your telephone.

Reflecting on Wilkins' list, as a fluent educated native speaker, I am a little surprised to find that I appear to be somewhere between levels 3 and 5.

The Cobuild project has contributed enormously to our knowledge of natural language use. In the *Cobuild English Grammar Exercises* (page 41) Shaw invites the student to list four different ways of, for example, asking someone if you can make a phone call or offering someone a cup of tea. The implication seems to be that level involves knowing **more** ways of saying the same thing. This is unsatisfactory, for if they are pure synonyms there is little point in learning more than one, and if they are not, it is precisely the **differences** between them which matter.

e. Different kinds of content. Some kinds of content are intrinsically easier to express than others. We can readily identify at least four: **fact, opinion, attitude and self.** Very approximately, and with a large degree of overlap, this sequence expresses the relative difficulty. It is comparatively easy to exchange information, more subtle to show opinion, and even more difficult to indicate the attitude we have towards the opinion or fact we express. Lexis, structure and intonation interact in highly complex ways — certainly in ways which are much more complex than any linear sequence of structure or vocabulary could express. Many language learners are at least unconsciously aware of one of the most profound difficulties involved in language learning — one of the primary purposes of language is to allow us to express our personalities and ultimately **ourselves.** Inability to do this inhibits many learners who can convey fact and opinion, but only in a way which they feel conflicts with their self-projection. This entirely holistic perception of language ability is of great importance to the psychology of learning, but can in no way be accommodated on a linear model. Newmark[3] takes such a holistic view when he says: *An important test of our success as language teachers, it seems reasonable to assert, is the ability of our students to choose to say what they want.*

f. Successful communication. Language is most adequately assessed on a scale of communicatively successful/ unsuccessful, rather than right/wrong. At least four factors contribute to effective communication: **fluency, confidence, imagination and accuracy.** On all known methods of teaching and learning, accuracy is the last objective to be fully achieved. It is therefore surprising that it is frequently put as an early, or even primary objective in language learning. Once again building-brick, behaviourist views inhibit. Students can improve their language performance, and pragmatic effectiveness, by improving **any** or **all** of the features just mentioned. A student who needs to give a presentation in English may benefit more from classroom work which increases confidence and fluency rather than accuracy; another person, who feels embarrassed by mistakes, may base their confidence on accuracy, in which case different classroom strategies will be appropriate. 'Improvement' means different things to different students, and to different teachers. A consciousness of the multi-dimensional nature of level and improvement allows the teacher to pursue a range of options, rather than being restricted by any linear sequence.

2. Difficulty is non-linear

The difficulty of much language material is intrinsic to it; short texts of simple sentences are intrinsically easier than long texts consisting of sentences with embedded clauses. Similarly, some tasks performed with language are intrinsically more difficult than others, often for social rather than strictly linguistic reasons. Another factor, however, affects the difficulty of language teaching material — the design of those materials. Regrettably, many exercises are made more difficult because they are badly, or even perversely, designed. While language puzzles may have a role to play in teaching, exercises should not be constructed **as** puzzles simply to make them more difficult. A recent advanced vocabulary book asked the students to add two letters at any place in each of the following to form a new word using the clue: AGE (keen); ALE (part of the body). The answers are *eager* and *ankle*. The exercise is quite difficult, but the language practised is trivial. This is not advanced, but perverse. Can you identify the following sentences, from which the vowels have been omitted: WHTTMSTPLS? FSHRLLSKHR?

It is relatively easy to see the first sentence is *What time is it please?* The second, *If I see her, I'll ask her* baffles most people because one of the omitted words consists **only** of a vowel, and others **begin** with vowels. The second example is a great deal more difficult than the first, but only because of the poor construction of the example. Sadly, in my experience it is not unusual for teachers writing their own excercises to deliberately try to trick students in this way.

More seriously, many of the fill-in and even Cloze practices found in books are rendered unnecessarily difficult through thoughtless, inappropriate or perverse deletions. The basic construction of most English text moves from known to unknown material. Unsurprisingly, if early items are deleted the student must read the whole sentence, and mentally return to the beginning, reconstructing a thought-train backwards. This is unnatural, and although it is more difficult than an exercise based on deletion of early items, there seems no pedagogical justification for obliging students to engage in the necessary mental gymnastics. If this difficulty were confined to puzzle-like activities it would be unimportant. Unfortunately, it is common in supposedly serious, clearly focussed language practices. Consider the following examples:

Complete each of the following sentences with a phrasal verb using *down*:

1a. We . . . . on the motorway, that's why we are late.
2a. Don't . . . . the difficulties — the problem is more serious than you are admitting.
3a. I . . . . with a cold last week, so I was off work for a few days.

1b. Sorry we're late, but I'm afraid we . . . . on the motorway.
2b. The problem is more serious than you are admitting — there is no point in . . . . the difficulties.
3b. I had to have a few days off work last week, I wasn't very well. I . . . . with a cold.

The first three examples are more difficult than the second, simply because the deletion occurs relatively near the beginning; the whole context has to be grasped before any prediction can be made. When the context is clearly established first, although the language level is identical, the exercise is easier. Anyone who writes exercises — textbook writer or teacher, needs a clear understanding of the nature of text, and context (see page 103) if they are to avoid making exercises more difficult without making them more advanced.

3. Syllabus is non-linear

In the restricted definition we have given for this term, syllabus refers to the content of a learning programme. Typically, in addition to content, most syllabuses specify sequence. As such, they are intrinsically linked to the concept of level. The multi-dimensional nature of level, necessarily implies a multi-dimensionality of syllabus. This is reflected in many modern textbooks, particularly those associated with Swan and Walters, which explicitly claim to be based on 'a multi-syllabus approach'. Chapter 6 will discuss syllabuses much more extensively. Here it is sufficient to note that no step-by-step linear syllabus can be remotely adequate.

4. Discourse is non-linear

Much language teaching is based on the study of isolated sentences, but naturally occurring language only very rarely occurs in this form. Typically, language occurs as part of discourse — extended printed text, conversations, lectures, jokes, novels etc. None of these naturally occurring text-types is linear. Nattinger and DeCarrico[4], discussing the use of what they call macro-organizers have this to say:

> Up to this point, macro-organizers have been analysed as though they appeared in linear order in a discourse. Transactional discourse, however, whether spoken or written, does not typically proceed in a linear fashion.

Neither encoding — speaking or writing — nor decoding — understanding the spoken language or reading — proceed in a linear fashion. We do not process discourse word-by-word. If I wish to ask my wife about the children, so produce the sentence *Have the children . . . ,* it is clear that even though I produce the plural verb form first, it 'agrees' with the plural subject only because some holistic conception of the sentence must have preceded my uttering the first word. Similarly, if you read the following: *As soon as I read . . .* there is an ambiguity which is retrospectively disambiguated after reading the following *. . . I knew/I am reminded . . . .* Cloze procedures sometimes permit forward prediction, and sometimes require retrospective adjustment, a feature which arises because of the non-linear nature of discourse.

Discourse differs from a mere sequence of sentences precisely in that organising principles at a higher level are at work. Although this matter may appear rather theoretical, it has important implications for both syllabus and classroom procedures if students are to be helped to both decode and encode efficiently. Students confronted by holistic tasks such as understanding a lecture or writing an essay will find these difficult if their teaching has been primarily based on the study and production of individual sentences.

4. Formality is non-linear

There is a tendency among teachers, and even reference books, to label language more or less formal, or more or less polite. As far as reference works are concerned, this is to some extent inevitable but teachers should recognise that the formal/informal or more/less polite terminology is again an over-simplification.

Which is 'more polite' *Would you like some more tea?* or *More tea?* The question is, of course, meaningless as asked — formality or politeness does not inhere in language. It depends upon **who** says it, **to whom** and with what **intention.** Both formality and politeness are multi-dimensional. The complex of ideas which lies behind what linguists call 'appropriacy' is common to all known language communities, though of course linguistic realisations of, for example, superior/inferior relationships, or neutral versus insistant language differ from language to language.

Learners have an innate awareness that different language is appropriate depending on situation, participants and intention. In those circumstances, it is regrettable if teachers reduce language explanations to the banal and untrue by using such shorthand as '*Could* is more polite than *can.*'

The exponents suggested by Wilkins in *Notional Syllabuses* suggest 'more formal' or 'more polite' means longer. This is untrue, but not an unusual belief. Too often, 'advanced' is equated with obscure or convoluted. The Lexical Approach suggests that increasing competence and communicative power are achieved by extending the students' repertoire of lexical phrases, collocational power, and increasing mastery of the most basic words and structures of the language. It is simply not the case that 'advanced' users of the language use ever more complex sentence structures.

5. Meaning is multi-dimensional

Chapter 4 will explore different kinds of meaning and their relevance to language teaching and methodology. Here I wish only to establish one very basic point — meaning is a multi-faceted idea, another non-linear concept. Some words carry more meaning than others — they are semantically weaker or stronger. This has important consequences for syllabus and methodology. Oral practices can be more or less meaningful, and meaningful in different ways. This has implications for the kind of language practice which is consistent with the Lexical Approach.

Most importantly of all, understanding is not a binary, *Yes/No* concept; more or less meaning is created by an inter-personal process of interpretation, negotiation and response. Those very words reveal the multi-faceted nature of the concept of meaning. Primitive classroom procedures (*What does ... mean? Let's look at the comprehension questions*) diminish what is most central to language — meaning. The Lexical Approach is based on recognition of the centrality and multi-faceted nature of meaning.

PART 3 — Aspects of Language

Language lies at the very heart of the way we identify and express ourselves. Without language there would be no coherent thought, and human society could not evolve. Language allows us to cope with the world, and even to control others. Not surprisingly, it can be a very emotive topic. Here are some quotations — how do you react to them? Do you agree or disagree? Do you perhaps find some of them mysterious or annoying? Which do you think have any relevance for language teachers, or even students of a second language?

Without language we would not be able to think.

A language expresses a culture.

Language is power.

A language is a dialect with an army.

Language is essentially instrumental.

Language arises only from social interaction.

Humanity is diminished if minority languages are allowed to die out.

English is becoming the world language.

Written language is not spoken language written down.

In a literate society, we tend not to take the spoken language seriously.

More viewers complain about bad language than violence on television.

Non-native speakers should learn to speak **with** natives, but not **like** natives.

As the range of quotations clearly illustrates, our attitude to language enters almost every corner of our personal, social, educational and political life. We may see language in at least four different ways, as:

— An idealised system
— A practical skill
— A personal asset
— A means of exercising control

This list is in no sense comprehensive, but immediately suggests several important perspectives.

1. Idealised System

Language may be seen in very abstract terms, as in Chomsky's idea of competence. Language as system, particularly grammar system, remains the basis for many state school syllabuses. Language is assumed to be a body of knowledge, to be mastered. Brumfit, in a telling phrase, has pointed out that English as an idealised system means that even the most proficient L2 learner is on a 'deficit curriculum', where emphasis is always on what the learner **cannot** do. Many teachers, particularly non-natives whose own English is excellent, tend to be preoccupied by the deficiencies in their students' English. Covertly, they treat English as an abstract, idealised system to be mastered. Such a view of language is seriously inhibiting to successful language learning.

2. Practical Skill

Language is essentially for use, a means to an end, not an end in itself. In the modern world English is rapidly becoming the lingua franca needed by many for purely practical purposes. For many people, even highly deficient English is useful, or even essential. If language is conceived as a skill, the criteria for evaluating it become very different — it is successful communication rather than conformity with the code which assumes paramount importance.

There is a considerable body of literature on skills training from other fields. If we conceive of language as skill, this literature can contribute useful strategies for the language classroom.

3. Personal Asset

Language is an important tool of self-definition, a powerful creator of identity, whether national or individual. Within the European context, most countries have 'a language problem', where the preservation or active use of a language has enormous symbolic value, so powerful that in some cases it is closely associated with civil disobedience and even terrorism.

Within this wider, social context, a centrally imposed language, or language norms can be seen in terms of political power or cultural imperialism. Socio-political considerations of this kind are important in considering the kind of English which is the target, or goal for non-native learners. Mutual intelligibility is obviously necessary, but this can too easily move into an assertion that non-native speakers should not only be able to speak **to** native speakers, they should also speak **like** native speakers. As we shall see below, native-speaker-like ability is not a well-defined concept, and begs more questions than it answers. A tiny number of non-native users of English will achieve, and wish to achieve native-like proficiency, but these will be exceptions. Native-speaker-like ability may be a model but it is very rarely a target. Abbott[5] endorses this view in these words:

> If international — perhaps even national inter-ethnic — intelligibility is to be achieved and maintained, there will need to be some kind of common model. Since the standard Englishes of Canada, U.S.A., U.K., Australia and New Zealand maintain a high degree of mutual intelligibility, any one of them is suitable as a model, none being subject to strong mother tongue interference. It should be stressed that the chosen standard will be a model, not a goal.

Teachers need to be sensitive at all times to the fact that learners can use English for instrumental purposes, without in any sense wishing to become British, Australian, American or whatever. They may wish to acquire English as an additional personal asset, without allowing this to effect any change in their social and cultural identity.

4. Personal Identity

In addition to social identity, language is the primary means for our own personal self-definition. The language we use helps other people, and most importantly ourselves, to understand who and what we perceive ourselves to be. Eric Heffer, veteran left-wing M.P., was described as a man 'whose political vocabulary remains resolutely the same'. Nigel Kennedy, a gifted classical violinist who refused to conform to the image of a classical musician describes his own confusion:

> At one point I was like a cameleon. If I was eating at Chequers or Downing Street I would talk in one way; and when I was with my friends I would talk in another way. I am now stuck in a language where I feel comfortable.

Though definition of this kind, is centred primarily in our mother tongue, it applies also to second or subsequent languages. Knowledge of a foreign language can, in a few cases, allow an individual to be a fully integrated member of a society different from the one they were born in. While this is rare, many people have learned a foreign language and find that the ability to use it genuinely enriches their lives — they can talk to more people, visit more places, get a better job, enjoy new literature and genuinely feel themselves more fulfilled as individuals. Few subjects on the school timetable have the potential to make such a contribution to the student's life.

Language helps us to define who we are, but this presents an immense challenge to language teachers. Ultimately, the language each of us uses is our own, but it is derived from the language of others around us, in particular the language presented by our teachers. For the teacher, the language you are teaching to students is **your** language, but ultimately if you are successful, the language the student uses will be uniquely **his or her own**.

In the hurly-burly of the classroom it is easy to lose sight of these larger issues, but it is almost certainly true that an opportunity for real personal development is being lost every time a teacher emphasises language as system rather than practical skill or personal resource.

5. Language as Coping

Language does not exist in a vacuum. People use it, as a means to an end, to achieve particular purposes. The range of purposes is enormous, coincident with what it means to be human. Examples of purposes achieved through a language include the transactional (buying a train ticket), emotional (expressing anger), creative (writing or reading a poem), but they all have one thing in common. They mediate the relationship between the language user and the external world. Language allows us to express, and thereby cope with, many of our human needs. Nothing could illustrate more powerfully the multi-dimensional nature of language than the central fact that it empowers the user.

Summary

The primary purpose of language is the creation and exchange of meaning. Basic, or proto-language essentially involves nominalisation — naming of concepts — and is lexical rather than grammatical. Language consists of grammaticalised lexis, not lexicalised grammar. It is necessary to repeat this leitmotif precisely because it conflicts so starkly with much received opinion and practice about language teaching.

Language sometimes appears in textbooks purely for the purposes of exemplification; this is language confined to signification and usage. All naturally occurring language, however, exhibits a range of features among which we can usefully list:

Spontaneous	Immediate	Contextualised
Individual	Interpersonal	Interactive
Holistic	Purposive	Organic

Any course which does not adequately reflect these features is severely defective.

A metaphor of language

In an important analysis of the nature of the acquisition of the grammar of a second language, Rutherford attempts to revolutionise the metaphor which underlies our perception of the nature of language. He describes the standard view in these terms[6]:

> We tend to think of a language as somehow 'put together' and that to know something of how it 'works' we have to 'take it apart'. Language professionals find it useful and convenient to try to understand the nature of language by unravelling it, disassembling it. We break language down in order to build it up, and we call the resultant debris 'building blocks'. The very terminology that we employ in analysing and describing language, in other words, reveals that our general concept, at least to some extent, is one in which language is a complex thing with many edges, with attached and moving parts — that is, a *machine*.

His alternative metaphor is quite different[7]:

> There is another side to language that is not very machine-like at all. Language is constantly in the act of change and growth, whether it is the historical development of a language over a time span measured in millennia or in 'historical' development of an idiolect from the age of two to five. Growth of course is quite unmachine-like, or alien to that which we can conceive of in purely mechanical terms. The apt descriptive term for 'growth' then is not 'mechanic' but 'organic'. Thus, although language has characteristics that lend themselves to the 'machine' metaphor, it has a great deal to it that also suggests very aptly the metaphor of *organism*.

The shift of metaphor is important. An organism grows holistically, not linearly. It develops, rather than being built. Most importantly, the totality is much greater than any assembly of the supposed constituent parts.

Rutherford develops the 'language as organism' metaphor fully and rigorously. The shift of metaphor is a powerful example of the importance of work in applied linguistics making a valuable contribution to potential classroom procedure by encouraging a fundamental shift in the teacher's mind-set.

Native speaker English

Consider the following sentences. Can you imagine yourself saying them, not as examples in a language lesson, but as a natural part of your own daily life?

That's a bloody silly suggestion.
My aunt passed away over the weekend.
That problem is outwith my remit at this stage.

That's not a road I want to go down.
The approach is existential, rather than metaphysical.
We wasn't even there.

There can be no doubt at all that all these are natural, native speaker sentences. Many readers, however, including native speakers will have rejected more sentences than they have accepted as part of their own English. Many factors influence the language used by a particular individual — region, cliché, taboo words, education, and the more difficult to define but important *I don't talk like that.*

Every native speaker in an entire life time uses only a small percentage of the vast unrealised potential which is 'the English language'. For all that, many language teachers would like to talk about the language of the educated native speaker, whom I have christened the dreaded Edna, as if this was a well-defined and useful concept. Many non-natives of my acquaintance speak English which is closer in general style and content to my own than the correspondence between my English and that of many native speakers. This may be largely a matter of education, but is also influenced by job, interests, social attitudes, and many other factors. Regrettably, in my opinion, even highly competent non-natives tend to defer in matter of linguistic judgement to native speakers on the precise ground that they **are** native speakers. This is a mistake; it is certainly not the case that native speakers are always the best judge of what is, and is not possible or likely in their own language — even the dreaded Edna may be socially and linguistically insensitive, or just plain unobservant. Educated non-natives, who have studied English objectively and are interested in the subject must have the confidence to recognise that their introspective judgements are as valid and well-based as those of many, if not most, native speakers. Too often they under-value their own vast linguistic experience because they perceive it as falling short of some abstract, and wholly unattainable ideal.

On a practical level, if mutual intelligibility is to be a criterion, there is a strong case to be made for native speakers learning something about English as a foreign language. Many natives, particularly perhaps those who use English in the business community, are stunningly insensitive to the fact that English as used by native speakers to native speakers is, in world terms, a rather specialised idiom. English is no longer the possession or preserve of its native speakers. It is rapidly becoming the world's *lingua franca*. Native speakers and non-native speakers alike have differing degrees of ability to use the language more or less effectively in a narrower or wider range of situations. The distinction is not essentially between native and non-native users, but between different levels of linguistic competence *per se*. The non-native may need to become accustomed to understanding language used **by** native speakers **for** native speakers; some non-natives may want or need the ability to speak **to** native speakers even if not **like** native speakers; a minute percentage may learn to speak English **like** a native, though even they will not use it **as** a native. The native speaker has one single advantage over the non-native — greater exposure to the language. That is unquestionably a small objective advantage. In many situations other factors are of equal or greater importance. For the foreign teacher a realistic awareness of their own ability in English — including any possible limitations — is a help; any instinctive feeling of inferiority to Edna is counter-productive.

In the modern world, English is the way the world communicates. This means increasing numbers of non-native speakers use it more and more widely. It also implies that its native speaker users must become increasingly aware of, and able to communicate effectively with, the vastly more numerous group of users of English as a second or foreign language.

First and second languages

Almost everyone is able to speak at least one language, their mother tongue. Chomsky has argued that a language acquisition device is innate, and certainly the evidence suggests that human beings who do not suffer from a mental disorder acquire one language comparatively effortlessly, and over a relatively short period of time. Does this imply that learning a second or subsequent language (L2) is a similarly straightforward task? If so, why does language teaching engage in some of its present contortions? If not, how is second language acquisition different? Strongly held views on this topic are common, but reliable evidence is difficult to come by. Firstly, we note that Ellis, in his survey *Understanding Second Language Acquisition (1985)*, observes[8]:

> Second language acquisition refers to all aspects of language that the language learner needs to master. However, the focus has been on how L2 learners acquire grammatical sub-systems, such as negatives or interrogatives or grammatical morphemes such as the plural **-s** or the definite and indefinite articles. Research has tended to ignore other levels of language. A little is known about L2 phonology, but almost nothing about the acquisition of lexis.

Two points may be made:

a. It is intrinsically more likely that L2 acquisition is **similar** to L1 acquisition, rather than that the two should be totally distinct processes.

b. Although the two processes are probably similar, they cannot be **identical,** precisely because a second language is involved.

In acquiring L1, the learner must relate language items in precisely two ways, externally to the real world, or internally to other items of L1. Self-evidently, many lexical items will have meaning attributed to them through ostensive definition, through a relationship of the signifier to the real-world signified. Acquisition of the sub-systems of the language (what is roughly thought of as 'the grammar') will be acquired partly through existential, deictic realisation of meaning, and partly by an increasingly developed awareness of the system of internal contrasts within L1.

For the L2 learner, part of the 'out-there real world' is the pre-existent knowledge of L1. In acquiring L2, therefore, L2 items may be directly related to the real world, and an increasing awareness of L2/L2 contrast can develop so that L2 acquisition resembles L1 acquisition. On the other hand, L2 can also be related to L1, in ways that are either positively helpful or confusing. In this important way L2 acquisition must differ from L1 acquisition.

A moment's introspection into the interlanguage of an L2 learner rev
it exhibits precisely the characteristics we would expect if the three p
were involved. It is possible to be able to name an object, or perform a
pragmatic function in L2 which lies outside your L1 repertoire, so it is
possible to relate L2 directly to the real world. The fact that an L2 can be
mastered clearly indicates the role of the developing perception of L2/L2
contrasts. The role of interference — both structural and in the form of
lexical false friends — is also well recognised. One important shift of
emphasis, however, is that the terminology here — interference — carries an
intrinsically negative connotation. This is unfortunate, as students are as
likely to draw **successful** inferences by referring L2 to L1 as they are to draw
unsuccessful ones. The student's L1 is as much a resource as any other aspect
of the student's real world knowledge; attempting to marginalise it, or reduce
its role is both impossible and undesirable.

Almost everyone acquires L1 'naturally'; many people have successfully
acquired an L2 in precisely the same way, so such a process is clearly
possible. Most second language acquisition, however, occurs in classrooms.
Very often this has resulted in over emphasising the **differences** between L2
and L1 acquisition. There is a substantial case for making language use in the
classroom resemble, rather than be different from, 'real' language use.

PART 4 — Aspects of Learning

Learning is a process, non-linear in character. Whatever you are learning —
how to ride a horse, French, gardening — you do not make progress through
a series of instant, irreversible steps. In this respect, learning makes a
mockery of teaching which often claims to aid learning precisely by selecting
and sequencing the subject matter into small, manageable steps.

Reflect, for a moment, on two learning experiences of your own, one
connected with a foreign language, the other with a quite different topic,
subject or skill. Do you recognise the following features of learning as
intrinsic to both experiences:

Planned/unplanned	Overt/covert	Conscious/unconscious
Receptive	Experimental	Reflective
Experimental	Provisional	Cyclical
Individual	Holistic	Involving

Many of these features are in no need of further explanation, but a few
comments may help:

a. Sometimes you try hard, but cannot learn; at other times, things seem to
come automatically, without effort.

b. All learning, by definition, comes from outside ourselves but it is
frequently not enough to be told something, or even for something to
happen. True learning seems to result from a continuous symbiotic
relationship between experience, reflection on that experience, and eventual
holistic internalisation of it.

c. All knowledge is, in an important sense, an illusion. Learning is essentially provisional and cyclical, based on endlessly repeating the cycle Observe (O) — Hypothesise (H) — Experiment (E). This O-H-E learning paradigm contrasts sharply with the misguided P-P-P paradigm which still influences language teaching.

d. Learning is essentially organic and involves connecting new material to what is already known, by extending or adapting previously perceived knowledge. This process may not be obviously active, but it is essential that you are both cognitively and emotionally involved. (Cognitive and emotional involvement can, of course, also inhibit or prevent learning. The learner can object, intellectually or emotionally, to new material or new experiences in such a way as to render them alien and subjectively useless).

e. Different learners make differential use of the same material or experience. For intellectual or emotional reasons they prove more or less able to integrate new material into the totality of their present knowledge.

A great deal is known about teaching, and teacher behaviour, much less about learning. What is clear is that learning is not a simple, linear irreversible process. It is more elusive, provisional, holistic and individual than is convenient for teachers. In this respect some of the characteristic features of learning reflect the characteristic features of language.

The list above was prepared from a methodological perspective. Encouragingly, it reflects many of the items listed by Rutherford[9] working from a linguistic point of view. He contrasts the mechanic and organic views and in addition to the points listed above, draws attention to the following contrasts which endorse, overlap with, or develop my own list:

Mechanic	Organic
Grammar as an end	Grammar as a means
Exhaustive	Selective
Agglutination	Fusion
Increasing complexity	Progressive re-analysis
Speeding up (time needed for production)	Slowing down (time needed for reflection)
Cadential (lock-step learning)	Chaotic (differential learning)

Paradoxically, this list is at the centre of Rutherford's argument for a grammar-centred approach — but self-evidently he uses this term to mean something very different from the traditional, mechanical-grammar view. He highlights the paradox himself: *Though it may seem paradoxical, what is to be taught in the kind of grammar-centred approach we have been discussing is not grammar at all.*

If learners are actually 'taught' anything, we would have to say that they are taught 'how to learn' or, better still, 'how to manage their own learning'. Rutherford's argument for a grammar-centred approach is thus also learner-centred, and supports, and largely reflects, the emphasis on grammar as a receptive skill which is consistent with the Lexical Approach.

Finally, we should recall that in contrast to learning, teaching is frequently:

> Linearly organised   Uni-directional   Selective
> Decontexualised   Unspontaneous   Teacher-centred

Of course teaching cannot be completely spontaneous, random and based on the whims of the moment. Every teacher who has given a completely un-prepared class admits that, despite occasional successes, it is not the best way to proceed on a regular basis. Teachers must choose what to put in and what to leave out, decide in advance some sort of teaching sequence, and recognise the artificial nature of the classroom. But good teachers use these factors as a flexible framework not a straightjacket. If the teaching is unidirectional, both in the sense of a linear syllabus and the sense that all initiatives come from the teacher, the nature of both language and learning are violated. Such an atmosphere disempowers the learner, while the whole nature of language and of learning is to facilitate the empowerment of the individual. In language learning no single idea is more important than this.

References

1. English Observed, p33.
2. Current English Grammar, p7.
3. In Brumfit and Johnson, p163.
4. Lexical Phrases in Language Teaching, p95.
5. See *English a World Language* Nr 1.
6. Second Language Grammar, Learning and Teaching, p36.
7. ibid p36.
8. op cit p5.
9   op cit p154/5.

Chapter 3

The Wider Context

Every day teachers make decisions which genuinely, and sometimes deeply, affect the lives of their learners. In such circumstances, to shun theory is unprofessional. From time to time it is necessary to think in the wider context, and to question everyday classroom materials and methods in the light of more theoretical considerations, and the whole intellectual and social context within which the teaching takes place. Theory can be sterile, but it can also provide valuable insights.

PART 1 — Philosophical Problems

1. There is no definable target.

Chomsky's competence referred to 'ideal' speakers in 'homogeneous speech communities'. No such speakers or communities exist. There is no way we can define 'perfect English'. Idealisations have been central to Western thinking for at least 2,000 years. Only in this century have people questioned the value of a concept which, by definition, does not exist. 'She speaks perfect English' is neither more nor less than a social, personal judgement. People who are prone to making judgements of this kind would like their pronouncements to have a higher, more objective status. They delude themselves.

2. There are no objective linguistic norms.

This is an embarrassing corollary of the previous point. For language teaching, it is tempting to suggest that students should be taught 'standard English'. This excludes extreme regional varieties, and seems a reassuringly safe idea. Unfortunately, it is not. As Brumfit[1] points out:

> 'Accuracy' is a relative term, based on a social judgement of the language used by a speech community. When, for the teacher, an idealised accuracy is set up, it must be based on a model devised by a descriptive linguist. Such a model . . . always involves a strong degree of idealisation.

'Standard English' is an unrealised, idealised abstraction. Whose standard? Standard for what purposes? Less superficially suspect, but equally doubtful, is the concept of the 'educated native speaker'. Widdowson has pointed out that this concept is not only ill-defined, it is non-definable. Which native speakers? Educated in what fields? To what level, and whose standards? With which sub-varieties of English at his or her disposal? The following interchange between uneducated native speaker student and teacher confuses no one:

S. We wasn't even 'ere.

T. Oh, we wasn't, wasn't we.

Although this is a natural utterance of an educated native speaker, we seek to explain why it does not conform to our expectations of 'standard' English. The definition becomes circular — if an educated native speaker uses language which is not standard, then it is not the language of an educated native speaker.

'Standard' or 'educated native speaker' English are both theoretically indefensible reifications. Linguists, writers and teachers must choose the language which is to be available to their students. No theoretically defensible objective norms exist. Practically, we must accept subjective choice, demanding only that the reasons for the choice be as informed and open as possible.

3. There are no absolute criteria for language use.

Language is essentially pragmatic in character — situational, contextualised, and purposive, not intended to **be**, but to **do**. Real world language which achieves its pragmatic ends may be deemed successful, but no criterion of 'correctness' is applicable. Real world language is not used in attempts to conform to a code, exemplify, or realise norms. It comes as something of a shock that if we accept these inevitable features of real world language, the whole concept of 'correctness' becomes an illusion.

Codified language was an abstraction; abstractions readily permit the concept of idealisation, and by implication conformity or otherwise with the ideal. In a world of pragmatics, no such absolute criteria can be established. *I got my message across* is both a necessary and sufficient condition for 'successful' language use.

Again, this is neither casuistry nor irresponsibility. It does not necessarily imply either the lowering of standards, or a disregard of accuracy. It is better that a message be conveyed efficiently, rather than laboriously; a speaker who makes too many 'mistakes' may successfully communicate the content of the message, but also convey an irresponsible, or anti-social attitude which is also part of the meaning which is conveyed. 'Correct' language is a deceptively precise term, devoid of real meaning. 'Successful' language is a more useful and creative term, precisely because of its intrinsic ambiguity.

4. Language is not limited to what has been said before.

Paradoxically, all the language reference books in the world are retrospective, recording and describing language which has already 'happened'. This is paradoxical, precisely because language is not essentially about meaning, but about **meaning potential**. As the external world changes, all creative individuals see the world in new ways; new words and combinations of words become possible, perhaps even current or established. In our own field, *communicative competence* was an incomprehensible collocation 50 years' ago (for too many teachers it remains so!).

Mayfly words, which exist only briefly, on particular occasions of use are just as much 'real English' as established sentences of the *Oh dear it's raining again* variety. The essential dynamism of linguistic potential rather than any static, canonical view is not confined to vocabulary, idiomatic expression or the spoken language. Around the moment of writing, it is clear that a grammatical item as central to English as its basic pronomial system is in a state of flux to an extent which irritates or embarrasses many of its native speakers in widely contrasting, and even opposing ways. Some contemporary writers who are highly linguistically conscious still use *he* as a generic pronoun; some writers for language teachers favour *she* as a generic pronoun, on the grounds that most language teachers are women. I have just read a book in which the generic pronoun alternated between *he* and *she* from chapter to chapter, and another[2] in which the Introduction concludes with the following:

> In this book the pronouns used to refer to 'learner' and 'teacher' are 'he', 'his', and 'him'. They have been chosen as a stylistic convenience and are intended as unmarked forms. To those readers for whom this convention is not acceptable, I extend my apologies.

Important social, political and personal issues are at stake here. Language is meaning potential, and here it expresses the potential for change, hence the zeal, derision or fury aroused by the issue just referred to. Linguistic meaning is essentially metaphorical, and highlights, but only at the expense of repression.

Look at your language teaching books — textbooks and grammars. Do they show verb paradigms? Is the 'third person' represented as *he/she/it*? Where are generic pronouns discussed? Is any reference made to the use of *she* for ships or cars for which one has a special affection? Is this more or less important than generic pronouns?

To return to the paradox — codified meaning is based on language which has already been used; novel language which ignores codified meaning will be incomprehensible. True, but while language may be restricted **by** its former uses, it is not restricted **to** its former uses. Native speakers are allowed to use it creatively. Who would deny non-natives the same privilege?

5. Meaning is intrinsically ephemeral.

The codified meaning of language is derived retrospectively from earlier uses of the language. Any particular occasion of language use is constrained by signification and usage; constrained by, but not limited to. Any actual occasion of language use, is uniquely contextualised by situation, speaker, interlocutor, attitude and many other factors. Any actual occasion of language use is essentially ephemeral. Chapter 4 discusses the nature of meaning, and recognises that fixed meanings, signification and usage, are resources which both restrict and facilitate the creation of evanescent, negotiated occasion-specific meaning. Paradoxically again, if 'real' meaning is to be found anywhere, it is in the multiplicity of individual, evanescent meanings. There is more meaning in people talking to each other, however unsuccessfully and inadequately than is to be found in the largest library of unopened dictionaries. Language **acquires meaning in use**, and use, however embarrassingly, is like breath on a pane of glass.

6. Individual language items cannot be objectively defined.

Despite our everyday feeling of 'knowing the meaning of a word', it is not the case that individual words are in one-to-one relationship with real world objects. Some part of the meaning which we regularly attribute to particular words is derived from the relationship of the language item to the real world. Language teachers have exploited this fact by holding up a pen and saying *This is a pen*. Apparently obvious and unambiguous, this procedure is severely flawed. The student may think *pen = anything you write (on paper) with* but this is not the case. *Pen* may need to be distinguished from *pencil*, and no consideration of a single ostensive definition, in isolation, will reveal that difference. Meaning is essentially differential — based on contrast(s) between language items. You cannot know the meaning of *booklet, brochure, leaflet, flier,* and *pamphlet* without knowing the way each differs from the others. Although I have chosen a lexical example, similar considerations apply to the meaning conveyed by particular grammar structures. The essentially contrastive nature of meaning is taken up again in Chapter 4.

From a philosophical point of view, the contrastive nature of meaning raises a real difficulty about the nature of communication itself. Communicative meaning on a particular occasion is partly determined by the signification of an item, but also by its contextual value, which is derived partly from contrast with items which are **not** used. If the two speakers have differential knowledge — one has a much larger vocabulary than the other — each will be referring to a different set of contrasts, expressing or interpreting more or less meaning than the conversational partner. Even with good will, cheerful approximation is the best that can be accomplished. All of us get through life like this, on partly shared, partly missed, and partly misunderstood meaning. It is an inevitable, but slightly disconcerting fact. One of the purposes of special fields of discourse such as that of science is to attempt to define all terms in mutually agreed ways, thereby generating a relatively highly developed mutual reference system which in turn maximises mutual intelligibility. Language fields such as pragmatics, and cross cultural communication reflect a concern that meaning can only be made by reference to agreed frameworks.

This apparently rather abstract point has considerable methodological implications for language teachers, suggesting that certain types of **contrastive** presentation are **essential** to the establishment of certain types of meaning, and mutual intelligibility. Some single items cannot be understood **except** in contrast to other items.

7. Absolute explanation and definition is impossible.

Grammar books and dictionaries codify language items. Clearly, such codifications are possible and useful. But they are much less absolute than is often assumed. In Britain people not infrequently write to the quality press to complain that language has been used 'wrongly' (usually by a prominent person with whom they disagree for other reasons). As 'proof' of the crime they cite a dictionary definition, asserting confidently that this is 'what the word really means'. In fact, language is a matter of meaning potential, which means new uses are always possible, and particular occasions of use may deviate slightly or substantially from the codified norm. Reference books are inevitably retrospective and statistical; they tell about previous occasions of language use, and about what is often, usually or sometimes the case.

As a brief aside, I would draw attention to the enormous importance of the Cobuild dictionary project not only in providing a uniquely innovative and useful series of dictionaries, but, perhaps as importantly, in changing perceptions of the kind of information which dictionaries contain. Traditional dictionaries define; the defining style is invariably philosophically suspect on several counts:

a. It is often based on a false ideal of synonymy.

b. It largely ignores contextual and collocational restrictions.

c. The definitions themselves use or contain a specialised metalanguage, undefined for, and usually unknown to, users.

This combination of factors tends to inhibit dictionary users, and objectify the definitions in ways which cannot be justified by evidence.

The Cobuild project has developed a completely new defining style which largely avoids these difficulties. Their style is more descriptive, contains more information, and is, as far as I know, the only dictionary which acknowledges explicitly, within the defining style, the **statistical** nature of the evidence. The importance of the statistical nature of linguistic data, both theoretically and for practical classroom activities, reappears in later chapters.

The last two philosophical difficulties are concerned with the nature of language learning, rather than language itself. Both question, but do not necessarily refute, existing practice.

8. There is no evidence that explicit knowledge helps performance.

Language teaching claims to facilitate, and make more efficient, the process of language learning. A number of classroom procedures and strategies are well-established — teachers or textbooks providing explicit rules or explanations, students being told why a particular piece of language is 'wrong'. Such strategies in general give the student knowledge **about** the language; in Krashen's terms, they are contributions to language learning, rather than acquisition. Such activities occupy a significant percentage of class time for many teachers. It comes as a surprise, therefore, to discover that there is no empirical evidence that explicit knowledge of the kind encouraged by such procedures is any help to spontaneous language production. The philosophical difficulty arises because it is difficult to see how such empirical evidence could be obtained.

If English is just a school subject it can, perhaps, be reduced to separate items of knowledge which can be tested — the spellings of particular words, irregular past tense forms — but knowledge of this kind is not language, which is essentially purposive, holistic and spontaneous; it is primarily about **doing**, not knowing. It seems that, by its very nature, language is ill-suited to be a school subject!

For teachers teaching monolingual classes who have a knowledge of their student's L1, some matters can be discussed in L1, in the same way as students discuss with their history or physics teachers. Unfortunately, for native speakers teaching multi-lingual classes, this is not a possibility, and a further philosophical difficulty arises. Ability to explain difficulties you are having with the language, is itself a language problem. This presents in an obvious and extreme form one of the central problems in teaching — if students do not understand something, they cannot explain what it is that they do not understand. The temptation then, as we have just seen, is for the teacher to provide a standard explanation on the assumption that this kind of explicit knowledge helps. Perhaps it does, but that it does is a statement of belief, without empirical foundation.

9. We do not understand the relationship between intermediate and terminal behaviour.

Frankenstein made the mistake of believing that if he assembled all the right parts, the final whole would be of a particular kind. Much, if not most, language teaching is still conducted on the basis that the totality which is a student's English is assembled bit by bit, from small pieces. Such an assumption is highly questionable, indeed probably untrue. Two points may be made:

a. Viewing language as a skill, behaviour which is seen as defective as terminal behaviour may be seen as successful as intermediate behaviour. Few schoolteachers think in terms of intermediate and terminal behaviour, seeing things much more in terms of particular lessons, or at most, the objectives of a particular semester or year. Teachers in private language schools, particularly where students' objectives can be relatively precisely specified, will find the terminology more familiar, but the problems scarcely less.

b. Methodologically, we simply are not sure how best to help students towards successful production of a macro-linguistic item such as a talk or essay. If it is your objective to give a 20 minute talk, is it better to follow an intermediate stage of a 5-minute talk, followed by talks of 10 minutes, 15 minutes and finally 20 minutes, or would you be better to do a very poor 20 minute talk, followed by a slightly improved version, another slightly improved version and so on? Do you learn to write essays by writing bad ones, and improving, or by learning to write sentences, and then paragraphs, and then how to link paragraphs? The truth is we do not know, and again it is difficult to see how we could get evidence.

I stress that these last two points **question** certain practices, but definitely do not dismiss them. Since, however, a number of classroom procedures are based on unsupported belief, it seems reasonable to suggest that they should be used sparingly, as part of a battery of procedures rather than exalted to the status of pedagogic principles.

PART 2 — Psychological Problems

We turn now to psychological factors which may encourage or inhibit effective language learning. We identify three different potential areas — students, teachers, and the participants viewed as people.

1. Teachers need to feel successful.

There is nothing to be ashamed of here; it is natural to wish to be valued, to succeed rather than to fail. It is, however, possible to base this feeling of success on quite different criteria — money, power, knowledge, the service of others, popularity. Each reader can make a personal list, and will doubtless feel strongly, both positively and negatively, about the list I have suggested. The basis of our self-esteem can differ from person to person, and individually we can change our priorities through life.

Some teachers derive their self-esteem from their knowledge of the subject and classroom ability, a few from the control and power they exercise. The thinking of this book is based on quite different criteria — the democratisation of knowledge and the empowerment of the learner. A reader who is unsympathetic to these — my — values will almost certainly also be hostile to many of the detailed suggestions.

2. Language is identity, with a consequent fear of loss.

We remind ourselves that language is a powerful badge of group or individual identity. A new language can widen horizons and be personally enriching — but not necessarily so. A new language — especially if imposed — can threaten identity. Any perceived threat will have a profound influence on the student's openness to the new language.

3. Language enables us to cope, and failure is uncomfortable.

We have already recognised the importance of language in helping us to cope with the world around us, and it is all too easy to recognise the uncomfortable feeling that comes when we cannot get what we want, say what we mean, or explain a difficulty.

Many activities in the traditional language classroom do not put the student in the position of using language in this way. The activities are, from the student's point of view, much 'safer' — listening to a teacher explanation, doing a de-contextualised sentential grammar practice. These activities may not necessarily contribute to the student's long-term language ability, but in the short-term they do not represent a psychological threat. It comes, therefore, as no surprise that students frequently **ask** for such activities. Very few of us consciously and deliberately place ourselves in situations where our inadequacy, and inability to cope is tested and revealed. Unfortunately, language learning activities which more closely resemble real-world language use, are not of the safe risk-free variety. Some resistance to this kind of activity is to be expected, and respected. At the same time, it would be disappointing if teachers merely fell back into explanation, correction, grammar practice and other safe activities.

4. Students need to experience regular success.

Many students, particularly children, enjoy the early stages of language learning — there is a feeling of doing something new, and a feeling of progress. Soon, however, many students seem to stagnate on 'the plateau'. Progress becomes imperceptible, and students become demotivated. The truth is that any individual lesson at any other than beginner level, makes very little contribution to the overall ability of the student — how many 45 minute periods are likely to be of immediate **perceptible** value, **and** contribute to long-term language improvement? Obviously, not many. But a feeling of progress and success are psychologically essential, a necessary condition for effective learning. This need has one over-riding methodological implication — students should be required to do **quite different things** at different stages in their learning programme.

It is a matter of some surprise that a low-level language textbook looks remarkably like an advanced level course. There are differences — the advanced course is more dense on the page, and the texts longer; usually, there are fewer pictures and, in some sense at least, the content is more 'difficult'. Methodologically, however, the range of activities to be found in the books exhibit more similarities than differences. It is easy to see the reasons for this — within a state school system teachers tend to teach students of particular ages and stages, and they frequently remain relatively ignorant of what has happened in the language classes before their students come to them, or what will happen to them in subsequent classes. In private language schools, most teachers meet an almost unending stream of 'intermediate' students. Unfortunately, these are ideal circumstances for a rather generalised, undifferentiated methodology to evolve. In fact, if elementary and advanced students are to be given any chance of feeling success, they should be doing quite different things and, even within the broad intermediate band, radically different emphases should be placed on the teaching at different levels.

5. Introspection is not always reliable.

One of the most remarkable aspects of humanity is self-consciousness — the ability to observe and reflect not only on the external world, but also on ourselves. Introspection is powerful, and invaluable. It is not, however, infallible. No educated person in the contemporary world can deny the existence of the unconscious which, by definition, influences us but lies beyond our power of introspection.

This matter is important, for many language teachers are willing to assert, often forcefully, that they know how they themselves mastered language — in particular, they are adamant that explicit knowledge of rules helped. Here we have another statement of belief, without empirical foundation, which may or may not be true. Introspection into how we ourselves learned, or for example into what particular language items mean, needs to be treated with a degree of scepticism. It may help; it may even be true, but it is an inadequate basis for dogma.

6. Arbitrariness and difference are threatening.

Most of us are comfortable with the familiar and cautious about anything we perceive to be new or different — we feel more comfortable with friends than strangers, more relaxed in our own country than abroad. Carried to extremes this need leads to xenophobia, prejudice, and irrational conservatism, but in moderation it is an entirely normal reaction.

Similarly, faced with what is new our only strategy for making sense of it is to relate it to our previous knowledge and experience. In this way we make the unfamiliar familiar, with a consequent lowering of our anxiety. Arbitrariness defies this procedure and, seemingly irrational and uncontrollable, is threatening and anxiety-raising. Non-native language teachers can feel threatened by naturally occurring language items which conflict with the rules they were taught at university 30 years before; all teachers can feel threatened by new content or methods, particularly by proposals that suggest a change in their own role in the classroom. Students may feel perplexed, alienated and threatened by language patterns which are totally unlike anything they have met in L1. Students are often threatened by, and hostile to, radical shifts in methodology — if they have been brought up in a rigid, teacher-dominated classroom, a task-based participatory classroom may seem anything but liberating.

Each of us likes to feel we have a coherent world view which, while perhaps evolving, is fundamentally stable. We like 'to know where we are'. Anything which challenges our current coherent image can be perceived as a threat and, in consequence, easily provokes hostility.

7. Received wisdom is not always true, but changing is painful.

The history of human ideas shows enormous changes in received wisdom — the nature of the Heavens, the cause of illness, the role of women. Individually, most readers will recognise in their own lives radical shifts between the way they viewed some aspect of the world at one particular point in time, and the way they view that same matter now. Collectively and individually the stable, status quo, changes. Such change seems to be made up in two distinct ways — a process of evolution of a particular idea, and a relatively instantaneous acceptance of the new status quo. Change is neither the evolutionary process nor the decision, but some combination of both. The key point, however, is that however this change occurs, it is troublesome, turbulent and painful. It begins with unease or anxiety, at least a suspicion that things could be different. Arguments for or against emerge. Conflicts between the two are inevitable, an intrinsic part of the way we form and change our ideas. Many people have an intuitive sense of this, and resist change precisely because they wish to avoid the conflict which is an inevitable part of the process. Teachers need to bear this in mind for two reasons:

a. As far as they themselves are concerned, changes of content and methodology challenge their previously held views. If those views were well-informed and coherent, a threat to the part is a threat to the whole. Suddenly questions are more apparent than answers, and certainties evaporate. If you have ever experienced this feeling, be reassured — the only people whose minds cannot be changed are those who resist the turmoil of questioning, contenting themselves either with blind dogma or a wishy-washy *I suppose it's alright; I've never really thought about it.*

b. Conflict may be inevitable, if the teacher wishes to influence (= change) students' attitudes. This may be to the content of what they are learning, the methodology, or the sociology of the classroom. It is important to realise that such conflict is central to the evolution of ideas. Conflict tends to be a word with negative connotations for most people. It is essential to recognise that it need not be destructive, but can be the very essence of creativity.

8. Growth involves risk.

This point develops the last. Growth is the name we give to personal change — change is uncomfortable and painful, growth involves risk.

To some extent, this appears to conflict with Krashen's assertion that we acquire best in low-anxiety situations. Teachers need to be sensitive to individual students — no risk, no development; but if they are pressurised into risking too much, this will be counter-productive.

9. The human mind prefers security.

Asked to choose between security and insecurity, most of us would unhesitatingly choose the former. Unfortunately, the human mind appears to prefer even false security to insecurity. Some young birds would die of starvation in the supposed security of their nest. They need to be kicked out, and risk the fact that they may not be able to fly, if they are ever to learn to feed themselves.

If you are an experienced teacher and you always do things in the **same** way, what evidence do you have that you are doing things in the **best possible** way?

If students know what is going to happen in every lesson, how can you ensure their security does not turn to boredom? Stevick has pointed out that it is a matter of **balance** between security and insecurity, predictability and risk.

From a teacher's point of view, have you lost your curiosity, and the adrenalin which flows when you do something different ... *I wonder what would happen if I* ... Next time the students look lost, and you are tempted to intervene and 'help', could you wait and see how they handle their uncertainty and how it evolves? It might help, and if not you can repair the damage later. But a word of warning — we are thinking of psychological problems ... from your point of view it would only **be** a risk, a state of insecurity, if it didn't 'feel good'. If you **know,** and are **sure** you can put it right, that won't do. You have to wonder, and feel a **real** sense that maybe this time you **won't** be able to regain control at will.

10. The human mind tends to make meaning.

Having discussed problems, and insecurity, discomfort and danger, we can conclude this section with one startlingly positive assertion — human beings are essentially, incorrigibly, meaning-making. Shortly after birth babies learn to focus their eyes, and soon instead of seeing they watch. Later, as every parent knows, life becomes an incessant stream of *Whys*. Faced with tragedy, people ask *Why did this happen to me?* The whole edifice of human science and technology is based on the premise that we **can** understand, **can** make sense of the world around us. Which of the following seems to you to be the odd one out: *Banana, bus, sea, coffee, clouds?* In fact, I selected those five words more or less at random (at least consciously) so the 'question' has no 'answer' — but almost certainly you started to look for similarities and differences: what do the words mean, how many letters are there in them, do the things move? Meaning doesn't inhere, humans make it. That is perhaps a central insight which should inform any activity which claims to be educational. It is profoundly encouraging — making meaning is natural, compulsive and satisfying.

PART 3 — Contiguous Fields

The philosophical and psychological factors already considered highlight one idea as permeating many, if not all, the individual points — the move from supposed absolute 'knowledge', to criteria which are much more pragmatic and relativistic in character. Far from being confined to language teaching, this trend is much wider and has enormous implications.

Literature and art

At particular points in history the creation of a serious literary or musical work was constrained by what, at the time, were seen as necessary rules. In Shakespeare's early plays, the lines are rigorously end-stopped; in the later plays, as he discovers he can say more by breaking the rules than keeping them, this constraint disappears. *Othello* is notorious for breaking the rules of Aristotelean unity, but in performance it can be profoundly moving. Attempts to contain musical composition within strictly formal, rigorous rules, have failed as composers have disregarded formal constraints in the interests of **emotive power**.

Western painting went through a period of highly formal technical discovery, particularly to do with perspective. It developed into what, at the time of its production, was seen as increasingly accurate representation. At a particular period this 'accuracy' and naturalness were highly valued, and seen as central to the purpose of painting. With the advent of photography, the idea of accurate representation was challenged and overthrown. Impressionism, with its attempt to catch what is ephemeral rather than permanent, arose. All modern artists, even those using a strictly representational style, are conscious that what is central to their activity is the search for **expressive power**. For some, this is best achieved through abstraction and pure design; for others, rigid, almost obsessively accurate representation serves the same purpose. They all know that they are not 'telling the way it is', they are interpreting.

The camera cannot lie — not long ago this statement was accepted as both obvious and true. Nowadays, it is easy to see that its apparent objectivity is an illusion. The camera is directed, and the print can be selective. It is a different discipline, but as subjective as painting. It presents not fact, but interpretation. Like metaphor, it selects at the expense of suppression, and objectifies at the expense of simplification. 'The Enlightenment' did not 'happen'; the word (*enlightenment*) is a simplified reification of an enormously complicated set of changes in the mind-set of western culture. The word helps us to talk more clearly, perhaps even to **think** more clearly, about the development but it does not accurately name an event. It is worth having the term because it helps us to understand — neither more nor less than that. The famous picture of a young girl running in flames towards the camera during the Vietnam War was not **the** image of war, only **an** image. What makes it important is its **expressive power**, its ability to communicate.

In all these 'artistic' areas, codification is possible, and even helpful; there are rules of perspective; music is not merely a form of noise. Ultimately, however, they are concerned not with formal accuracy, but expressive power.

Science and mathematics

For most of us, at least those educated within a western tradition, there is a relatively sharp divide between the world of 'the Arts' and the world of natural science and mathematics. For several hundred years now science has been perceived as the pursuit of objective truth, 'real' knowledge. The influence of science on our everyday lives is obviously not in question; what is less obvious is the influence of science on our everyday thinking. Science proceeds through a cycle of hypothesis, observation, evaluation, re-hypothesising. A central tenet of science is that the hypothesis must be testable, and if refuted, rejected. It proceeds by a process of constantly purging itself of error. The corollary appears to be that it is constantly approaching 'the truth', an objective description of the real world. Its rigorous and explicitly empirical methodology has resulted in scientific knowledge being held in the highest esteem, and other, more subjective human activities have often been perceived as inferior to the objectivity of scientific knowledge. One of the greatest scientists of all time, Heisenberg,[3] observes :

> In classical physics science started from the belief — or should one say from the illusion — that we could describe the world or at least part of the world without any reference to ourselves. ... Its success has led to the general ideal of an objective description of the world.

A principal influence of scientific thinking has been to encourage us to value objective knowledge, and even to objectify knowledge where this procedure is wholly inappropriate. The two great advances in science in the 20th century — relativity and quantum theory — both totally undermine the philosophical basis of the supposed objectivity of scientific belief. Again, Heisenberg observes: *We have to remember that what we observe is not nature in itself but nature exposed to our method of questioning.*

For several hundred years the mathematical theory established by Newton was accepted by all. It corresponds closely to our experience of everyday life, and can be understood as a precise, mathematical statement of our normal experience. Almost all the technological advances of the last 300 years are based on applications of Newton's Laws. Not surprisingly, it was easy to equate such a powerful theory with 'truth'. But to scientists, what was important about the theory was not whether it was 'true', but that it was powerful. Scientific theories are estimated highly precisely if they exhibit **predictive power**. The value of Newton's Laws is not that they are true, but that they are useful — they predict accurately.

The two great steps forward represented by relativity and quantum theory were necessitated precisely because Newton's Laws failed to predict accurately in rather specialised situations — when distances were very large (relativity), or almost infinitesimally small (quantum theory). Until we had the power to observe events on very large or very small scales Newton appeared to have 'the truth'; as soon as our ability to observe improved, it became clear that his theory was 'wrong'. It retains its enormous practical usefulness but never again can it, or any other scientific theory, be given the status of truth. Scientists now recognise that empirical knowledge is created not discovered, and is essentially and irretrievably subjective.

Both relativity and quantum theory are, at a certain level, profoundly disconcerting. Both are counter-intuitive, and seem directly to conflict with our experience from everyday life. For all that, rigorous observation shows that both have greater predictive power than any alternative yet devised. The very name of relativity reflects the fact that the observer is involved in the observation; that any supposed objectivity of the observation is an illusion. The central tenet of quantum theory is even more disconcerting. It states, in a precise mathematical form, that it is impossible, not in practice but **in principle,** to know for even one single atomic particle exactly where it is and what it is doing at any time. It states, not as an emotional cry of despair, but in the most precise, carefully defined terms, that all our science is based not on certainty, but on fundamental uncertainty, uncertainty which cannot be overcome for it is **intrinsic to the nature of knowledge.** It is ironic that the knowledge which is still seen by most people as the most certain, 'real' knowledge readily acknowledges itself to be irretrievably uncertain. Accepting this has allowed scientists to explore previously unimagined areas, and to increase the usefulness — **predictive power** — of their work.

This century has seen another important development in the philosophy of science. Popper has pointed out the fundamental asymmetry between proof and disproof. It is quite impossible to prove the statement *All crows are black*, but a single white crow will totally disprove the statement. Science proceeds not by trying to prove, but by seeking to disprove. Ultimately, perhaps all theories are tested to destruction, and it is this process which advances our knowledge. However gratifying successful experiments may be, it is 'failures' which cause reappraisal, re-hypothesisation, and ultimately progress. It is in no sense paradoxical that in science it is only in failure that the seeds of success lie.

Chaos theory

This branch of mathematics is only 20 years old. It depends on number-crunching computers which have only recently been available. Stewart, in an entertaining and accessible account of the theory[4], points out that since Newton mathematicians have, by accident, been in pursuit of solvable equations so that they could solve them. In this they were quite successful, but at the expense of ignoring unsolvable equations. In the search for the regular, which could be understood and systematised, mathematics overlooked the irregular — the perceived exceptions. In fact, these points (discontinuities) are of great importance in the real world — the cable breaks or the last straw is added to the camel's back. Because many such discontinuities presented apparently unsolvable problems, they were either ignored or idealised. Such a procedure produces short-term benefits, but as recent chaos theory has shown, its fundamentally distorting nature is, in the end, a restriction. Cheating, wittingly or unwittingly, doesn't help.

Categorising what **can** be categorised and ignoring or idealising 'exceptions' is very reminiscent of the procedures used in the development of many grammar books — but if the exceptions are exceptions only to the rules that we have created, it is at least as likely that the **rules** need to be questioned rather than the exceptions ignored. In passing, we may note that speech frequently appears less ordered, more chaotic, than writing. Difficulties of observation, and apparent difficulties of categorisation have led to it being treated as in some way defective. The truth is of course different — what was defective was not the spoken language, but our technology and conceptual framework. Even now, teachers and even linguists are too ready to dismiss real-world language data. This may be more comfortable and convenient than questioning the conceptual framework, but it only delays and inhibits real understanding.

The belief in the objective, absolute nature of scientific knowledge reached its height in the late 19th century. At that time, most other forms of knowledge aspired to the same supposed absolute, objective character. Sadly, many grammar books still perpetuate this outdated view of knowledge. 20th century science has recognised three important characteristics in its own subject matter:

- Scientific observations are essentially statistical
- Observations are inherently subjective
- Progress is made by refutation, not proof

Attempts to study language objectively are very recent; the discipline of linguistics is still less than 100 years old. (It is usually dated from Saussure). It deals with a very complex personal and social phenomenon. To some extent, it inherited its terminology and categories from a time when language was not regarded as a possible subject for objective study. In those circumstances, we should hardly be surprised if some substantial re-evaluations, and re-categorisations are necessary as our technology and conceptual frameworks become more rigorous and highly developed. Within the broad scientific context, this has indeed been the case. The central achievement is, perhaps, Heisenberg's — he has freed science forever from the belief that it is the pursuit of certainty that was its legitimate, indeed intrinsic, aim. The consequences are enormous — to make technology as authentic a discipline as pure science; to emphasise the pursuit of progress rather than the pursuit of knowledge; to emphasise pragmatic utility rather than abstract accuracy. An essentially abstract, theoretical breakthrough has resulted in renewed emphasis on practical utility. Language studies could usefully make a similar change.

Skills Training

Language may be viewed in different ways, with correspondingly different emphases when we consider how it can best be taught. Language is at least partly a skill. (Though this conflicts with Chomsky's view that language is unique in human skills and the only way to study language acquisition is to study language acquisition. There is little evidence for the assertion that language is unique in this way.) There is a substantial literature discussing how skills are acquired and improved. If language is a skill, this literature should provide insights into appropriate classroom procedures. Johnson[5] takes up precisely this point by referring to his own experience of learning to ride a horse. The central distinction is between **knowledge about**, and **knowledge how to**. This latter is sometimes called **procedural knowledge,** and involves the ability to **perform under real operating conditions**. Part of the ability of a championship golfer involves being able to chip the ball accurately up to the pin not only in a practice round, but when also being watched by a large crowd and the television cameras. In the same way, a language learner needs to be able to **use** the present perfect at the lost property office, not simply to complete a fill-in exercise in a quiet classroom without time constraints. Knowledge about is a small part of procedural knowledge, which is a much more all-embracing concept.

This matter assumes great importance when we consider what teaching procedures are appropriate to improving the learner's performance. If the student lacks knowledge about, the teacher's role is self-evident — to inform or explain. If the deficiency is in procedural knowledge, the skills literature suggests that informing and explaining have a very small part to play. What seems to help the learner best in these circumstances is an **internalisation of what successful performance feels like**. This begs many questions — how does the internalisation take place? Feel in what sense? Nonetheless, the skills literature has something useful to say. Namely, that we can identify conditions for the kind of feedback a teacher can provide which are likely to assist the learner in the internalisation which produces improved performance. These conditions include:

a. The knowledge of what is correct (knowledge about).

b. Awareness that the performance **was** defective. In real operating conditions — doing something in the real world — it is not always obvious that something has gone wrong: the student who says *I don't can come tomorrow* and whose message has been understood, may genuinely not realise that anything was 'wrong'.

These two aspects of feedback are usually familiar to teachers — they regularly draw attention to mistakes, and give information or explanations about what would be 'correct'.

c. The learner needs to see (in the extended sense of develop an awareness of) correct performance. This is most likely to be achieved if the learner observes a competent performance — in the case of language students almost certainly their teacher. It strongly suggests that it is reformulation, in addition to or instead of any formal correction, which should be a teacher's principal strategy for dealing with 'mistakes'. This is discussed more extensively in Chapter 10.

Observing musical master classes clearly endorses this view. Young musicians rarely benefit from 'correction' but frequently say *Oh, now I see ...* simply as a result of listening to a brief demonstration from the 'master' taking the class. The Pakistani cricketer Imran Khan, describing his own career endorses this view quite explicitly:

> I improved as a player not because I received any coaching in England but because I had plenty of opportunity to play against world-class cricketers. My improvement came from watching and observing their techniques.

Nobody would deny the teacher's role in giving basic information — how to hold the racket when you play tennis. Throughout any learning programme teachers will need to give knowledge about, and make students aware of mistakes. The key, however, is that these elements are part, and only part, of the process of feedback. As soon as language is perceived as skill, teachers should abandon the (behaviourist based) **learn** — **perform** sequence, adopting instead that described by Johnson as **mistake-occurrence** — **corrective action** — **retrial.**

Linguistics

Regrettably, some teachers are ignorant of, or even hostile to linguistics. The objective study of language can seem remote from the classroom, and can seem to have the same effect on language as the biologist has on the rabbit when she dissects it to discover how its digestive system works. Linguistics can be an arid discipline, sorting and categorising in a manner more reminiscent of algebra than communication. Even so-called applied linguistics, and sub-disciplines such as discourse analysis can seem no more than intellectual games. But the subject matter of language teaching is language. There should be no doubt that rigorous study of the subject matter should concern any professional language teacher.

The general development of linguistics has mirrored that of the artistic and scientific fields mentioned in this chapter. Initially, linguistics concerned itself with language as a reified abstraction. This was both desirable and inevitable — the purpose was to avoid the highly subjective view of language which is intrinsic to the nature and study of literature. Early linguistics emphasised paradigmatics and syntagmatics; loosely, language needed to be organised. Not surprisingly, structural syllabuses reached their heyday. Later, the influence of pragmatics came to be felt, resulting in functional/communicative approaches. Many younger language teachers do not realise that what they regard as 'normal' is a startling development of the language teaching of the 50's, brought about by developments within applied linguistics.

Nowadays, socio-linguistics, and even ethnology make important contributions. These topic areas verge into sociology and politics. Such comparatively modern disciplines as discourse analysis involve examining language not as a reified abstraction, but as a means of communication between peoples. Cross-cultural communication is a natural development of the same thinking — language in use, as a purposive inter-personal instrument.

It will be noted that all of the above contiguous fields reflect developments in the same direction — from objective, abstract, systematic, search for 'truth' to a much more pragmatic, subjective, functional orientation. The different fields of artistic endeavour referred to move from the acceptance of formal norms to the **centrality of expressive power**. Science and the apparently ultra-objective mathematics, move from the search for truth to the **centrality of predictive power**. Skills training encourages us to think not in terms of objective knowledge about, but individual **ability to do**. Linguistics, while retaining its scientific method, has widened to reflect the individual, social, and inter-personal nature of language.

Together it is easy to see that at the heart of these fields lies a growing awareness of the profoundly subjective, individual nature of everything which we know and can do. Some people are defensive as the old, abstract, apparently objective certainties are swept away. In my view, they are wrong. The central theme of the thinking of our time is about personal, individual empowerment. Such an idea can be a source of anarchy, but equally of liberation. It is, however, the sign of our times. Language teachers can no more stand aside from it than anybody else. Abstract, absolute knowledge of system has had its day. The philosophical, psychological and historical time is right to emphasise the empowerment of the individual, and in language the **centrality of communicative power**.

L1 Learning

The single subject which is, perhaps, the closest to the acquisition of a second language is mother tongue learning. It is a matter of some dispute how similar or dissimilar the two processes are. What is surprising is that so little explicit reference is made in discussing second language acquisition (SLA) to what is known about the acquisition of a mother tongue.

Foster's survey *The Communicative Competence of Young Children* quotes research and evidence in support of a number of interesting ideas relating to mother tongue acquisition. Most noticeable among these are:

— The gradual preception of individual sounds appears to take place within the perception of an intonational envelope (p.47).

— Some children approach segmentation problems by reproducing whole phrases, such as *Whatsat, Whatyouwant.* (p.48).

— Some children as old as ten are unable to reproduce all sounds accurately, suggesting that some of these may be particularly difficult. (p.44).

— When morphemes are acquired, they may not at first be used everywhere they are needed. (p.78).

— Children both over-extend and under-extend the use of particular words, for example, calling all animals *doggie,* or only relating *cars* to **moving** vehicles.

— Often, not knowing the relevant word, children use the closest word they do possess. (p.52).

Several more general points are also worth noting:

a. Initially all communication is restricted to the immediate environment of, Here-and-Now; with the advent of language children can move outside the immediate situation, and with developing **grammatical** competence, they are increasingly liberated from the immediate context, and able to talk about past events, hypothetical situations etc. (p.25, p.66).

b. Morphology is only gradually mastered; in English, for example, children often assume that verbs that end /t/ or /d/ already have a past tense ending, so they may treat *ride* as already past. In contrast, they also produce over-regular forms such as *breaked* and *bringed.* Mastery of the system involves intermediate stages of mistaken hypotheses, which are subsequently corrected.

c. The size of mother tongue vocabulary is uncertain, but a recent estimate suggests that at 3:0 (3 years, zero months) it is almost a thousand items, and at 6:0 around fourteen thousand items. Assuming children start building vocabulary at around 18 months, one estimate suggests that they add on average nine new words a day from then on. This indicates the enormity of the task of mastering the vocabulary of a second language.

d. Research in mother-tongue acquisition naturally involves the observation of children at the pre-linguistic stage. Foster observes:

> Children at both the pre-linguistic and first word stage are clearly capable of carrying on quite sophisticated conversations, providing they have a willing adult as a participant. (p.67).

While the precise relationship between L1 and L2 acquisition is contentious, both concern the acquisition of language, and it is reasonable to assume **similar**, rather than totally different mental processes are involved. The L1 acquisition research at least suggests:

— Language is not 'built up' by learning sounds and structures, but by an increasing ability to break down wholes into parts which are at different levels, separable.

— Acquisition of the grammatical system is a process based on the Observe-Hypothesise-Experiment paradigm. Inadequate and wrong hypotheses have an important role to play as an intermediate stage towards mastery.

— It is possible to use effectively unanalysed, pragmatically useful wholes which are only subsequently analysed at, for example, phonological or morphological levels.

— The generation of meaning, and consequent development of acquisition, are both aided by contact with a 'sympathetic interlocutor' whose language level is more sophisticated.

Finally, we must observe that L1 research does **not** endorse the view that correcting the child's output speeds acquisition. Research in this area is inconclusive, but it is certainly not the case that research shows formal 'correction' of children's mistakes to be of value.

Summary

All the areas mentioned in this chapter share two characteristics, typical perhaps of contemporary thought — a distrust of dogmatism and certainty, and a respect for an approach to knowledge which is essentially purgative. The philosopher Cupitt identifies doubt, scepticism and self-criticism as the modern intellectual virtues. He further suggests that rather than attaching ourselves to any fixed deposit of truth, we should become consistently self-critical, revisionist and iconoclastic. Truth, in his view, lies not in a fixed position, but in the direction of movement.

We improve our ideas, as he puts it 'by the lengthy trail of broken images and abandoned illusions'. The certainties of language teaching are often false certainties; as in any other field of intellectual endeavour, we should remain self-critical, and willing to change as evidence and experience challenge our cherished positions.

References

1.   In Communicative Language Teaching, p.187.
2.   Second Language Acquisition, 1985.
3.   Physics and Philosophy, p43.
4.   Does God Play Dice
5.   ELTJ 42/2

Chapter 4
The Nature of Meaning

Human beings have a natural propensity to make meaning. The most highly developed system available for this is language. But not all language is equally meaningful, or meaningful in the same ways. An awareness of different kinds of meaning, and how meaning is made can be helpful for the language teacher.

Meaning is negatively and differentially defined

Few people ever reflect on how words or other language items such as lexical phrases or intonation patterns create meaning. The temptation is to think of a word as having a fixed meaning, and to assume that words are in some sort of one-to-one isomorphic relationship with 'reality'. However 'obvious' this may be, it is in fact totally untrue. Meaning does not inhere in words in this way; it is essentially defined by the **differences** between terms, and ultimately by exclusion — what it does **not** mean. These ideas may be counter-intuitive, but they have an impeccable pedigree, deriving directly from the work of the father of modern linguistics, de Saussure. In his famous Course, he says:

> When we say that these values correspond to concepts, it is understood that these concepts are purely differential, not positively defined by their content but negatively defined by their relations with other terms of the system. Their most precise characteristic is that they are what the others are not.

This point is self-evident if related to phonology. No two people pronounce words in exactly the same way, yet they remain mutually comprehensible. Culler, discussing de Saussure's work asks:

> We might approach the question by asking how far the actual noises produced could vary and still count as versions of the same signifier. (The answer is) the noises may vary considerably, and there is no essential property which they must possess, so long as they do not become confused with those of contrasting signifiers. We have considerable latitude in the way we utter *bed*, so long as what we say is not confused with *bad, bud, bid, bowed; bread, bled, dead, fed, head, led, red, said, wed; beck, bell, bet*.

In other words, it is the **distinctions** which are important, and it is for this reason that linguistic units have purely relational identity.

Saussure offers a concrete example — the 8.25 Geneva to Paris Express is the same train every day, even if the coaches and locomotive which make it up are different from day to day. It is still the 8.25 if it leaves late, and even if it leaves late every day. What matters is that it is not the 11.32 Geneva to Paris Express, nor the 8.25 Geneva to Milan Express.

Saussure's analysis has exercised considerable influence on linguistics, though from a practical point of view it is extremely difficult to avoid speaking of language items in positive terms. Many writers have argued that binary oppositions are not simply a methodological device for studying language, but are a reflection of the nature of language itself. This is plausible, as such oppositions are the most natural and economical way of creating differences which are essential to the creation of meaning.

The essentially differential nature of meaning implies that the individual language user creates meaning through the exercise of choice — selecting one language item at the expense of rejecting one or more others. The essentially negative nature of meaning means that the selected item is not that which most precisely codifies the speaker's meaning, but that which is **least unsatisfactory**, the best approximation. This consideration is of great importance when considering someone using a second language, particularly someone whose knowledge of L2 is very restricted. Using language which accurately conveys meaning in context, even if only an approximation to the words or structures a native speaker would choose, exemplifies the use of L2 in a way which fully reflects the real nature of language. Regarding language as 'successful' rather than accurate', is not a problem confined only to the L2 learner. All of us conduct our lives by choosing **sufficiently** accurate language from the repertoire at our disposal.

Central to the creation of meaning, then, is choice. This applies to phonology, words and other lexical items, and a wide range of language patterns and grammatical structures. Grammar is more extensively discussed later but here we must recognise that some grammar is a matter of fact, and some a matter of language-user's choice. Grammar as fact contributes little to meaning — using *womans* rather than *women* breaks the rules of grammar as fact, but does not convey less meaning. Grammar as choice — the speaker selects between two possible well-formed alternatives — creates meaning. Chalker[1] describes grammar as follows:

> The grammar is an interlocking system in which the grammatical choices themselves contribute to the communicative meaning. ... Choice of the passive, like choosing to mark for time or aspect, is the selection of a grammatical device that contributes to meaning.

Wilkins[2] endorses the same view:

> Past events may be encoded in the past tense or in the present perfect and the choice is made according to the speaker's emphasis and view of events.

Close introduces the idea as central to his *Teachers' Grammar* (LTP 1992) and it is the basis of my own study *The English Verb* (LTP 1986). Willis[3] confidently asserts *meaning implies choice*. The idea that meaning is created through the exercise of choice cannot be over-estimated.

Referential meaning

Not all meaning is of the same kind. What most people call 'the' meaning is technically *referential meaning*. The referential meaning of an utterance is confined to what philosophers call its propositional content. It is 'the basic facts', without interpretation or embellishment. Although this term describes the basic meaning, it is the one which we will find least useful in our subsequent discussion of the implications for language teaching.

Differential meaning

Language items are defined by **contrast** with other language items, rather than the inherent properties of the object or situation to which they refer. With this warning, consider the meaning of the following words:

cup	glass	plate
basin	bowl	dish
saucer	beaker	mug

Now consider the following features in relation to these words:

material	flatness	handles
shape	use	position

Now label these drawings with one or more of the words:

Are you still sure what a 'bowl' is or a 'plate'? Do you find yourself thinking of the individual objects in isolation, or are you approaching it by contrasting one object with another, searching for differences. Each object is defined, to a large extent, by **not being the others**. As the thesaurus shows, the list, and corresponding contrasts can be considerably extended — *pot, wine glass, chalice.*

Meaning is created by contrast. Explaining how a *bush* differs from a *tree* is easier and more useful than trying to 'define' *bush*. This has obvious methodological implications for teachers — instead of trying to say 'what a word means' it is easier and more valuable to present contrasting items. This applies as much to grammar as to vocabulary. The contrastive nature of meaning suggests contrastive methodology will have an important role to play.

Connotational meaning

Wine glasses, goblets and chalices are (perhaps) similarly shaped drinking vessels, but the words do not 'mean the same thing'. The speaker uses one word rather than another to give additional, connotational meaning. In a simpler example, a whole group of words can be substituted for *walked* in this sentence: *He walked down the street.* He could have *marched, staggered, strolled, bounced.* Each of these words contains the referential content of *walked* — he got himself from one end of the street to the other on his legs — but, in addition, each gives us a great deal more information about **how** he walked. Connotational meaning adds extra meaning and the pedagogical implications are similar to those mentioned above.

Contextual meaning

Ellis[4] defines context in the following way:

> The 'context' of an utterance can mean two different things. (1) It can refer to the situation in which the utterance is produced; this is the 'situational context'. (2) It can refer to the linguistic environment — the surrounding language; this is the 'linguistic context'. Both types of context influence the choice of language forms and therefore have an effect on output.

In this book I use the term **context** for situational factors, and **co-text** for the linguistic environment. In different fields of applied linguistics one or other of these factors may loom larger; it is co-text rather than context which is more helpful in determining the language selection and appropriate exercise types for language teaching.

Context has a part to play; we use different language in different situations, with different people. Most of us can greet our friends with a simple *Hi!* but could not use this to the Duke of Edinburgh with the same meaning (though perhaps his friends can). That language used in that situation would still have meaning, but not the **same** meaning. Language means different things depending upon the situation of use. This raises the embarrassing question of what language means when it is used only for the purpose of practising language, for example, the de-contextualised examples of a grammar exercise. Frequently it does not mean anything. Some applied linguists have gone so far as to deny that such language is language at all, coining instead the phrase 'language-like behaviour'. It is difficult to remember that the centrality of meaning to language was not always perceived to be important. In the 50's and 60's, orthodoxy dictated that the drilling of grammatical patterns was a useful, indeed indispensable, activity. Nobody thought this sequence remotely odd:

T   He's a big man, isn't he?
C   Yes, he's the biggest man I know.
T   He's a tall man, isn't he?
C   Yes, he's the tallest man I know.
T   That's a weird idea, isn't it?
C   Yes, it's the weirdest idea I know.

At the time, nobody thought this was a weird idea, just sensible, orthodox practice. Nowadays, such drilling is taboo and readers may be surprised that, in discussing grammar exercises in Chapter 9, I advocate a (modified) role for drills of this kind. Unfortunately, language teaching has too often suffered from a band-wagon effect, and particular orthodoxies have been accepted and discarded in too uncritical a manner. Drills of this kind have a **limited** role to play, for they truly exemplify important patterns of the language, but at the level of intonation rather than grammatical structure.

Although oral drilling, which retains real pedagogic value, has been discarded, grammar exercise books still consist largely of single, wholly de-contextualised sentences. These seem to me almost wholly inimical to the nature of language and the process of learning. In general, de-contextualised lexical items — words and phrases — retain the codified element of their meaning; fully grammaticalised sentences, other than those used as lexical items, are wholly devoid of meaning when de-contextualised. Context — situation, participant and purpose — are not optional extras in the creation of meaning; they are intrinsic to it. This has important implications for what actually constitutes 'a language practice'. It is not to go too far to say that it invalidates many of the so-called practices in widely available standard books. This is not to say that such exercises do not, at a certain level, 'work' — only that they are a pale shadow of what real language practice should, and can, be like.

Typically, words do not occur in isolation, but in the company of co-text. Choice is intrinsic to the creation of meaning. Co-text plays an important role in supporting, or limiting choice. Think again of the words listed earlier:

cup	glass	plate
basin	bowl	dish
beaker	mug	saucer

Which word(s) could you use to complete the following sentences? You may think one or more words fit, with varying degrees of ease and perhaps with slightly, or even substantially different meanings. (You may need plurals.)

1. You don't look well — shall I get you a .... of water?
2. She's cut herself — can you get me a .... of water so I can bathe her leg?
3. Let's do the .... I don't like leaving them in the sink.
4. If we are going on a picnic we'd better get some plastic ....
5. I'm not really hungry — a .... of soup is enough for me.
6. Oh, I forgot the cat. I haven't given him his .... of milk.
7. Take the strawberries into the dining room please. Just put the .... in the middle of the table.
8. There wasn't much to eat — just a couple of .... of fancy little sandwiches and a few .... of peanuts.

In the real world many things are possible — most people have seen a saucer used as an ashtray and, for the duration of that use, **called** an ashtray (ah yes, but it's **really** a saucer. Are you sure?). Perhaps in example 8 there were *saucers* of peanuts, but you are more likely to have selected *bowls* as the most likely word. The selection is made partly on the basis of real world knowledge, but also on purely linguistic grounds — we intuitively know which words frequently co-occur, so we expect their co-occurrence. This expectation suggests important pedagogical strategies. Instead of teaching, and listing isolated words it makes considerable pedagogic sense to present words in context, to work with them with their co-text, and finally — and this for many is an important step forward — to devise **recording formats** for new language which reflect the importance of co-text. Such recording formats will take the importance of co-text into account, in a way which no linear, item by item listing ('the vocabulary book') ever could.

Collocational meaning

The occurrence of certain words or structures predisposes us to expect certain other language items. The co-occurrence of words in this way is a matter of degree. Both *golden opportunity* and a *nice sweater* are natural collocations but while *golden* and *opportunity* collocate strongly, the linking of *nice* and *sweater* is much weaker. The linking between two items of a collocation is not equally strong in both directions: *rancid* almost demands to be followed by *butter*, while *butter* can be preceded by a wide range of adjectives. Collocation has many implications for both the content and methodology of language teaching. Here, we note that collocation has an important role to play in the creation of meaning. It is almost impossible to explain the meaning of the verb *bark* without reference to *dog*. To a large extent the meaning of *bark* is more or less completely expressed by the sentence *Dogs bark, but pigs grunt and ducks quack*. The combination of the collocation and the set of oppositions **constitute** the meaning of *bark*. An important element of the Lexical Approach is the perception of the central role of collocation in language and its meaning-generating power.

Pragmatic meaning

When we use language there is content, but language is not only a way of **telling**, but of **doing**. Wilkins[5] puts it this way:

> An account of the internal grammatical relations and therefore of the ideational meaning does not tell us much about the use to which a sentence is being put by the speaker. The speaker's purpose is no less a matter of what he is doing with the language than of what he is reporting through it. Although questions of use have not always been considered part of semantics, they are of great relevance to the language teacher who is preparing pupils for the process of communication.

A speaker may utter a sentence which is, for example, a positive, active statement, expressing a particular content. The listener may, however, interpret the sentence as a threat, or warning, as advice or contradiction. These interpretations are pragmatic meanings. In addition to the content expressed, the listener **interprets the speaker's purpose** in uttering the sentence. In some cases there is close congruence between the surface meaning of what is said and the intention behind what is said. But this is by no means always the case. *Can you lend me a pound?* is usually pragmatically equivalent to *Will you lend me a pound?*, but that does not allow us to conclude that *can* 'has the same meaning' as *will*. *I'm afraid he is in a meeting* may pragmatically mean *He's not available to talk to you*.

All known speech communities use utterances where there is little or no congruence between the apparent referential meaning and the pragmatic meaning. It is not, however, the case that all cultures use the same kind of linguistic devices to express the same kinds of pragmatic meaning. Different cultures may recognise different degrees of directness in expressing disagreement; in addition, they may encode these differences using different linguistic strategies. Here is fertile ground for international misunderstanding, and the field of cross-cultural communication has largely come into being as attempts are made to describe pragmatic meaning and make language students aware of the inherent dangers.

Idiomatic expressions convey pragmatic meaning which is very different from surface meaning. Traditionally idioms have been regarded as marginal to the language but modern research suggests that native speakers may have an enormous repertoire of learned utterances which belong on a Spectrum of Idiomaticity varying from the colourful *He was running round like a headless chicken* to the quasi-transparent *Could I just say a few words* ... Some contemporary grammarians have suggested that situation-specific learned utterances provide the basis for the generalisations which ultimately provide the L1 learners' grammar. These theoretical advances have clear implications for L2 learning, and within the Lexical Approach, as we shall see in Chapters 5 and 8, institutionalised realisations of pragmatic meaning have an important role to play.

Many linguistic factors contribute to the pragmatic meaning of an utterance — lexical selection, structure, stress and intonation. Some of these — most notably intonation — usually form a very small part of a language learning programme but intonation plays an important role in signalling speaker intention, and therefore pragmatic meaning. Many foreign learners of English with a high degree of structural knowledge remain hopelessly perplexed when confronted with informal conversation containing the kind of 'question tags' which are not, pragmatically, questions. Two problems arise — first deciding on the basis of intonation whether the utterance is intended as a question, and secondly, if it is not, determining an appropriate response which is different from the 'answer' to the (unintended) question.

Pragmatics has, in recent years, played an important part in determining language teaching syllabuses. The structural syllabuses of earlier years were essentially based on syntagmatics, and the abstract study of language in relation to itself. Nowadays, most language teaching books include units specifically labelled with pragmatic, i.e. functional, headings. Teachers need consciously to incorporate the question *What was he doing when he said ...?* rather than *What did he mean when he said ...?* Recognising the speaker's intention, and being able to express your own intentions, are central to effective language use.

The pragmatic opposites of utterances are frequently not obvious from a knowledge of lexis and syntax. But it is at least as important to be able to refuse an invitation as it is to be able to accept it, to disagree as to agree. Teachers, particularly at intermediate and advanced levels, need constantly to be aware of the potential difficulties students may have in generating pragmatic opposites. Again, the methodological implication is clear — teachers need to be constantly challenging their students by asking *And what would you say then if you meant Yes/No instead of No/Yes?*

Discourse meaning

The meaning of a word may change because of the words with which it co-occurs — *a bright light, a bright idea*. But the value a word has may also change because of the more extended context in which it occurs:

It's lovely to see you again. I've brought you a few flowers.
— Oh how nice! Daffodils! They're so cheerful at this time of year.

(Later)
Now, where do you think I should put the flowers …?

In the last utterance *flowers* means *daffodils*, and what is normally considered a hyponym has become a synonym. This is not optional, for the utterance *Now, where do you think I should put the daffodils* sounds distinctly odd unless I emerge from the kitchen with a vase of daffodils **and** a vase of tulips. In natural discourse the value of a word may change from its signification.

The above example shows that we make our meaning only as clear as is **necessary for effective communication.** If it is necessary to distinguish the daffodils from the tulips, both words would be used; if there is only one vase, *flowers* is clear and *daffodils* seems over-explicit. This suggests one important implication for language teaching — increased attention to general words — *stuff, things,* which effectively function as pro-forms. In connected, usually spoken, discourse, pro-forms constantly assume different values and allow the language user to achieve many pragmatic purposes with a comparatively restricted vocabulary. Years ago I remember the frustration of taking a job in France equipped only with my schoolboy French. My vocabulary of nouns for the objects which surrounded me was sadly deficient but my practical communication took a great leap forward with the acquisition of the French word *truc*. Learners of English need two words, *thing(s)* for countable nouns, *stuff* for uncountables. These words have enormous communicative power, and are in no sense sub-standard. Competent native speakers regularly use such sentences as *Where shall I put this stuff? Can you pass that thing please.* In discourse such sentences are meaningful and unambiguous. They could easily and naturally be used by teachers in class (*Have you brought your things? Where's the stuff we were doing yesterday?*). But these maximally useful pro-forms seem to be familiar to comparatively few L2 learners.

Factual meaning and modal meaning

This idea, which initially seems rather remote from the classroom, has considerable significance. In considering the nature of grammar and in particular the general meanings which can be attributed to different forms of the English verb. Wilkins[6] describes what a speaker does in the following words:

> While expressing his perceptions the speaker simultaneously expresses his own attitude towards what he saying (or writing). He vouches for the degree of validity that his statement has. He may represent it as simply an objective truth. On the other hand he may indicate that the ideational meaning is subject to some contingency, is desired rather than positively asserted or is potential rather than actual.

A difficult idea is involved here. In everyday speech the sentences *She speaks French* and *She can speak French* would be described as stating facts. Technically, however, this is not the case. When the speaker utters the first sentence, the speaker asserts the factuality of the statement; in Wilkins' description (s)he 'vouches for the degree of validity' of the statement, and in this case represents it as objective truth. The second statement is modal in character, and the speaker does not represent it as objective truth. It is not a matter of whether the state of affairs is or is not a **matter of fact**; what matters is the **degree of validity attributed to the statement by the speaker.**

There is a paradox lurking here — everything the speaker says is inevitably subjective. When I make modal statements I **explicitly acknowledge the subjective nature of my assertions**. There are, however, linguistic forms — in English the present simple and past simple — which the speaker selects when wishing to **claim** objectivity for the statement.

Non-factuality or modality can be expressed lexically — *Perhaps she speaks French* — or grammatically — *She may speak French*. Different languages have different ways by which speakers can distance themselves from the propositional content of what is said. In some fields of discourse, such as scientific writing, the speaker tends to choose exactly those language forms which objectify the propositional content. In political or business negotiation, forms are frequently chosen deliberately to distance the speaker from the propositional content: *How would you feel about* ... rather than *How do you feel about ...,* *I would need to consult Head Office* rather than *I need to consult Head Office*. Effective language use is a great deal more than crudely 'saying what we mean' and the meaning we make is a great deal more than the expression of propositional meaning.

In the particular case of teaching English, the past simple and present simple are precisely the forms with which the speaker represents the content as objective fact. Traditionally, language teaching has seen these language forms as essentially associated with the expression of present and past time. As I have argued in *The English Verb*, this connection is not valid and is, indeed, the source of a great deal of confusion. It is the case, for example, that almost all reference to future time in English is modal. Any attempt to develop in students an awareness of which verb forms will be appropriate for the expression of future time in English is likely to be unsuccessful, or at least unnecessarily laborious, unless the essentially fact-stating quality of past simple and present simple is recognised. They do not simply express meaning in a different way, they express a different kind of meaning.

Negotiated meaning

The discipline of literary criticism exists because a literary text cannot decisively be said to have a single meaning. All that exists is the text but this is not to be emptied of its meaning like a sponge being squeezed dry. The meaning does not inhere in the text, it is created by the interaction between text and reader. Different readers, who bring different life experience, knowledge and opinions to the text, will quite legitimately claim that the text 'means' different things. This can, of course, be infuriating. Many of us have come out from a performance of Shakespeare complaining that the director's interpretation 'is not what the play is really about'.

But of course we are wrong, for the text is not 'really about' anything. It is just there, and, perversity apart, the director may quite legitimately take from it a different meaning from what you or I assert it is really about. Literature, perhaps the most self-conscious use of language, does not produce text which contains meaning waiting to be discovered, only text which has the potential to allow its readers to create meaning.

It might seem that informal conversation is of a quite different character but Nattinger[7] and DeCarrico suggest:

> The language that makes up social conversation asserts primarily an interactional function of expressing social relationships and personal attitudes, but it also serves a secondary, transactional one of expressing 'content'. Conversations are joint productions, in which the participants constantly take account of one another and adjust their speech to fit the contours of the social situation in which the conversation is taking place. Conversational language thus mirrors the way speakers check on how well they are being understood, claim and prove their understanding of what is being said, and how both keep the conversation going.

The key phrase is 'joint production'. Just as author and reader create interpersonal meaning by a process of negotiation, so conversation exhibits a much more obvious negotiation. Meaning is created by the interaction of one language user with the other. In this sense, no single language user expresses what he or she means, but simply participates in the creation of negotiated meaning.

In real-world conversation where one participant is significantly more linguistically able than the other — mother and child, native speaker and foreign visitor — a very considerable degree of communication is possible because the more competent language user helps the less able in many ways — guessing intention, providing unknown words, ignoring surface error, interpreting the less able language user's effort generously to maximise the possibility of effective communication. This sympathetic strategy facilitates communication which would otherwise be impossible. It appears also to facilitate long-term language acquisition.

It is disconcerting, therefore, to realise that many teachers often adopt precisely the opposite strategy — requiring students to create finished products such as essays with no interaction during the process of creation, requiring students on their own to struggle to say what they mean rather than the teacher acting as a sympathetic interlocutor. Bizarrely, foreign students are sometimes required to encode their meaning in a vacuum in a way which is rarely required of native speakers.

It will be noted that the negotiation of meaning necessarily implies that it is not possible to separate the four language skills — listening and speaking, reading and writing — in the decisive way we sometimes think. Signalling our agreement, confusion, or need for clarification through speech is an important part of listening; perceiving misunderstanding, and consequently paraphrasing is an important part of speaking. Language and learning present themselves as holistic entities. Teaching may involve breaking things down into stages or skills, but if this dissection is carried too far, it violates the nature of both language or learning.

The most important consequence of negotiated meaning for language teachers is that it is highly desirable to arrange classroom activities which involve real attempts by students to communicate meaning and where the success of the activity is judged by the success of this communication. Yet again we return to the priority of successful over accurate language and to the centrality of communicative power.

Top-down and Bottom-up meaning

What do the following words mean: *serious? pentek* (Hungarian)? By now, we approach a question like that with great suspicion — it is impossible to attribute meaning to isolated, de-contextualised tokens. Consider now the following:

The Chancellor predicted there would be serious consequences for interest rates and employment prospects.

Pentek, Szombat, Vasarnat (*Szombat* is Hungarian for Saturday).

The second example suggests that *pentek* is a day of the week, probably Friday (It is). I know this because I was given a beautifully illustrated Hungarian calendar. On the calendar one day of the week is printed in red. My real world experience tells me that that is almost certainly Sunday, and since I know the order of the days of the week I can decode *pentek* = *Friday*. I decoded the word — gave it meaning — by what is sometimes called a **top-down** process — I used my knowledge of the real world, in particular of calendars and printing conventions. Relating the unknown item to the **whole of my knowledge** allowed me to attribute provisional meaning. In a real situation I could then check, and if necessary modify my assumptions. In the first example above, I attribute meaning both to the single word *serious* and to the overall content of the sentence in a similar way — by bringing my real world knowledge to bear and interpreting — and that is the key word — the sentence in such a way that it 'fits' my overall world view. Widdowson[8] describes this process in the following way:

> Literary critics have come closer than linguists to an understanding of the communicative function of language and the ways in which discourse is made. Their approach to language acknowledges at least that meanings in discourse are to be worked out by active interpretation and are not a simple function of correlation, but this interpreting ability depends on more than just a knowledge of pre-formulated rules ... (It stresses) the elusiveness of exact meaning, the creative aspect of interpretation, the importance of involvement.

This is another way of looking at negotiated meaning, but has important implications for language teachers, particularly those who are teaching adult learners. Adults have a vast repertoire of world knowledge which allows them to interpret (= understand) material which contains words which they do not understand. Indeed, any process which concentrates on the words which they do **not** understand is diametrically opposed to the process by which we normally understand text. So much for teachers who present adult students with a text and ask *Are there any words you don't understand?*

Such teachers are unconsciously assuming that meaning is made **bottom-up**; you understand a bit, and another bit, and another bit and put the bits together like a jigsaw to create the whole picture. This is partly true — **one** of the ways in which meaning is created. It is not, however, **the** way that meaning is created.

The parallel with a jigsaw puzzle is helpful — when you begin, particularly if you do not have a copy of the finished picture, it is extremely difficult.

Rather despairingly, you may be willing to try any green bit with any other green bit — perhaps they fit. Contrast this with the situation when only a few pieces remain to be fitted — despite the gaps, the whole picture is clear. This insight should suggest to many teachers better ways of handling texts than any which concentrates on unknown words.

Referring again to the example above, it is possible to make sense of the Chancellor's prediction of serious consequences by contrasting it with what else he might have said — *very serious / some / some slight / no consequences.* Subconsciously we make meaning not only by recognising what the speaker has said, but by **contrasting** it with what has **not** been said. When I remark that *I am living in Brighton*, it contrasts with the more obvious *I live in Brighton.* The additional meaning is created through the contrast, but equally, when I remark *I live in Brighton* you assume that I intended precisely this meaning, by covertly contrasting with what I did not say, *I am living in Brighton.*

In summary, meaning is made in three ways, by an implicit system of **contrasts; bottom-up**, a synthetic process of adding bits to each other, and by **top-down interpretation**, incorporating detail into an overall view based on previous, real-world (including language) knowledge.

The process of productive creation of meaning — speaking and writing — proceeds in the same ways — the selection of the **least inappropriate** items from those known, building meaning bit by bit, and relating the bits to an overall assumed framework. Most language uses, of course, are neither uniquely productive or receptive, but a combination. Each participant makes meaning using the processes just described, and together they employ the same processes to create negotiated meaning. Far from being static and objective, meaning is intrinsically more subjective, inter-personal and evanescent.

Since the purpose of language is the communication of meaning, language teaching activities should invariably be meaning-centred. The brief survey of this chapter demonstrates that meaning is a complex concept. This suggests that, methodologically, different kinds of activity, acknowledging the different aspects of meaning should be a natural part of the language classroom. Too often, signification and usage, with a nod in the direction of the occasional function are the only kinds of meaning students meet in their language classes. That repertoire diminishes the nature of meaning and provides far from optimal conditions for language acquisition. Within the Lexical Approach, a much wider range of meaning-based activity is essential.

References

1. Current English Grammar, p.7.
2. The Communicative Approach, p.87.
3. The Lexical Syllabus, p.3 and passim.
4. op cit p.7.
5. op cit p.22/3.
6. op cit p.22.
7. Lexical Phrases in Language Teaching, p.113.
8. Explorations in Applied Linguistics, p.49.

Chapter 5

The Nature of Lexis

PART 1 — Introduction

We begin by repeating our refrain, Language consists of grammaticalised lexis, not lexicalised grammar. Lexis is the core or heart of language but in language teaching has always been the Cinderella. Carter and McCarthy in a seminal collection of papers on the subject, warn of the 'apparent chaos' of the lexicon. They go on, however, to say:

> Language practitioners need not shy away from lexis as a boundless chaos; organisational principles are available and simply wait to be more fully exploited. (Page 38)

We have already seen that language teaching has traditionally developed an unhelpful dichotomy between the generalisable, pattern-generating quality of grammar and the apparently arbitrary nature of individual vocabulary items. The reality of language data is more adequately represented by a Spectrum of Generalisability upon which grammatical or vocabulary items may be placed. This chapter, however, is about the nature of lexis, not vocabulary. The terminology is not a matter of pretention or pedantry, but represents a radical and profound change in the way we see and analyse language. Loosely, if you 'have a big vocabulary' you 'know a lot of words'. More precisely, you have access to a huge store of lexical items some of which are quite different in kind from others. What are we to understand by the term 'lexical item'? The question is in some ways as profound as asking the nature of language itself for, at its heart, it concerns the nature of the 'bits' which constitute language.

In a powerfully influential paper, Pawley[1] and Syder distinguish clearly between what is memorised and what is lexicalised:

> Not all sequences memorised by individual speakers are lexicalised. What makes an expression a lexical item, what makes it part of a speech community's common dictionary, is firstly, that the meaning of the expression is not (totally) predictable from its form, secondly that it behaves as a minimal unit for certain syntactic purposes, and third that it is a social institution. This last characteristic is sometimes overlooked, but is basic to the distinction between lexicalised and non-lexicalised sequences.

It is worth identifying, and reflecting on the three characteristic more fully. For them, lexical items are such that:

— Meaning is not totally predictable from form.
— Each is a minimal unit for certain syntactic purposes.
— Each is a social institution.

The first of these is the primary perception of linguistics — many, perhaps most, lexical items are neither more nor less than individual words so it is no surprise that the fundamentally arbitrary nature of the sign must apply.

Language can be sub-divided in many ways — sentences, turns, morphemes, phonemes. For different purposes different items constitute minimal units. It is not meaningful to ask what constitutes 'the' minimal units of language, only the minimal unit for a particular analytical purpose. Because something **can** be analysed, it does not necessarily follow that it is always useful **to** analyse it. 'Lexical items' are the minimal units **for certain syntactic purposes** — this has two important consequences, sequences larger than lexical items are too large, but equally importantly, shorter sequences are too small. The immense importance of this point will emerge shortly.

Language is a social phenomenon, socially rather than individually defined. Many sentences which are possible if generated by the supposed rules of native speaker competence can immediately be recognised as improbable, or even downright bizarre. There is a vast difference between what we could say and what we do say. This is one of the puzzles Pawley and Syder are addressing — the problem of nativelike selection. It appears that of all the sentences which might be produced by a native speaker, some occur with a much greater frequency than we might expect while we are certain that some possible sequences will never occur unless a linguist produces them for the purpose of demonstrating their implausibility or impossibility!

Lexical items, then, are **socially sanctioned independent units**. Many are words, but many consist of multi-word units. The existence and importance of formulaic many-word units is discussed by many commentators:

> . . . much native speaker language is formulaic; it is simply that the native speaker usually has a vastly greater range of formulae to call upon for use in a wider range of strategic domains. (McCarthy)[2]

> . . . The existence in a language such as English of very many institutionalised units perfectly serves the needs of adults (native speakers as well as foreign learners) who are predisposed to store and re-use units as much as, if not more than, to generate them from scratch. (Cowie)[3]

> Many early researchers thought these prefabricated chunks were distinct and somewhat peripheral to the main body of language, but more recent research puts this formulaic speech at the very centre of language acquisition and sees it as basic to the creative rule forming processes which follow. (Nattinger and DeCarrico)[4]

The centrality of the repertoire of lexical items is increasingly recognised, and Cowie succinctly highlights their most important use: *their economising role in speech production.*

These multi-word units can be analysed, but modern research suggests that speech may be processed more rapidly — both receptively and productively — if the units are perceived as single, unanalysed wholes. Cowie suggests that many items which are learned as wholes can later be analysed into their constituent parts as, redundantly but usefully, native speakers retain the ability to produce the item in its unanalysed form rather than generating items 'from scratch' on every occasion. Rather than relying on the generative power of grammar:[5] *Users rely on a vast store of fixed phrases and pre-patterned locutions by which they routinely manage aspects of interaction.*

Nattinger has written extensively about the value of lexical phrases (his term) in language teaching. He provides the following taxonomy:[6]

1. **Polywords:** short, fixed phrases whose meaning is often not analysable from the regular rules of syntax. They include idioms, euphemisms, slang, two- and three-part verbs.

2. **Phrasal constraints:** short relatively fixed phrases with slots that permit some variation.

3. **Deictic locutions:** short to medium length phrases of low variability whose function directs the flow of conversation (*as far as I know, for that matter, further to my letter of*).

4. **Sentence builders:** phrases up to sentence length, highly variable containing slots for parameters or arguments. (*If I X, then I Y; the ... er X, the ... Y*).

5. **Situational utterances:** complete sentences, amenable to the regular rules of syntax and highly dependent on social context. They provide the framework for particular social interactions.

6. **Verbatim texts:** entire text with extremely low variability, used for quotations, allusion, aphorisms, proverbs etc. Some are general units, used by everyone in the speech community, while others are more idiosyncratic and ideolectal.

This taxonomy was proposed some years ago by Nattinger and provides only one possible listing. I suggest a somewhat simpler analysis.

PART 2 — Different Kinds of Lexical Items

Words

The most basic kind of lexical item is also the most familiar — the individual word. Little needs to be said about the nature of such items, though they do pose pedagogical problems concerned with selecting, sequencing, and learnability.

The criteria most frequently used in establishing the relative usefulness of words have been frequency of occurrence, range of text-type in which the item occurs, availability, familiarity and coverage. The last refers to those items such as hyponyms which can substitute effectively for a wide variety of alternative, usually more specific, terms.

The most useful distinction we have noted so far in the search for words which will be useful pattern generators within a lexical approach is between words with zero or low information content (*with, of*) and those of high information content (*book, advert, oscillate*). The Cobuild lexicographic project was extremely successful in analysing words by taking an ultra-naive view that all words were similar, and that identical forms represented identical words, albeit different senses of the same word. They were less successful in basing language teaching material on the same criteria, precisely in my view because words with different degrees of informational content require different pedagogical procedures.

Willis, describing the basis of the Cobuild course is explicit that the primary analytical unit is the word:[7]

> Instead of specifying an inventory of grammatical structures or a set of functions, each stage of the course would be built round a lexical syllabus. This would specify words, then meanings and the common phrases in which they were used.

> If one starts by listing words and their behaviour, one can generate automatically the structural environments and the words which are likely to occur within them.[8]

This theoretical position provides a number of insights. There is, for example, no justification for teaching *would* as part of the **structure** of English, while other modals are treated lexically. Willis convincingly demonstrates that *would* is more accurately and economically dealt with by asking what the individual word means. Similarly, the Cobuild word-based approach suggests a radically different grammar of the word *any* from that traditionally taught. In contrast, however, the project acknowledges lexical items other than words only rather grudgingly:

> Also annotated in the database are common phrases with *way* which are found so frequently that they function almost like lexical items in their own right; *By the way* this visit of Muller's is strictly secret; *In a way* these officers were prisoners themselves.[9]

> We probably carry in our minds 'chunks' of language incorporating the word *thing* in these grammatical frames:
> *The (adjective) thing is that … ; The (adjective) thing is to … ; It's one thing to X and quite another to Y*[10].

The caution is noticeable: phrases function 'almost' like lexical items in their own right; we 'probably' carry chunks in our mind. There is considerable research evidence which endorses the view that a great deal of language is stored in units larger than the individual word. The rigorous theoretical position espoused by the Cobuild team produced a major breakthrough in dictionary making, but the language teaching materials based on the same criteria were seriously inhibited by a resistance to other types of lexical item.

Multi-word items

In contrast to individual words there are many hundreds of thousands of lexical items which are multi-word units, each recognised as having an independent existence, even if they could be further analysed into components. These multi-word units can usefully be sub-categorised, but any categorisation will involve marginal cases and overlapping categories. Despite this, looking at groups of lexical items is revealing. The two most important groups are **collocations**, which are message-orientated, and **institutionalised expressions**, which are essentially pragmatic in character.

Polywords

This is the least novel, and 'messiest' category. Like single words, these are frequently found in dictionaries. They are usually relatively short — two or three words — may belong to any word class, and the meaning of the whole group may range from immediately apparent or totally different from the component words. Only one kind of polyword, phrasal verbs, has featured prominently in language teaching. Others deserve increased attention. Here are some examples:

taxi rank	put off	of course	by the way
record player	look up	on the other hand	the day after tomorrow
continuous assessment	look up to	all at once	in his element

Immediately we see that the categorisation is fuzzy edged, and a matter of interpretation rather than objective fact. Perhaps *continuous assessment* is more usefully categorised as a fixed collocation (see below); if *the day after tomorrow* is a lexical item, what about *at the weekend* — perhaps that is best treated as a fixed item rather than *at + the weekend*. Finally, even if *in his element* is a polyword it permits some variation: *in her/their element*. We fortunately, are not looking for rigidly defined categories, only useful ways of grouping. We have already noted that almost all grammatical categorisation has fuzzy edges; it comes as no surprise that attempts to categorise lexis raise similar problems.

Collocations

Collocations describe the way individual words co-occur with others. The pairs of words which can co-occur are, of course, almost infinitely numerous. Variation is possible on both syntagmatic and paradigmatic axes:

prices	fell
incomes	rose
unemployment	stabilised
. . . .	. . . .

Possible two-word combinations vary from the totally unexpectedly novel — free collocation — to the rigidly institutionalised or ossified form — fixed collocation. As we have now learned to expect, this is not a dichotomy but a spectrum between fixed and free poles. We have already seen that the pattern generating power of a word is inversely proportional to its informational content; a similar consideration applies to collocations. Nattinger and DeCarrico[11] put it this way:

> As collocations become less fixed, that is as more variation becomes possible along both axes, predictability lessens and meaning increases.

Fixed collocations are one kind of polyword. Free collocations are, by definition, entirely novel and therefore lie towards the creative, grammatical competence-based pole of language. Like words with varying degrees of informational content, collocations at different ends of the fixed/free spectrum suggest different pedagogical procedures.

One element of a collocation pair may strongly, perhaps almost uniquely, suggest the other element, but this degree of fixedness is non-reciprocal. Nattinger cites *rancid* as almost uniquely determining its collocate *butter*, while *butter* certainly does not suggest the preceding adjective with anything like the same degree of certainty. This lack of reciprocity will have an important pedagogical implication — if we wish to use words as pattern generating items, it will be important to identify those which most rigorously and helpfully predict collocates.

Bahns[12] has pointed out that some collocations translate directly whereas some do not. Not unreasonably, he suggests that it is those which do not which cause most learning difficulties for students. Unfortunately, he offers no guidance on what categories are most or least likely to be translatable. The problem is similar to that of the translation of individual words — if a word has very high, for example technical, meaning-content it will tend to have a close or exact equivalent in another language. Words of relatively low meaning content, and in particular de-lexicalised words, with their complex patterns, are much less likely to exhibit one-to-one correspondence. In the case of verb + noun collocations, it is precisely those involving relatively de-lexicalised verbs which need most attention on a comparative basis. Again different pedagogical procedures are needed.

Collocations, like individual words, are neither pragmatically tied, nor pragmatically identifiable; in this, they differ from institutionalised expressions, discussed below. Words and collocations are intimately associated with the **content** of what the language user expresses rather than what the language user is **doing** — complaining, explaining, contradicting etc. In a balanced lexical approach, this insight will be of more than theoretical interest, enabling us to produce a more comprehensive and balanced range of lexis for the learner.

Institutionalised expressions

Characteristically, these allow the language user to manage aspects of the interaction; they are pragmatic in character. Their use means that the listener or the reader quickly identifies what the language user is doing. Once what is being **done** has been identified, linguistic processing can concentrate on what is being **said,** on specific content. These institutionalised multi-word units ensure the efficient processing both receptively and productively, in both speech and writing. Despite their essential role, and wide applicability, they remain largely unidentified in language teaching, and the least exploited of potential linguistic resources for students. Broadly, these fixed items may be categorised under three sub-headings:

— Short, hardly grammaticalised utterances: *Not yet. Certainly not. Just a moment, please.*

— Sentence heads or frames — most typically the first words of utterances, serving a primarily pragmatic purpose: *Sorry to interrupt, but can I just say ...; That's all very well, but ...; I see what you mean, but I wonder if it wouldn't be better to ...*

— Full sentences, with readily identifiable pragmatic meaning, which are easily recognised as fully institutionalised. It is these sentences — characterised by their typicality in native speaker usage which were the principal concern of Pawley and Syder's paper. They suggest[13]:

> The number of memorised complete clauses and sentences known to the mature English speaker is probably many thousands. Much more numerous still, however, is a class of phraseological expressions each of which is something less than a completely specified clause.

Elsewhere in the same article they claim[14]:

> The stock of lexicalised sentence stems known to the ordinary mature speaker of English amount to hundreds of thousands. In addition, there are many semi-lexicalised sequences, for just as there is a continuum between fully productive rules for sentence formation and rules of low productivity, so there is a cline between fully lexicalised formations on the one hand, and nonce forms on the other.

By 'a nonce form' they mean a totally novel, speaker-generated utterance. It is at the opposite end of the spectrum from fully institutionalised sentences. The enormity of their claim — that there are hundreds of thousands of such utterances — is only now beginning to filter into language teaching, although even the least experienced teacher is at least partially aware of the problems — a good knowledge of the grammar of English, and an extensive vocabulary is not sufficient to ensure that the learner speaks English like a native, or even speaks English well, or effectively. If students have been exposed largely to written language and formal grammar they may experience considerable difficulty in understanding native speakers; worse still, much of the language they produce, or know, while formally 'correct' will deviate to such an extent from what is natural as to cause serious problems of comprehension.

Institutionalised expressions will be a help to any non-native learner. Clearly a repertoire of such phrases is an important part of fluency for the intermediate and more advanced learner. For elementary and lower intermediate students some phrases of this type will have immediate practical utility, a fact which has been recognised traditionally by tourist-style phrase books, and in slightly modified form, by the enthusiasm with which functions — that is, pragmatically identifiable utterances — were taken up as teaching became more 'communicative'. Institutionalised expressions provide a way of increasing the elementary student's communicative resources rapidly, and at the same time provide accurate and natural data against which other novel utterances may be monitored and a valuable resource contributing to the acquisition of competence.

Lexis as the basis of language

The shift in terminology from vocabulary to lexis can seem pedantic and pretentious. Although collocations and the various institutionalised expressions offer obvious additions to any conventional syllabus, they do not appear to represent a radical challenge to the status quo. Increasingly, however, as Nattinger and DeCarrico have noted, lexical phrases as they call them, do represent a major shift with profound theoretical and practical implications. In the preface to *Lexical Phrases and Language Teaching*, they observe:

> One common pattern in language acquisition is that learners pass through a stage in which they use a large number of unanalysed chunks of language in certain predictable social contexts. They use, in other words, a great deal of 'prefabricated' language. Many earlier researchers thought these prefabricated chunks were distinct and somewhat peripheral to the main body of language, but more recent research puts this formulaic speech at the very centre of language acquisition and sees it as basic to the creative rule-forming processes which follow.

This view represents a complete reversal of the traditional structuralist position. Structuralism asserted that the learner mastered the 'rules' of the system, and was thereby able to generate correct sentences. It now seems plausible that an important part of language acquisition is the ability to produce lexical phrases as unanalysed wholes or 'chunks', and that these chunks become the raw data by which the learner begins to perceive patterns, morphology, and those other features of language traditionally thought of as 'grammar'. Within such a model, phrases acquired as wholes are the primary resource by which the syntactic system is mastered.

Language can be analysed at many different levels but, as we have observed elsewhere, this does not necessarily imply that it is always useful to analyse it, nor, more importantly, that mastering the language involves 'assembling' it from its smallest component parts. Language teaching — often obsessed with teaching rather than learning — may have introduced counter-productive methodology by insistence on this essentially synthetic approach. Cowie is of the opinion that native speakers have the possibility of producing the same language items from two independent resources — generatively using their acquired competence, or by recalling sentences as learned wholes. He believes that despite the obvious redundancy involved, the advantages to language processing in real time are so substantial that we retain a vast repertoire of learned utterances, recallable as wholes, even after we have fully mastered the ability to generate the same utterances from scratch. Nattinger and DeCarrico, quoting and endorsing Pawley and Syder agree[15]:

> ... Prefabricated patterns 'form a high proportion of the fluent stretches of speech heard in everyday conversation ... Coming readymade (they) need little encoding work', and the speaker can 'do the work of constructing a larger piece of discourse by expanding on, or combining ready-made constructions'. Thus, although grammatical competence encompasses the knowledge of the lexical forms and their internal syntax, pragmatic competence accounts for the speaker's ability to continue to access these forms as pre-assembled chunks, ready for a given functional use in an appropriate context.

In short, correctly identified lexical phrases can be presented to L2 learners in identifiable contexts, mastered as learned wholes, and thus become an important resource to mastering the syntax. I wholly endorse this view, which precisely mirrors my own concern with the way in which we understand, and master central elements of the verb system. Traditionally, students 'learned' the difference between, for example, the *'ll* and *going to* futures and then 'practised them', often using single sentence de-contextualised examples. As is widely acknowledged, this fundamentally flawed methodology did not work, yet it remained, implicitly and explicitly, in many textbooks and classroom procedures. It is far more likely that students will be helped by being presented with a sufficiently large number of adequately contextualised (situation + co-text), archetypical examples of, for example, the *'ll* forms and, in due course, a similar range of well chosen examples of *going to* forms. Students can be encouraged to use these without employing any formal verbalisation of 'the difference'. In the short term, mistakes must be tolerated as students recall correctly, recall incorrectly, begin to experiment, and, over a period of time, converge toward standard use. If this procedure is to be maximally effective, the choice of examples is critical, and as far as possible from the artificially created examples of old-fashioned structuralism. The examples should:

— Be readily accepted by native speakers as institutionalised utterances.

— Reflect instantly identifiable pragmatic meaning.

— Exhibit different degrees of variability from fully fixed sentences to those exhibiting limited paradigmatic substitution (see below).

— Cover a representative range of possible (grammatical) subjects, reflecting frequency of occurrence in real world data.

The identification and organisation of examples of this kind is a central task for researchers, materials writers and teachers. It applies *mutatis mutandis* to both spoken and written language, and to both ESP and general language.

Given below is a proposed set of archetypical utterances exemplifying the use of *'ll* (all, of course, representing the spoken language). The reader might care before consulting my list to collect a dozen or so utterances so that you can then compare your list with mine.

Once such a list has been identified, it becomes the task of the materials writer to ensure that these utterances are introduced into the classroom adequately contextualised to make their pragmatic meaning clear — notice the radical shift of emphasis, the material must be contextualised so that the meaning of the **whole utterance** is clear **in relation to the discourse in which it occurs**. This naturally suggests the extensive use of listening materials, and classroom dialogues; probably both naturally occurring and quasi-natural scripted dialogue will provide the most effective mix for pedagogic purposes. The most radical change is unquestionably the shift of emphasis from the analysis of the component elements of the utterance to the primary focus shifting to the meaning of the utterance as a whole. Analysis will occur only later — and this 'later' may not mean as the next classroom activity; analysis may be delayed for several days or even weeks depending on the intensity of the teaching programme. Patience of this kind represents another challenge to the teacher's mind-set but, if the grammatical system of the language is acquired, the proposed methodology maximises the student's exposure to carefully chosen data and, in more adequately reflecting the nature of language and the nature of acquisition, maximises the benefit to the student in the medium, rather than short, term.

Archetypical utterances containing *'ll*

> I'll get it.
> I'll give you a ring.
> I'll drop you a line.
> I'll be in touch.
> I'll get back to you as soon as I can.
> I'll be back in a minute.
> I'll see what I can do.
> I'll see you later.
> Take my word for it — you'll regret it.
> You'll never get away with it.
> Be careful — you'll make yourself ill.
> It'll be alright.
> It'll take time.
> That'll do.
> That'll be the day.
> She'll be six in June.
> (I'm sure) somebody'll be able to help you.
> Nobody'll even notice.
> There'll be hell to pay.
> We'll see.
> (I'm sure) they'll be pleased to see you.

It is immediately noticeable that many of these, readily recognisable as institutionalised sentences, seem much more natural than the language we often associate with elementary textbooks. They are much more idiomatic than textbook 'EFL-speak'. Does the idiomatic nature of many of these utterances debar them from use in language teaching, or at least relegate to upper-intermediate and advanced classes? I suggest not — it is rather that we must reconsider the nature and role of idiom in language teaching.

PART 3 — The Spectrum of Idiomaticity

The concept of idiomaticity is, for most people, rather ill-defined. 'Un-idiomatic' speech suggests the use of utterances which are grammatically possible, accurate but unlikely to occur in native speaker speech; in second language learning, 'an idiom' usually suggests rather picturesque expressions: *It's raining cats and dogs*; *He threw in the towel*.

Technically, an idiom is a particular kind of lexical item, defined by the fact that the meaning of the whole is not immediately apparent from the meanings of the constituent parts. It is unsurprising that the transparency of idiomatic expressions is a matter of degree — there is a Spectrum of Idiomaticity. Traditionally, picturesque idioms have been seen as appropriate for relatively advanced students — a sophistication, marginal to the serious business of mastering the central grammatical system. Similarly, the selection of idiomatically appropriate rather than formally accurate utterances has been seen as 'advanced' language teaching.

Once again we need to revise our view in the light of modern corpus linguistics, discourse analysis, the increasing awareness of the difference between the spoken and written languages, and contemporary attempts to accord the spoken language its natural place as the primary, and most natural medium of language use.

Modern linguistic research suggests that metaphor, far from being a literary device, is intrinsic to the nature of everyday language. The corollary is that language is intrinsically less literal than we have always assumed; this, in turn, implies that idiom is also intrinsic to everyday language use — in some cases the meaning of an utterance will be derivable directly from the meaning of its constituent parts, but in many cases the meaning of the whole will either have a conventional pragmatic meaning **additional** to the surface meaning, or, as in the case of what are traditionally thought of as idioms, the whole will have a meaning radically different from the parts. Although not traditionally thought of as idioms, all of the following demonstrate aspects of this spectrum:

He fell off a ladder while he was cleaning the windows.
Demand fell in the New Year as the dollar rose.

I broke that vase your mother gave us for Christmas this morning!
Somebody broke into the car while we were at the theatre.
We broke down on the motorway.
I need a full breakdown of the cost before we can make any decision.

We keep a fairly low profile but we are very active in the market place.
We're not out of the wood yet, but things are picking up a bit.

Excuse me, can I just say something.
(Claps) ... Could I just say a few words ...

The metaphorical/literal and transparent/idiomatic nature of most of the above examples has long been recognised. What is new is recognition of those features in examples such as the last pair. The first of these is conventionally used to interrupt a meeting to give a short message; the second is used to call for silence at a social gathering in order to propose a vote of thanks. Both are institutionalised expressions whose pragmatic meaning is not apparent simply from the words used. *Could I just say a few words* has a pragmatic meaning not associated with *Could I say some words*, or *Could I say something*. Despite the fact that the others are well-formed English sentences, they are not idiomatic utterances if calling for silence in a small social group. The utterance is highly idiomatic, although in no sense resembling the 'raining cats and dogs' type idiom. These more natural idioms should play an important role in language teaching, even at elementary and intermediate levels. This will particularly be the case in courses aimed at adult learners anxious to increase their communicative power rapidly.

Institutionalised sentences or holophrases of this kind are very numerous. Pawley and Syder have suggested that mature English native speakers have a repertoire of 'many thousands'. They list some hundred which they claim are the result of only a few minutes reflection, and my own experience when introducing this idea to groups of native speakers bears out their suggestion A group can usually agree on a list of twenty such utterances within a few moments. A few examples:

I see what you mean
I'll go along with that!
The damage is already done.
It's funny you should say that. It reminds me of . . .
I think we are at cross purposes here.
Yes, but it's not as simple as that.

It is at least plausible that native speakers regard sentences as well-formed or otherwise largely on the basis of their resemblance to the stock of learned idiomatic utterances of the kind just listed. In the notes on the Pawley and Syder paper the editors say: *It is suggested that the grammar of a language contains, in addition to productive rules, a 'phrase book with grammatical notes'*. Peters, has concluded:

> Any sharp distinction between vocabulary and syntax collapses into a dynamic and fluid continuum, ranging from the completely fixed to the completely original.

Pawley and Syder make explicit[16] the possible resource-value of lexicalised sentence stems:

> It has been pointed out that lexicalised sentence stems may be 'inflected' or expanded', except for a minority of expressions that are completely rigid in their form. In order for a speaker to derive (partly) novel forms using a given lexicalised sentence stem, it is necessary for him to know the grammar of that stem. A novel sequence would be native-like at least to the extent that it consists of institutionalised sentence stem + permissible variations. It appears, however, that each such sentence stem has more or less unique grammar; each one is subject to a somewhat different range of phrase structure and transformational restrictions.

This suggestion is almost staggeringly radical — many thousands of individual sentences, first learned as wholes, each have their own grammar. Everyone is familiar with language produced by non-natives which is grammatically accurate in the sense that it conforms to the general generative rules of the language, yet the sentence sounds odd or 'foreign'. Clearly, restrictions apply to particular sub-patterns, or individual sentences. These have often been dismissed as matters of style or register and, as several commentators have pointed out, this has allowed linguists to avoid studying such restrictions. If we are to take a lexical approach to language teaching it is clear that some of these sentences, grouped and chosen for archetypicality, must be introduced relatively early in the learning programme. Grammar will, to some extent at least, be acquired through generalising, and learning the restrictions on the generalisation from these sentences. In this way lexical phrases — a particular kind of lexical item — will provide the basis for a lexically, rather than grammatically driven syllabus. The problem of selection has not yet been fully solved, but it provides the direction in which we must move if an approach is to be developed where the central role of lexis, and correspondingly subordinate role of grammar, are recognised.

PART 4 — Lexical Density

Lexical density is the ratio of content carrying words to total running words. As Halliday[17], in his comprehensive survey *Spoken and Written Language* observes:

> (It) is a characteristic difference between spoken and written language (that) written language displays a much higher ratio of lexical items to total running words.

He goes on to describe written language as 'dense', in contrast to spoken language which he calls 'sparse'. Several attempts have been made to analyse the linguistic features which underlie the contrast. We are all implicitly aware of it in that it is relatively easy to identify a piece of language presented on paper as coming originally from a spoken source. Broadly, written language achieves lexical density, and the resultant density of information, by using a relatively high proportion of complex noun phrases and subordinate clauses. The difference in lexical density between spoken and written language has at least three important pedagogical implications:

a. If students are only presented with language in one medium (spoken or written) their acquisition will be biased, and in relation to mature native speaker language, defective. Although, as I have argued extensively elsewhere, the spoken language must have priority, all courses (except for very young children) should contain a proportion of written language.

b. Certain grammatical items — notably complex noun clauses and subordination — are **characteristic** of the written language. If, as I have suggested elsewhere, students' courses are heavily biased in favour of learning to speak English through the use of spoken data, such students will, quite reasonably be relatively poor if they are required to write extensively. Testing students who speak English well by requiring them to write paragraphs or essays is quite simply testing something different. It is necessary constantly to keep in mind Halliday's dictum that written language is not spoken language written down.

c. If students in particular fields — notably academic English or those preparing for written examinations — need to be able to write essays, reports and the like, specific training will be needed. Interestingly, even highly educated native speakers may remain unable to write coherently and effectively in L1. The ability to write may be subconsciously acquired through extensive reading of text similar to that which you wish to produce; in this way, the grammar of written English may be acquired in Krashen's sense of the term in the same way as the grammar of spoken English, through extensive exposure to the right kind of comprehensible input. In sharp contrast to the grammar of spoken language, which I believe is essentially and uniquely acquired through comprehensible input and acquisition, the grammar of written English can, in Krashen's sense, be learned. This is precisely because the process of producing written text is often a highly self-conscious, reflective, non-spontaneous activity. Even competent writers think of the content, formulate it linguistically, and frequently re-formulate it, before putting a single word on the page. Because this process is conscious, it is an area of language where learning can contribute directly to more effective performance, and ultimately to acquisition. This is a distinction which I do not believe Krashen has made, at least in his published work.

As usual, the written/spoken distinction is a spectrum rather than a dichotomy. Very formal speech, notably lectures or presentations, exhibit characteristics of both informal spoken language and lexically dense written language. Competent lecturers and presenters are precisely those who maintain a good balance between these two styles — 'reading a paper' at a conference can be too lexically dense for an audience to follow; 'conversational' lecturing or presenting can give an impression of unpreparedness or time wasting. Because conscious choices are involved between alternative 'correct' ways of expressing the same propositional content, academic writing, lecturing, and linguistic presentation skills all lend themselves to explicit teaching. Clearly, this has important implications for the content of courses aimed at academic or business English.

PART 5 — Vocabulary Size

Whatever definition of 'vocabulary size' is adopted, it is clear that the mature native speaker has an enormous repertoire. It is usual to distinguish between active and passive vocabulary; native speakers recognise a huge number of items which are not part of their everyday production. Research into lexical phrases, however, suggests that they know a huge number of items — individual words, fixed collocations, sentence stems, and institutionalised sentences. Commentators' estimates vary in assessing the number of items known to the mature native speaker, but are never less than tens of thousands and Pawley and Syder[18] claim:

> The number of single morpheme lexical items known to the average mature native English speaker is relatively small; a few thousand. The number of morphologically complex lexical items is much greater running into hundreds of thousands. A very considerable proportion of the total body of (relatively) well-defined complex lexical items consists of what we will term here 'lexicalised sentence stems'.

McCarthy claims that much native speaker language is formulaic and the native speaker has a 'vast range of formulae'.

If these claims are correct it suggests a severe deficiency in most contemporary language teaching materials. Even if we confine ourselves to a much narrower concept of lexical items — what are normally thought of simply as words — the problem of what constitutes a minimum adequate vocabulary remains. The central problem is that words are of different kinds — the traditional word classes — and that the most frequent words usually have low information content, while high-content-bearing words are relatively rare. The question of 'minimum adequate vocabulary' is much more complex than simply knowing the most frequent words of the language — it is a question not only of how many words, but **what kinds** of words. Sinclair and Renouf[19], for example, identified a particular problem:

> The conventional view of the words in a language is that they either have lexical meaning or are confined to syntactic functions in the sentence. Hence uses which are discoursal or pragmatic, which carry out functions to do with the larger patterns of text, are often missed. For example, the humble and exceedingly frequent word *to* has a discourse function which is important and valuable to the user. It often occurs at the beginning of a move or sentence, and indicates that the comment which it introduces is an evaluation of the main part of the utterance. Some of these uses have become familiar phrases, like, 'to be honest', 'to cut a long story short', and the contrast between this function and the use of *to* as if it were 'in order to', can be seen in the ambiguity of the following (constructed) example: *To be fair, Tom divided the sweets evenly.*

Some would argue that expressions such as *to be honest* are polywords, and should be identified as such for students. Sinclair prefers a word-based approach, identifying a particular pragmatic meaning for *to*. Whichever view one takes, the essential fact is that traditional vocabulary teaching found no place for items of this kind.

The vast majority of the words of any language are, of course, nouns. Traditional vocabulary teaching has recognised this, but frequently only at the expense of other word categories. Picture dictionaries lend themselves to the depiction of nouns, but, although action and change can also be depicted, verbs remain greatly under-represented. Vocabulary teaching materials, exercises, and classroom procedures are almost exclusively directed towards nouns. My own investigations show that many intermediate students have quite large repertoires of nouns which they are unable to use effectively because they do not know the other words which co-occur with the nouns — most importantly they lack an adequate vocabulary of verbs. Furthermore, even if they know a verb, they may be wholly unaware of its connotational range — students can open doors, windows and books but may be unaware that you can *open a letter*. Such collocation is not obvious, and can be acquired only through extensive contact with the language, or formal teaching. (The opposite of *opening the door* is *closing the door*, but the opposite of *opening a letter* is not *closing a letter*). If you wish to talk about a noun it is precisely words in **other** word categories which are needed. Often, vocabulary teaching is almost exclusively directed to naming more and more objects, rather than encouraging the ability to talk about things.

An effective and balanced vocabulary involves knowledge of a sufficient number of verbs (with their collocational ranges), adjectives, and adverbs. In the latter case these must not be restricted to adjective-adverb pairs of the *beautiful/beautifully, careful/carefully* kind; sentence adjuncts and polyword adverbials are at least as important. In addition to those word classes, traditionally associated with vocabulary teaching and content, at least five word classes traditionally associated with grammar and function words are needed. These are **connectors, intensifiers, auxiliaries, determiners**, and **prepositions**. These categories are frequently dealt with only from a grammatical point of view but they are words in their own right, and in common with other words do have signification, de-contextualised meaning. Most obviously, prepositions of place have readily apparent signification, which is consistent and logical. It will be noted that several of the word categories which have been under-represented in traditional vocabulary teaching — most notably adjuncts and connectors, but also intensifiers, auxiliaries and determiners — are characteristic of language at the level of discourse rather than individual sentence. Once again we see that language teaching's preoccupation with the formation of correct sentences has had a distorting effect on what has been included, and more importantly excluded, from teaching materials.

PART 6 — Context and Co-text

Learning theory has quite properly suggested that words may be more effectively learned if they are presented systematically, in rich contexts rather than randomly. This helpful insight has unfortunately led to two methodological distortions. Firstly, many teachers assume that words can **only** be learned when contextualised, and that **any** form of 'putting the word in a sentence' represents contextualisation. Both these assumptions are false — words may be perfectly adequately contextualised by learners in terms of their real world experience or imagination. Conversely, simply putting the word into a sentence may **not** contextualise — it may need to be realised in an utterance, not a sentence, that is as part of a coherent text so that its discoursal features are apparent. Contextualisation means noting the **situation** in which the word may occur, but most importantly noting **the co-text with which it can regularly occur**. If context is seen as situation + co-text, it is the latter — co-occurring language — which is more important for language learning.

This insight relates directly to the second absurdity — vocabulary teaching which uses as its primary organisational principle what are often called semantic fields. Even Wilkins, in *Notional Syllabuses*, suggested on several occasions that the vocabulary content of learning would be largely determined by topic, a term which some prefer to semantic field. The idea is seductively simple — students learn the words together which cover a particular topic or situation. There is nothing wrong with this as a principle, but its pedagogic implementation has usually resulted in vocabulary teaching totally dominated by a process of nominalisation, resulting in word lists consisting almost entirely of nouns. Gairns[20] and Redman, confidently assert:

> Items commonly associated with ... With this type of relation we are drawing on our knowledge of the world. Ask a native speaker what items he commonly associates with 'kitchen' and he will probably list the appliances, gadgets and general contents illustrated in the picture.

The picture in question presents about fifty words — all of them nouns. The authors talk about 'items' associated with the kitchen, and unfortunately the term is usually taken as synonymous with 'things', rather than 'linguistic items'. If vocabulary teaching is to be based on topics or semantic fields, it is essential to consider different word classes — again most importantly verbs — and to think about the language used to **talk about the topic**, not simply to name the objects associated with the topic. Once again, what is of central importance is co-text.

Summary

It is difficult to grasp immediately the enormity of the changes implied by the perception of lexis as central to language. It is much more radical than any suggestion that there are a few multi-word items which have in the past been overlooked. The primary perception is that historically we have studied language by breaking it into the wrong bits — words and structures. A few polywords were recognised but the integrity of most multi-word items has been ignored. More seriously, the whole analysis of language has been seriously distorted, as a simple traditional 'structure' rarely coincides with a single lexical item, so the boundaries between chunks have been distorted or unrecognised. A parallel may help clarify the radical nature of the shift in perception — imagine English analysed by syllables, rather than words. All words are made of syllables, and the analysis of monosyllabic words would be unchanged. But the larger unit — the word — is unquestionably a more powerful analytical tool than the syllable for most purposes. The change from word to lexical item is on this scale — some individual words are lexical items, but lexical items present a more powerful analytical tool than words. Multi-word lexical items are independent units, and the ability to chunk language successfully is central to the theoretical understanding of how language works. It is also a strategy and technique with important pedagogical implications. Students need to be made more aware of lexis, and helped to identify, practise and record lexis in the most efficient and helpful ways. The pedagogical implications are the subject of the next two chapters.

References

1. In Richard and Schmidt p.209.
2. Discourse Analysis, p.122.
3. In Carter and McCarthy p.136.
4. Lexical Phrases in Language Teaching p.xv.
5. In Carter and McCarthy p.61.
6. In Carter and McCarthy p.76.
7. The Lexical Syllabus p.15.
8. ibid p.52.
9. ibid p.31.
10. ibid p.39.
11. op cit p.21.
12. ELTJ 47/1 Jan 1993.
13. op cit p.205.
14. op cit p.192.
15. op cit p.13.
16. op cit p.214.
17. op cit p.61.
18. op cit p.210.
19. In Carter and McCarthy p.153.
20. Working with Words, p.29.

Chapter 6

Lexis in the Syllabus

Syllabus in this chapter is interpreted in what Nunan calls the 'narrow' sense — the content of the teaching programme. Willis, in *The Lexical Syllabus*, observes that an approach involves both syllabus specification and methodology, and that syllabus and methodology are not discrete options; indeed, syllabus may be specified in terms of goals, performance objectives, or other criteria such as Prabhu's procedural syllabus. Here, I am concerned with the contribution lexis may make to the specification of content. Historically, syllabuses were structural; the Communicative Approach introduced functions, and certain re-orderings. The question naturally arises as to what similar changes are called for by the Lexical Approach. The search for a **strictly** lexical syllabus is likely to be frustrating for theorist, teacher and student. Widdowson has observed that a strictly lexical syllabus would begin with one word texts each complete in itself, proceed to two word texts, and so on to ever more complex texts but where, at all times, any grammatical complexity was obligatory as the language user's meaning became increasingly complex, and **demanded** additional grammaticalisation. Even if such a syllabus were possible to devise, it is difficult to imagine it being pedagogically acceptable.

Similarly, the attempt by Cobuild to define a lexical syllabus around the most frequent **words** of the language has not, despite its fascinating theoretical base, met with widespread acceptance. Some of the reasons I perceive for this are discussed below. I emphasise that my own concern is to look at the **contribution** which lexical items of different kinds can make in determining content.

Educational Syllabus

Language teaching is part of a wider whole, the education of individuals. Every learning experience should contribute to the development of mature individuals. Although educational experiences will differ in the way they contribute for every participating individual, effective educational experience should increase **curiosity, wonder and awe, confidence** and **self-worth**. In addition it should increase the individual's ability to **concentrate, appreciate, argue a case, tolerate, take responsibility** and **co-operate**.

There is in all education a hidden agenda which seeks to develop particular intellectual skills, the most important of which are involved in:

1. Identifying problems.

2. Collecting information, data and evidence.

3. Classifying data, by recognising similarity and difference.

4. Ranking, making hierarchies, separating more from less important.

5. Evaluating evidence and argument.

6. Estimating, so that the plausibility of an answer may be evaluated.

7. Taking decisions — based on complete or partial data.

8. Communicating results effectively.

It will be noted that much traditional language teaching is in direct conflict with some of these objectives. The P-P-P paradigm, repetition, and controlled pattern practice are elements of this kind. A task-based methodology, and an O-H-E paradigm are in sympathy with the wider educational syllabus. This is important, for nothing which happens in the classroom should conflict with the educational ideals which the above summary expresses.

The single most distinctive feature of the Lexical Approach is that it proposes a fundamentally different attitude to the treatment of text. Firstly, it is suspicious of de-contextualised language, recognising the importance of co-text, and therefore preferring extended text or discourse. Secondly, it proposes a range of awareness-raising activities directing students' attention to the chunks of which text is composed. Texts play a role in introducing interesting content, but also act as a major linguistic resource from which students can **extract** lexical items for study, expansion, and recording in appropriate formats. A basic classroom strategy will be helping students to avoid becoming preoccupied by grammar or vocabulary, concentrating instead on different kinds of lexical item.

Syllabuses are normally thought of as listing, and perhaps sequencing, course content. In fact, three factors are important: inclusions, exclusions and sequencing.

Inclusions, Exclusions and Sequencing

As all teachers know, courses are invariably too short. Although a case can be made for including any language which is new for the student, a principal role for the syllabus is to provide principled ways of **including** only **maximally useful** items. What is maximally useful is not intrinsic to the language, but relates to particular courses, and even particular students. A primary distinction is between long courses — perhaps over several years in school — and short intensive courses intended to have a high surrender value. Too many courses are constructed on the implicit assumption that they are intermediate stages on the way to full language competence. Only rarely is this the case; most students will remain intermediate and this should influence the language selected for inclusion.

Within the Lexical Approach:

—All low level courses will give students a large vocabulary, even if they are initially unable to grammaticalise it.

—Pragmatically useful lexical items, particularly institutionalised utterances form a significant component of all courses.

—A balance will be maintained between (relatively rare) words carrying considerable meaning, and (relatively wide and frequent) patterns with low meaning content.

Three principal reasons may be identified for **excluding** material: it is **not identified**, **not valued**, or **not prioritised**. In the days of structural syllabuses, mastery of structure was regarded as synonymous with language learning; the consequent emphasis of structure within syllabuses was wholly to be expected. When the influence of pragmatics was felt in language teaching, functions became a familiar term to teachers. As a result *Would you like ...?* was re-identified as *Offering*; its re-identification allowed it to be re-valued, and re-placed, much earlier in courses. Within the Lexical Approach different kinds of lexical item may be identified, or in relation to traditional language teaching, re-identified. Examples are treating *would* as a single word lexical item, rather than part of 'the conditional' (see below), or the recognition of fully institutionalised utterances which may be introduced and treated as unanalysed wholes contributing to, rather than derived from grammatical competence.

The tension of syllabus v language and learning

Most language syllabuses still list discrete items; this listing naturally, but misleadingly suggests that language may be learned in a similar way, by 'accumulating entities'. Nunan[1], in his comprehensive survey *Syllabus Design* remarks that 'there are general arguments against grammatical grading of content, whether this grading be based on traditional criteria or on more recent criteria stemming from SLA research'. And he quotes Widdowson as observing, as early as 1979:

> Inventories of functions and notions do not necessarily reflect the way languages are learned any more than the inventories of grammatical points and lexical items. This comment reflects Widdowson's claim that 'Dividing language into discrete units of whatever type misrepresents the nature of language as communication'.

The tension between language as communication and the supposed necessity for discrete item listing for language syllabuses is reflected in Willis' comment:[2]

> An approach which itemises language seems to imply that items can be learned discretely, and that the language can be built up by an accretion of these items. Communicative methodology is holistic in that it relies on the ability of learners to abstract from the language to which they are exposed, in order to recreate a picture of the target language. The lexical syllabus attempts to reconcile these contradictions. It does itemise language. It itemises language minutely, resting on a large body of research into natural language. On the basis of this research it makes realistic and economical statements about what is to be learned. But the methodology associated with the lexical syllabus does not depend on itemisation.

Wilkins distinguishes between synthetic and analytical syllabuses, the former being 'a process of gradual accumulation of parts until the whole structure of language has been built up', while in the latter, Nunan[3] suggests:

Learners are presented with chunks of language which may include structures of varying degrees of difficulty. A starting point for syllabus design is not the grammatical system of the language, but the communicative purpose for which the language is used.

Prabhu[4], describing his well-documented Bangalore Project describes its origins:

A strongly-felt pedagogic intuition that the development of competence in a second language requires not systematisation of language inputs or maximisation of planned practice, but rather the creation of conditions in which learners engage in an effort to cope with communication.

Prabhu, Widdowson, Nunan, Willis and indeed many others would concur with Nunan's judgement that[5]:

Evidence from second language acquisition research suggests that learning does not occur in a simple additive fashion.

Syllabuses tend to isolate, divide and sub-divide. The tacit assumption is that macro-skills are a synthetic assembly of micro-skills; that larger units of discourse are assembled from words and structures. These assumptions are almost certainly untrue but this raises pedagogical difficulties. The implications are that we should adopt a more holistic view of language, and a task-based approach to learning but, as Willis[6] observes:

A shortcoming of task-based approaches is that they make it difficult to specify syllabus content, and as teachers we cannot be sure what has been learned in the course of a given language activity or a given unit.

There is a fundamental conflict between the teacher's natural desire to give clearly focused and effective lessons, and the non-linear nature of language and learning. Although there is substantial theoretical support for task-based goal-orientated syllabus specification, most teachers continue to demand much more specific linguistic objectives for each lesson. While endorsing and encouraging a methodology based on tasks and skills, rather than specifically linguistic criteria, we can identify explicitly linguistic changes which are consistent with the Lexical Approach.

Content-Specifying Lists

One of the most influential attempts to specify content was the Threshold Level, which attempted to develop in detail the work summarised in *Notional Syllabuses*. Somewhat surprisingly, whilst claiming a primary focus on meaning, Wilkins[7] had a rather cavalier attitude to vocabulary:

But it is therefore with the general aspects of meaning and use that the categories presented here are concerned, though they are not less significant for being general in character. This also explains why no attempt is made in this framework to account for a lexical content of learning. This is probably better approached in terms of subject-matter and situation. At the same time, lexical aspects cannot be entirely excluded since grammatical and lexical devices often interact significantly.

To a certain, though limited, extent the semantico-grammatical categories themselves have applications for the lexical content... The lexical content of learning, therefore, can be largely derived from an analysis of the typical topics which occur in the language use of a given group.[8]

Wilkins's view is, thus, that however important vocabulary may be, it has no **defining** role to play within syllabus design.

In contrast, Willis[9], developing Sinclair's ideas, regards vocabulary, and quite specifically **words**, as the key to syllabus specification:

> Sinclair advanced a number of arguments in favour of the lexical syllabus, but the underlying argument was to do with utility and with the power of the most frequent words of English. . . . We decided that word frequency would determine the content of our course.
>
> Instead of specifying an inventory of grammatical structures or a set of functions, each stage of the course would be built round a lexical syllabus. This would specify words, then meanings and the common phrases in which they were used.[10]

It will be noted that, despite the reference to 'phrases in which they occur' Sinclair and Willis largely equate the lexical syllabus with a **word-based** syllabus. Inherent in this interpretation are three problems which manifest themselves in the course described in Willis's *The Lexical Syllabus*:

1. The most frequent 'words' are frequently items previously regarded as structural and, ironically, words of low semantic content. These largely de-lexicalised words are highly frequent precisely because they often have several meanings, and their pattern profiles are extremely complex. Mastery of words like *to, with, have* is considerably more difficult than mastering a vocabulary item with higher meaning content: *accident, soot, slump*.

2. The word-based syllabus introduced words with both their highly frequent and much rarer meanings together. A preoccupation with the word as a unit, meant infrequent meanings of highly frequent words were given preference over highly frequent meanings of rather less frequent words within the corpus. Some of these rarer meanings of high frequency words appear as of relatively low utility, and a relatively high confusion-factor for elementary students.

3. Multi-word lexical items are under-valued and under-exploited.

The Lexical Approach I propose avoids these dangers. It is specifically **not** a lexical **syllabus**, and explicitly recognises word patterns for (relatively) de-lexical words, collocational power for (relatively) semantically powerful words, and longer multi-word items, particularly institutionalised sentences, as requiring different, and **parallel** pedagogical treatment.

The old structural syllabuses specifically restricted vocabulary to the level necessary to exemplify structural patterns. Ironically, Willis in his word-based approach explicitly espouses the same principle:[11] *We set out to achieve the best coverage we could with as little extraneous lexis as possible.* (i.e. extraneous to the most frequent 700, 1,500 and 2,500 'words' which they selected as the basis for Parts 1, 2, 3 of their course). In contrast to their urge to restrict vocabulary at low levels, I advocate encouraging the **learning** of a comparatively large repertoire of high-meaning content nouns, adjectives and verbs. Although the words learned will inevitably be in corpus terms comparatively low-frequency, by definition they carry meaning. But words carry more meaning than grammar, and if it is communicative power which is the primary objective, increased vocabulary will play a larger contribution than additional mastery of even the most highly frequent patterns of high frequency words. There is an additional, pedagogical advantage. Willis observes that 'profiles become less complex as one moves down the frequency scale'. This means that from a naive, student point of view the words are easier to learn, and any L2 = L1 equivalence, which students almost inevitably make, is more likely to be accurate. 'Learnability' and communicative power are at least as important in selecting words for inclusion as frequency.

Lexis contributes as a syllabus component in the following ways:

1. Certain words deserve lexical rather than grammatical treatment

These are typically high frequency, de-lexicalised items. Those items which enter into the widest range of patterns, and are thus usefully if not maximally generative, are words which themselves carry least meaning. De-lexicalised verbs — *have, get, put, take, make, do* — represent an important sub-category. Function words, often thought of as prepositions — *of, with, for, by*, are another. The modal auxiliaries, including *would*, are a third. Most importantly, *would* should be dealt with early in a course **from a lexical point of view**. *Would* was treated in structural courses as 'the conditional'; functions moved it to an earlier, but comparatively marginal, non-generative position. It deserves high priority as a one-word lexical item. Interestingly, it is one of the items which merits fullest discussion in *The Lexical Syllabus*.

2. Increased attention to the base form of lexical verbs

A preoccupation with grammar and structure has obscured the importance of the base form of the verb in English. Willis comments on courses which 'spend an inordinate amount of time on the verb phrase', that is, on the **structure** of the verb, and so-called tense formation. In fact, the simple present is about eight times as common as the present continuous in naturally occurring English and is, with the marginal inconvenience of the third person **-s**, identical with the base form. The Lexical Approach advocates the need for a large repertoire of verbs in their base or lexical form with increased attention to the highly frequent present simple.

3. De-contextualised teaching of semantically dense items

Communicative power is most rapidly increased by expanding students' vocabularies, meaning their repertoire of lexical items, but particularly simple high-content **words**. There is no need for over-elaborate contextualisation in the early stages of learning; simple identification of signification, although in no sense mastery of the word, is an appropriate and valuable basis for increased communicative power.

4. Collocations

As soon as the inadequacy of the grammar/vocabulary dichotomy is recognised, it becomes natural for collocation to assume an important syllabus-generating role. This applies particularly to relatively high content nouns. When these are introduced, it should be natural to introduce **with** them verbs and adjectives which form powerful or relatively fixed collocations. The statistical evidence of corpus lexicography here clearly reveals the necessity of acknowledging both literal and metaphorical meaning. Often it is the latter which is more frequent.

5. Institutionalised utterances

Traditional grammar exercises usually include a sample sentence which provides the model for students to produce 'similar' sentences. Modern research into both grammar and learning suggests that students could usefully be offered a **group** of sentences for comprehension and reflection. These would not exemplify 'the grammar', but be pragmatically identifiable institutionalised utterances which students could **both** use immediately to increase communicative power, and as a **resource** the analysis of which would provide a basis for the gradual perception of pattern.

6. Sentence heads

These are very similar to institutionalised utterances. Sentence heads can frequently be identified and provide both an immediate increase in communicative power, and a resource to aid acquisition. These sentence heads frequently lie somewhere between grammar and function on a conventional syllabus. 'Grammar' in grammar practices frequently tried to cover all elements of the paradigm, consciously introducing first, second and third person subjects, singulars and plurals; in functional practice a single sentence head *Would you like to ...* requires students to complete the sentence in different ways. Introspection or statistical data, however, both reveal that some combinations of, for example, a particular modal and a particular person are much more frequent than others; compare *Could you ...* and *Could she ...* ; contrast *I might ...* and *Might I ...* ? *Do you think you might ...* ? and *Do you think I might ...* ? Paradigms exemplify the **possible** sentences of English; well-chosen groups of sentence heads exemplify the **frequent** or **probable** patterns of English. Functions are all too often ungeneralisable, while sentence head groups are generalisable.

It is noticeable that the institutionalised utterances and sentence heads of spoken English are very different from those of the written language. McCarthy is only one of many to suggest that 'vocabulary work in spoken language requires separate and additional procedures from vocabulary teaching using written texts'.

7. Supra-sentential linking

Traditionally this has been practised only on a grammatical level, concerning tags, interested responses etc. In fact, supra-sentential **lexical** linking is an important cohesive device in spontaneous conversation, suggesting lexically, rather than structurally, based exercises would be more natural and more pragmatically effective. McCarthy[12] quotes data in which:

> People did not typically agree or disagree with phrases such as 'I agree' or 'I disagree' (beloved of English course book writers); rather, there seems to be a preference for simply using some sort of lexical relation between turns.

This suggestion is borne out in Willis's work, and he goes further suggesting that much spontaneous conversation is based on joint production, in which participants contribute matching, complementary or contradictory lexical items in the development of a single unit of meaning.

Supra-sentential linking of this kind is central to spoken discourse, but quite different, and equally important features apply to the creation of coherent and cohesive written text. A central requirement of the Lexical Approach is that language material should be text and discourse, rather than sentence based. Again Willis agrees constantly reasserting that 'only by drawing attention to occurrences in text' can learners begin to build up an adequate picture of language in use.

8. Synonyms within the existential paradigm

This is a particular example of supra-sentential linking. Observations of real data show that in spontaneous speech the ability to use alternative language items as value-synonyms, although they have different signification, is a key feature of fluency. These value-synonyms may be both individual words (*daffodils/flowers*) or fully grammaticalised utterances realising the same pragmatic function (*That has my full support./Absolutely, I'd go along with that*).

9. 'Synopsising' words

Traditional grammar taught so-called reported speech. As discussed elsewhere, this category is wholly untypical of naturally occurring data. Most often, the speaker reports a whole **event**, rather than manipulating the words that were spoken. The 'reporter' summarises or synopsises the whole event lexically and so requires an adequate repertoire of synopsising verbs.

10. Metaphorical patterning

Metaphor is often perceived as an essentially literary device. Modern philosophical and linguistic research reveals that far from being restricted to literary language, it is intrinsic to the nature of language itself. Lakoff and Johnson[13], in a seminal work belonging essentially to the field of philosophy, have demonstrated convincingly that there are many concepts which cannot be discussed except in metaphorical language. They give many examples but here a single example must suffice: TIME IS MONEY.

They point out that this is an English proverb, but more than that, it is impossible to talk about time without basing the conceptualisation on the metaphor TIME IS MONEY. They developed the idea as follows (in slightly abbreviated form):

> Time is money is a metaphorical concept. It is metaphorical since we are using our everyday experiences of money, limited resources and the valuable commodities to conceptualise time. This isn't a necessary way for human beings to conceptualise time; it is tied to our culture. There are cultures where time is none of these things.
>
> We are adopting the practice of using the most specific metaphorical concepts, in this case time is money, to characterise the entire system.

This is an example of the way in which metaphorical entailments can categorise a coherent system of metaphorical concepts and a corresponding coherent system of metaphorical expressions for those concepts.

They point out that in English many of the words used to describe time can also be used to describe money: *spend, invest, budget, profitably.* Here are some of their examples:

How do you spend your time these days?
I haven't enough time to spare for that.
Is it worth your while?
You don't use your time profitably.
You are wasting my time.
This gadget will save you hours

Clearly, there is a pattern here which it is worthwhile to draw to the attention of students. Many of the words which are used to talk about money can also be used to talk about time. This is not fully generalisable, but it still constitutes a powerfully generative pattern system. The importance of Lakoff and Johnson's work is difficult to over-emphasise. It is essential reading for anyone interested in how language works.

When the Berlin wall was breached, at first a *trickle* of people came through. Later, as the gap was widened, people *flooded* through. There was a constant *stream* of people anxious to visit friends, or restore family contacts. Once the initial excitement wore off, the *flow* of people *dried up*.

The above passage represents my own observations of the language used by the B.B.C. News to report the destruction of the Berlin wall. An important metaphor is involved: crowds of people move like water. It is almost impossible to describe those events without resorting to 'water-words'. But notice, as Lakoff and Johnson constantly emphasise, metaphor highlights only at the expense of suppressing. People in movement may move like water, but they are **not** water, water does not re-establish family contacts. There is a useful linguistic pattern, but not an identification.

Editors on the Cobuild project were initially surprised at the preponderance of metaphorical usage — *torrents* are more likely to be of abuse or French than water. Lexicographic difficulties arise — if metaphorical use is more frequent than the literal, and therefore supposedly core, use should it be placed first in the dictionary? Their editors have observed, for example, the importance of plant-based metaphor in discussing abstractions such as government policy: *The problem has its roots . . . ; Since the beginning of the year, we have seen a flowering. . . .*

For language teaching, the importance lies in recognising:

a. That metaphor is a part of everyday language.

b. That such metaphorical usage is patterned, often in accessible, generalisable ways.

Functions and skills

The development of communicative power will be aided by incorporating a well-balanced range of lexically derived activities in the classroom. These must reflect the different kinds of lexical item. The change, however, is a matter of emphasis not revolution. Grammar retains a place, but a reduced one; lexis plays an increased role. Language content can, however, never be wholly separated from other elements of syllabus specification. Most functional syllabuses concentrate on micro-, rather than macro-functions and 'nice' rather than 'nasty' events. For many students such functions are *expressing irritation, expressing disbelief, distancing the speaker from the content of what is said, expressing condolence, telling and responding to jokes*, may be at least as important as *accepting and refusing invitations politely*. In a similar way, a lexical approach suggests that the skills syllabus needs to be broadened. Two skills central to the Lexical Approach are developing the students' ability to use the dictionary as a learning resource, rather than reference work, and, most importantly of all helping students to **identify lexical phrases** in text. This returns us, to the single most powerful methodological implication, namely a different attitude to, and use of, texts.

References

1.   Syllabus Design, p.34.
2.   The Lexical Syllabus p.*viii.*
3.   op cit p.28.
4.   Second Language Pedagogy, p.1.
5.   op cit p.30.
6.   op cit p.129.
7.   Notional Syllabuses, p.21.
8.   ibid p 76.
9.   op cit p.*v.*
10. op cit p.15.
11. op cit p.74.
12. Discourse Analysis for Language Teachers p.71.
13. Metaphors We Live By p.7ff.

Chapter 7

Lexis in Language Teaching

PART 1 — Lexis in the Classroom

The theoretical literature of language teaching is littered with claims by many writers that more attention must be paid to lexis than has traditionally been the case:

> There have been changing trends — from grammar translation to direct method to the communicative approach — but none of these has emphasised the importance of the learner's lexical competence over structural grammatical competence (Summers).[1]

> Functions without lexis are no better than structures without lexis. Referential lexis is a vast field — it certainly makes up the bulk of the learning load for any general purpose language course. (Swan).[2]

> The more one considers the matter, the more reasonable it seems to suppose that lexis is where we need to start from, the syntax needs to be put to the service of words and not the other way round. (Widdowson, 1989).[3]

These comments are radically different from the position usually taken by language teaching. For a long time Fries' view, that language learning involved mastering structure and that the vocabulary load should be kept to the minimum necessary to exemplify the grammatical structures held sway. Even today many textbooks are produced which take this minimal view of vocabulary. Linguists in Britain were predominantly interested in vocabulary selection and contrastive analysis; the idea that vocabulary should be restricted was accepted without question. Wilkins was one of the first to propose an increased role for vocabulary[4]: *Without grammar very little can be conveyed, without vocabulary nothing can be conveyed.*

Recently, students' needs — both practical with the increase in ESP courses and psychological — have joined with the theoretical insights of corpus linguistics and discourse analysis to emphasise the importance of vocabulary at all stages of learning, including the earliest. But if vocabulary — or more precisely lexis — is to be introduced effectively into programmes — how is it to be done most successfully so that students do not drown in the 'apparent chaos of the lexicon'?

We begin by summarising some of the key ideas:

1. The grammar/vocabulary dichotomy is a false one. Often when 'new words' are introduced into the class it will be appropriate not simply to present and record the word but to explore the grammar of the word — at

least noting its principal collocates, and perhaps one or two institutionalised sentences containing the word.

2. Lexis may be learned as well as acquired. Even Krashen, the principal proponent of the learning/acquisition distinction, clearly uses the term acquisition in relation to the gradual mastery of underlying **systems**. Swan has pointed out that the distinction does not apply to lexical items, including individual words.

3. De-contextualised lexis carries meaning, so that items can be learned de-contextualised. Learning their signification in this way does not ensure mastery of the item, but it does provide an important linguistic resource, as well as being psychologically satisfying. In the past, students have frequently been unable to say what they wanted to say until comparatively late in learning programmes — being able to say it badly, or inadequately, is therefore a step in the right direction.

Brumfit has remarked that to teach lists rather than systems runs counter to everything we know about learning theory. It would not, therefore, be appropriate simply to ask students to learn de-contextualised vocabulary lists. It is clear, however, that there is a strong case to be made for making clear to students in the early stages of learning a large number of items which may be presented pictorially, allowing students to label pictures, and thus establish signification without, in these early stages, the initially unnecessary confusion of co-text.

4. Ungrammaticalised, or inadequately grammaticalised lexis carries meaning. If we are anxious to build student's communicative power this necessarily implies a large, inadequately grammaticalised vocabulary in the early stages of learning. Partially grammaticalised lexis — acceptable pidgin — must be perceived as successful elementary and intermediate behaviour, rather than defective. Nattinger[5] has explicitly endorsed this position:

> One way to promote fluency is by encouraging 'pidginization', urging students to put language together the best they can and avoid the self- monitoring that would inhibit its use.

5. 'Activities' as well as objects can be named — so that verbs as well as nouns may be taught lexically. Common irregular past tense forms — *went, came, said* — can be learned **as vocabulary items, before** they are mastered as elements of the grammatical system. Verbs, particularly as collocates of nouns, deserve increased attention as elements of vocabulary, rather than grammar teaching.

Cobuild data reveals that 11 irregular past tense forms — *was, had, got, said, did, made, came, thought, went, looked, used* — are among the most common 200 words in their corpus.

6. Time is a lexical concept, and time expressions can and should be taught as such. Traditionally, time is taught grammatically, through tense. This has an unnecessary inhibiting effect on what students can say in the early stages of learning.

7. Early learning should ideally be centred on listening; early production should be almost exclusively directed towards spoken rather than written English. But lexical density differs considerably between spoken and written text so, if students are to develop sufficient vocabulary even in the early stages of learning they will benefit from **extensive** reading of vocabulary-rich material. While over-load must be avoided, students should be familiar from the early stages of learning with the idea of extensive, rather than intensive reading. As far as possible the tendency to stop at every unknown word must be discouraged, and conversely, contextual guessing and top-down as well as bottom-up understanding should be encouraged. If teachers of elementary students promote bad reading habits — asking about every unknown word, expecting complete detailed comprehension — students' language learning, and more generally their love of reading, can be permanently inhibited.

8. Archetypical examples should be introduced as un-analysed wholes, and students encouraged to use them both before, and parallel with any analysis of them. Unanalysed sentences whose pragmatic meaning may be understood from context must be valued as a resource aiding mastery of, rather than produced by, grammatical competence.

9. The generative power and collocational range of a word is approximately inversely proportional to its informational content. This means there are different kinds of words which will require different kinds of treatment in the classroom. Treating all words similarly will lead to chaos; exploiting different kinds of words in different ways and spending more time on some than others, using different recording formats for different kinds of words represents precisely the 'organisational principles' referred to above by McCarthy.

10. 'Learning vocabulary' involves a great deal more than simple memorisation. If grammar/vocabulary represents a continuum rather than a dichotomy, although conscious learning of a vocabulary item may help, it too must ultimately be acquired — integrated fully into the learner's linguistic resources so that it is spontaneously available when needed. Vocabulary learning and acquisition can be aided through classroom procedures which:

— Help students identify lexical items correctly.
— Encourage recording in helpful, non-linear formats.
— Encourage transfer from short-term to long-term memory.

Formal 'vocabulary' teaching

Vocabulary teaching has rarely been systematic. Frequently it is assumed, either explicitly or more covertly, that students will 'pick up' the necessary vocabulary by reading, and while concentrating on the serious business of mastering the grammatical system. Formal vocabulary teaching has tended to be either random, in response to a particular student question for a particular word or based on formal presentation of the words associated with a particular topic or field. A lexical approach requires a much more principled system of introducing and exploiting lexis, and even simple vocabulary, in the classroom.

Random vocabulary teaching

As every teacher knows, the need often arises in the classroom for words which have not been anticipated by any formal programme. Students ask for words; unexpected difficulties arise in texts. More or less explicitly the questions *What does ... mean?* or *What is the word for ... ?* arise. Sometimes it is appropriate to supply the needed word and simply continue with the main topic of the lesson. On other occasions the opportunity can be taken to supply, explore and record the word systematically. All too often students merely record the new word with an L1 'translation' in a vocabulary book, only to add a different, and wholly unrelated word a few minutes later. Listing of this kind, where the student has no possibility of retrieving the item, and the manner of their recording has no pedagogic value, is simply pointless. Stevick memorably observed *If you want to forget something, put it in a list.* Teachers and students could usefully bear this dictum in mind.

Although vocabulary which is random and unexpected will be needed in the classroom, that does not mean that it cannot be **exploited and recorded in principled ways**. All students children or adult, general or ESP, should have a good quality book, ideally with an alphabetical thumb index, in which to record selective new lexis. Often students have an attractively produced four-colour textbook and a tatty, dog-eared vocabulary note book. Potentially it is the latter which is more valuable. Its physical size, quality and organisation should endorse this, and encourage students to see it as a personal resource of lasting value. It is of little value unless the material in it is organised in such a way that the student can retrieve what is recorded in it efficiently — hence the alphabetic index. Its pages should be formatted, often by the students themselves so that the **process** of exploring and organising has pedagogic value. A number of appropriate formats — columns, boxes, displays and mind maps are discussed below. Randomly-occurring vocabulary is intrinsic to language teaching; random **listing** of vocabulary should be rejected.

Topics or semantic fields

This is, perhaps, the main way of organising lexical content. Because there is an explicit organisational principle, and coherent real world context it has obvious advantages over randomly occurring vocabulary. As already observed, however, unless considerable care is taken it easily becomes noun-dominated. If asked about the 'words you associate with ...', most people think visually, and name the 'things' they can 'see'. Even when explicitly aware of this it is difficult to break from visualisation and nominalisation — think of the language you associate with the kitchen, your desk or office, your car. Nouns, a few adjectives and perhaps verbs but what about phrasal verbs, institutionalised sentences, sentence heads, adverbial expressions? If semantic fields are to prove anything other than a primitive organisational principle, it is essential that the teacher looks for words from different word categories, most frequently by looking for those words which collocate with the ever-obtrusive nouns. It is essential to remember that in order to talk about any noun it is words in other categories which are needed, and not just any other words — adjectives that occurred **before** the key noun, verbs which occur with the noun **as subject**, and other verbs which occur with the noun **as**

object (*tap; hot/cold; Can you turn the hot tap off, please; That tap is dripping again*). Language teachers must become more self-consciously precisely that — **language** teachers. Naming the objects to be found in a kitchen is closer to the kind of activity we associate with primary school teaching, expanding childrens' knowledge and understanding of the world around them. Language teaching is about helping students to see what **language** properly belongs with other **language** items — in other words it is centrally and intrinsically about collocation.

Collocation

Collocation, by concentrating on linguistic environment rather than real-world environment, provides the most powerful organisational principle for language teaching, and for arranging for the efficient recording of new items. Language teaching has tended to organise things paradigmatically or vertically:

In my free time I really love | to play tennis.
| to go riding
| to go swimming

Collocation moves the emphasis to syntagmatic or horizontal organisation.

Vocabulary teaching has also tended to concentrate on **extracting** in order to examine and record them. Collocation involves explicitly trying to **insert** words with co-text. In many cases extracting words from context destroys meaning, and thus violates the nature of language itself. In many cases collocation is a principal characteristic by which words may be located or even defined. 'Knowing' a word involves a great deal more than being able to establish a one-to-one relationship between words and real-world objects, or between words in L1 and L2. A major element of being able to use a word — having practical procedural knowledge of it — involves mastering its collocational range and restrictions on that range. A class being taught for Cambridge Proficiency would be surprised if they were asked *Do you know the word 'book'?* They would interpret it as *Have you met the word 'book'?* As such, the question would appear ridiculous. But it is unlikely that even such advanced students have fully mastered the grammar of the word. Would they produce: *I've just read an absolutely infuriating book about the situation in the Soviet Union by some screwed up American who is still in love with the Cold War.*

It is difficult to recognise that this sentence is essentially constructed by a detailed knowledge of the grammar of the word *book*. Readers might like to complete the following table, supplying up to five items for each column — but not just **any** five items which could occur. Try to find items you think you might actually want to use to talk about books you have read, know about, haven't read, wish you had read etc. Avoid random lexicalisation, and the challenge is considerable at all levels of proficiency.

Verb	Adjective	
....	....	
....	....	
....	....	**Book**
....	....	
....	....	

It is also obvious that when first meeting the word *book* rather than making an L1/L2 entry in a vocabulary book, it would be much more helpful to record the word-grammar pattern:

a(n).......................... book about .... by ....

This kind of horizontal, collocational awareness is not 'advanced' language; it can be introduced from the earliest stages.

It is not always straightforward to identify collocations because the words are not always immediately adjacent to each other, and in some cases the hyponomous category is more useful than an individual word. Consider these examples:

The police arrested the burglars while they were still on the premises.
Many burglars are juveniles, who, even when they have been arrested, cannot be charged.
More suspected drug smugglers have been detained during the first six months of this year than were arrested during the whole of last year.

The flight takes about three hours.
It has taken me twenty minutes to find a parking space.
It takes a long time to even begin to understand another country.

Arrest (a criminal), and *take (a period of time)* are appropriate, and generalisable collocations. Both teachers and students need practice in identifying patterns of this kind in naturally occurring text. It is the gradual perception of pattern which underlies the development of competence, and what is usually thought of as 'grammar'. Chunking — breaking continuous text into useful component 'bits' is an intrinsic part of the Lexical Approach. Learning to identify collocations, and the underlying patterns which individual examples exemplify is one aspect of helping students to obtain maximum benefits from the input to which they are exposed.

Neither the difficulty of this chunking for students, nor the contribution which teachers can make in helping students chunk more effectively, should be underestimated. Students have a tendency to read text word-by-word; even **identifying** any multi-word chunks is difficult without appropriate awareness raising activities. Phrasal verbs, particularly if separable (*They take extra staff on for Christmas*) are perhaps the most familiar example of multi-word items which students find difficult for the simplest of all reasons — they are frequently unaware of their existence. Training in pedagogical chunking, and particularly the identification of multi-word items provide a new and important activity for teachers within the Lexical Approach.

Institutionalised expressions or Lexical phrases

We may divide these into sentence heads or frames and institutionalised sentences. The latter, which should always have readily identifiable pragmatic meaning, will typically be presented in dialogues, ideally in oral rather than written form. Students must be made aware that they are to understand the **whole phrase**, without necessarily analysing it grammatically. They must also be trained to note it accurately. This is more difficult than it seems. Usually we listen to language to understand the message, paying little attention to the precise words used to express it. In Wilberg's words we eat the sweet but discard the wrapper. With language material intended to present lexical phrases for learning, students must be trained to recognise the importance of the wrapper — the **precise** words used to express a particular pragmatic function. We have already noted that, for example, *Can I just say something* and *Can I just say a few words*, despite their apparent similarity, are utterances associated with totally different situations. Teachers must frequently ask not *What does (s)he mean when (s)he said ...* but two questions to focus student's attention on the **precise words**, and **pragmatic value**. *What were the exact words ... used when (s)he . . .? Why did (s)he say that?*

Students should be encouraged to **record whole sentences** in their resource book, again arranged in such a way that they can retrieve them. It should not be unrealistic to expect students to accumulate several hundred sentences of this kind if their course is orientated towards spoken fluency. In many cases they should record lexical phrases with either an equivalent in their own language (an equivalent, not a crude translation), or a functional gloss, probably in their own language. Sometimes it will be appropriate to record together items expressing similar pragmatic functions, most notably a pair which represent positive and negative responses. Only rarely will the pragmatic opposites be expressed by simple grammatical negation.

I cannot stress too strongly the fact that if work in discourse analysis, and the suggestions of, for example, Pawley and Syder and Nattinger and DeCarrico are to be taken seriously, considerable emphasis should be placed on lexical items which are sentence heads or institutionalised sentences. The Lexical Approach demands that, in contrast to the present marginal role of idiom, and the set of banal functions associated with textbooks, idiom must assume a central role.

Chunking

This implausible term, coined by Nattinger[6], refers to the way in which lexical items are stored in the memory:

> Many theories of language performance suggest that vocabulary is stored redundantly, not only as individual morphemes, but also as parts of phrases, or even as longer memorised chunks of speech, and that it is often retrieved from memory in these pre-assembled chunks.

Many commentators endorse this view that native speakers retain (redundantly) many pre-fabricated formulaic items — chunks. Fluency is achieved largely by combining chunks, reducing processing difficulty. These matters relate to the way we naturally store and retrieve language but clearly there are enormous implications for language learning — if students break up the language to which they are exposed in unhelpful ways, and then store 'the wrong bits' the advantage of storing chunks will be lost and tremendous processing demands will be made upon them as they attempt to re-create from scratch. Self-evidently, it is essential to heighten students' awareness of the bits of which coherent discourse or written text is composed. Students' storage and retrieval will be aided, and a valuable resource provided for their long-term acquisition of the underlying patterns, by a process which could be called pedagogical chunking. A few tentative efforts have been made in this direction, but the procedure needs to be given much higher priority. Nattinger[7] has claimed: *A great part of the learner's task is to chunk unfamiliar material in meaningful ways and create more effective lexical phrases.* In other words, introducing the idea of chunking to students, and providing them with materials which encourage the identification of chunks should be one of the central activities of language teaching.

An embarrassing statistic

Estimates of the mature native speaker's vocabulary vary considerably, but are never less than 40,000 words. Pawley and Syder's much-quoted estimate of learned utterances would suggest double that total. If learned utterances are taken into account, the 'list' of **productive** items known to the mature native speaker must run to tens of thousands. Let us, rather arbitrarily, suppose it is 50,000. Gairns and Redman[8] suggest:

> It is impossible to be dogmatic about the number of new lexical items that should be presented in a sixty minute lesson. We would suggest an average of eight to twelve productive items as representing a reasonable input.

They suggest that this would produce 1,000 items over 125 hours of study[9]:

> In other words the students would possess the lexicon considered necessary to meet the level of 'general ability' defined in the Threshold Level. How realistic is this goal? Professor van Ek states that the original intention had been to establish the height of the threshold level on the basis of 100 to 125 hours of study, but concedes that the aim was rather ambitious. Although there is no conclusive evidence to support this opinion we feel that most teachers will instinctively endorse the view that 1,000 items was beyond the capacity of most learners with 125 hours of study.

So, anything like native-like vocabulary would seem to need 6,000 hours of study — 8 hours a day, every day for two years. This chimes well with motivated intelligent people learning a not wholly unfamiliar language naturally in the environment in which it is spoken. On the other hand, it raises serious questions about what teachers are doing when they claim to 'teach' eight items in a lesson.

Elsewhere in *Working with Words*, Gairns and Redman happily suggest *treating individual items, taught as they arise, and emphasised according to their usefulness.* One must question the usefulness, or at least cost-effectiveness of devoting more than a very small part of class time to the formal 'teaching' of individual lexical items. Much of their methodology suggests applying to vocabulary or lexis the Present-Practise-Produce paradigm of traditional structuralist grammar teaching. This is largely discredited even for teaching productive grammatical patterns. To suggest presenting, explaining, practising and exploiting individual vocabulary items in a formal, structured teaching sequence is methodologically naive and inefficient, and remains blissfully unaffected by the sheer size of the task of acquiring a minimum adequate 'vocabulary'. Acquiring vocabulary is a comparatively messy process; teacher-centred methodology with over-elaborate teaching sequences is likely to hinder rather than help it.

In passing, we note that elsewhere they say[10]: *There are certain features of vocabulary which defy methodology. A coherent and meaningful group of collocations is often difficult to organise and it may be better to teach these as they arise.* This is linguistically naive. It is precisely the task of the language teacher to provide ways of organising lexis so that items are **not** dealt with on a one-off basis 'as they arise'. The Lexical Approach clearly demands that teachers are aware of, and constantly influenced by, a set of principles which directs students towards precisely the 'coherent and meaningful groups' which Gairns and Redman so glibly dismiss.

Identifying Exercises

McCarthy, writing about academic English, and Wilberg devising materials for students of business English have both suggested that students approaching these new areas of discourse simply fail to identify the language items in the material to which they are exposed which would be of most benefit to them, both for productive use and as a general linguistic resource. McCarthy proposed exercises of the following type:

> Pick out the words in the following text which are strongly associated with either the problem-solution pattern or the claim counter-claim pattern. (He then gives an article from *New Society*.)

Wilberg and myself used the material on page 124 in directing the attention of business students towards collocation in business English.

Recording formats

Quite different kinds of lexical items are characteristic of spoken and written English, and of different fields of discourse. Spoken English has a high density of lexical phrases, used to indicate the speaker's intention, and to maintain and develop aspects of personal relationships. Discourse-management phrases are typical of both informal conversation and relatively formal (unscripted) lecturing, though naturally the phrases and functions differ. Written language, although using phrases which organise the discourse, has a much higher density of collocation, particularly relatively fixed collocations which make high information content noun phrases.

For any student whose language studies are orientated towards a particular field of discourse, teachers must look carefully at the kind of lexical item which is typical of that discourse, introduce examples of it into class (including transcripts of spoken material) and then ensure that students appreciate the usefulness of identifying, organizing and recording the most useful types of lexical item.

Although Buzan had written about mind-maps as a way of organising and recording thought in helpfully non-linear ways, it was I think Wilberg, in

Business English who first recognised the powerful role recording formats could play as a language learning technique. The principle may be simply stated — language should be recorded together which characteristically occurs together. This contrasts with the old vocabulary book which generated simple lists by de-contexualising items. Our purpose must be the opposite.— to take time to explore and evaluate a word or other lexical item, to think of its collocates, pragmatic force or whatever and record it in a format so that:

a. It can be easily retrieved (another defect of the old vocabulary book).

b. Its appearance on the page reflects aspects of the linguistic environment in which it most frequently occurs either in general, or taking into account the particular student's work, field of study or interest. Some examples of recording formats (for convenience greatly reduced in size) are given on page 125, see also 144. The three most typical varieties are **collocation boxes, pattern displays** and **discourse structures**.

Most **collocation boxes** will show adjective-noun, verb-noun, noun-verb, verb-adjective-noun groups. Within the 'adjective' category must be included nouns used adjectively. It is important to make this clear to students, as the most powerful noun phrases tend to be noun-noun combinations (*cost price*) rather than 'ordinary' adjective-noun (*high price*).

Notice that the most useful list-generating words are usually nouns. After extensive experimentation, I suggest boxes should **not have more than five entries,** even if more suggest themselves. Larger lists tend to cause more problems than they solve — they generate unlikely or impossible collocations, and create confusion. The purpose is not to list as many items as possible, but to identify archetypical and maximally useful items.

Examples 3 and 4 show patterns which suggest slightly different boxes. There are, for example, many patterns containing *of*.

The **pattern display** is most typically used with de-lexicalised words, particularly verbs such as *get* and *have*, and prepositions. It is best used in two stages — firstly, students simply record useful expressions containing the de-lexicalised word. Secondly, if patterns begin to emerge a new version of the spider is made where a hyponym, or descriptive category replaces the original expression. Once again indiscriminate listing is to be avoided; here the search is for archetypicality and generalisability. Ironically, within a lexical approach, de-lexicalised words have an important role to play.

Discourse structures are more typical of the written mode, and are frequently much larger units than individual words or sentences. If students identify the language which shows relationships such as cause and effect, generalisation and exemplification, it should be natural for them to record the 'discourse frame' as a whole.

Cloze procedures

Lexical items, with the exception of single words, are by definition relatively fixed multi-word combinations. It is immediately apparent that they can be practised, and the memory tested, by deleting part of the whole. The deletion

Collocation in business English

YOUR LANGUAGE NEEDS

A large part of this book will help you to identify and list **word partnerships** which are particularly useful for you. This page explains how and why learning word partnerships will help you.

Here is a simple, general example. If you think of football the first word which comes to mind is probably **ball**. If you think of more 'football words' you will probably choose **nouns** like **match**, **team**. Most people choose nouns. Often we start to think about a topic by starting with important nouns.

In business English you probably think first of words like **advert** or **sales**. But when we want to talk about something we need to know the **verbs** which often make a **word partnership** with the noun.

You can't talk about a game of football unless you know the words which are often used with **ball**:

head a ball   **kick the ball**   **pass the ball**
lob the ball   **throw the ball**

From **one** useful noun, we can identify **a group** of useful verbs.

Another kind of word partnership in English is made by making a partnership of two nouns:

football match   **football supporter**   **football ground**
football season   **football league**   **football club**

You can see that from one word we can cover a very wide area by identifying **word partnerships**.

It is the same with the business words:

place an advert;   **appoint an advertising agency;**
increase sales;   **a sales conference;**   **launch a sales campaign.**

Pages 57 to 76 will help you to create your own personalised **word partnership** lists.

From a few words, your teacher can help you to identify a lot of language you will find immediately useful to talk about your professional and personal interests.

Time spent identifying the language which is most useful for you is not wasted. The process of thinking about, and talking about your needs will help you to learn English efficiently.

VERB - NOUN PARTNERSHIPS

Choose your own texts. Use them in the same way as the text on page 48. List useful partnerships from the texts you choose here.

VERB	NOUN	VERB	NOUN

KEYWORDS INTRODUCTION 1

Many professional words are regularly used with a small number of other words. Instead of learning individual words you will find it much more useful to learn word partnerships. In the middle of the diagram is a **keyword**. Around it are **background words** of two different kinds. Underline them with two different coloured pens.

In this example you should have:

Verbs which go in front of the keyword: **sign** an agreement
Words which go **between** the verb and the keyword: sign a **temporary/trade** agreement.

Make a list of word partnerships. Find two word partnerships
(verb + keyword) or three-word partnerships (verb + adjective/noun + keyword)

Usually on the following pages we then suggest that you write some sentences about your own situation using some of the partnerships. As usual, this will help you remember the partnerships better.

KEYWORDS 11

The word in the centre of the diagram is the **keyword**. There are different kinds of words in the **background** words. Use different coloured pens to underline the background words so that you divide them into groups. Find some two-word and three-word partnerships. Look for some partnerships which include **the keyword** and **a verb** from the background words. Write four sentences about your own situation. Use coloured pens or highlight the word partnerships so you can check them easily later.

IMPORTANT VERBS 1

Often the words which you think are most important for you are nouns, for example, **meeting**, **sales**, **insurance**. But if you want to speak English you need to speak and write sentences. So, you need to know which verbs are often used with your important nouns and with word partnerships which include the noun. Here are some examples:

attend a meeting   **organise a meeting**   **postpone a meeting**
increase sales   **achieve a sales target** **launch a sales campaign**
take out insurance   **pay an insurance premium** **make an insurance claim**

These two and three-word combinations are often the basis of complete sentences in business English.

A good business English dictionary will help you with the important nouns but very often it does not help you to choose the correct verb to make important word partnerships. On the following pages is a list of some of the verbs which are often used in professional English. You can use the list in two different ways:

1. Take a key word. Look for verbs which are often used with the keyword. List the most useful word partnerships.

2. Choose an area of professional English, for example **banking**, **insurance**, or **exports**. Look for verbs which will make word partnerships connected with that area. Make a list, with equivalents in your own language.

On the opposite page you will see an example. All professionals need to talk about **meetings**. But which **verbs** do you need to help you to do this. The most important ones are listed.

Use the following pages to make similar lists starting from the key words or professional areas which **you** need.

IMPORTANT VERBS 2

Most professionals need to talk about meetings. You almost certainly know the word. But which verbs make word partnerships with it? A business dictionary and the verb list on pages 144 to 146 will help you to find partnerships and equivalents in your own language. Check later by covering the English column to make sure you can remember.

ENGLISH	YOUR LANGUAGE / EXAMPLE
address a meeting	
arrange a meeting	
ask for a meeting	
attend a meeting	
avoid a meeting	
be late for a meeting	
be tied up in a meeting	
call a meeting	
cancel a meeting	
chair a meeting	
close a meeting	
have a meeting	
interrupt a meeting	
organise a meeting	
postpone a meeting	
report on a meeting	
set up a meeting	
start a meeting	
take the minutes of a meeting	
wind up a meeting	

Pages taken from *Business English*, Peter Wilberg and Michael Lewis, LTP, 1990

Collocation boxes

(re) draft dictate go through get fax	confidential sales special offer urgent promotional	letter

Example 1

small nice classy reasonable popular	Italian Chinese Thai Indian Mexican	restaurant

Example 2

a sheet of (large, flat piece)	paper glass ice flame stamps

Example 3

a letter	of	complaint resignation acceptance ....

Example 4

Pattern displays

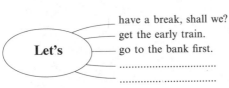

Let's	have a break, shall we? get the early train. go to the bank first. ....

Example 5

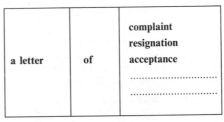
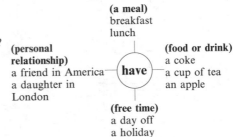

(a meal)
breakfast
lunch

(personal relationship)
a friend in America
a daughter in London

have

(food or drink)
a coke
a cup of tea
an apple

(free time)
a day off
a holiday
a break

Example 6

Discourse Structures

Greeting visitors to your workplace

Good morning (Ladies and Gentlemen). On behalf of........may I welcome you to........ . It is a great pleasure to have you with us today. I hope you enjoy your visit/meeting/the conference. If there is anything we can do to help, please do not hesitate to ask. Now, you don't want to listen to me all day so I'll hand you over to my colleague ....(who will show you...../take you to......).

Example 7

There is general agreement nowadays that .... Despite this, several objections can be raised. The most important of these is ....

Example 8

must not be arbitrary; the purpose is pedagogical, not a guessing game. It will be appropriate to delete individual words from collocations or fixed phrases, the beginning or ending from an institutionalised clause or sentence, discourse markers from whole text, and even whole sentences of identifiable pragmatic function from extended dialogue. Cloze activity can be used by students to test their memories, and in the classroom for awareness raising and linguistic sensitisation. They are, of course, not a way of **teaching** lexical items.

Cloze procedures may focus on the linguistic devices which make text cohesive. Such exercises have tended to focus on the function of closed-class grammatical words: *although, on the other hand*, pro-forms. Less attention has been paid to **lexical** cohesion within texts, although theoretical work, most notably by Halliday and Hasan, clearly indicates that lexical 'chains' play an important role in creating cohesion. Carter[11] believes that specifically targetted cloze exercises have an important role to play in raising student awareness:

> One limitation is that the emphasis is mainly on the function of grammatical words; there is little attention to the specific role of lexical words in the organisation of text. . . . although there is much of value in this domain which can be exploited by the teacher, it is within the semantic networks established by lexical cohesion that teachers might find more extensive ways of using Cloze to exploit the discourse structure of written language.

Grids, matrices and componential analysis

Because these exercise types are based on visual displays, it is perhaps necessary to state explicitly that I see no role for them within the Lexical Approach. Their purpose is explicitly analytic, atomistic and semantic, and specifically disregards the importance of collocation and other co-text. While elements of componential analysis such as whether a particular item carries positive or negative connotation, may be helpful in providing shorthand for use in the recording formats discussed above, as teaching material they have nothing to offer within a lexical approach which is holistically and discourse-orientated.

Lexical phrase drills

The heading is a curious combination of a language teaching buzz word — lexical phrases — with one of its more discredited methodological procedures — drilling. Ironically, the discredited 'grammar drill' may return — in modified and restricted form — to help students learn lexical phrases. Lexical phrases are learned as unanalysed wholes. Often, they are quite long and, in the initial stages of learning a language, difficult to 'get your tongue round'. Quite often they involve a degree of idiomaticity, so they may 'sound strange' to the student. People feel uncomfortable using in conversation something which seems implausible. If you know the fear meaning of *afraid*, and think *get = bring*, neither of *I'm afraid he's out* or *I'll get it* (= *I'll answer the phone/door*) will sound plausible. There is, thus, a strong pedagogical case for introducing lexical phrases into the classroom, and asking students to repeat them several times in a drill-activity and to use some of them in situational practices of a relatively controlled kind. This was first done by Keller in a series published in Canada entitled *Gambits*, now available as *Conversation Gambits, LTP, 1988*.

Nattinger[12] has specifically argued in favour of pattern practice drills for lexical phrases. Writing within the American tradition he is also fully aware of the dangers:

> The challenge for the teacher would be to use such drills to allow confidence and fluency, yet not overdo them to the point that they became mindless exercises, as has often been the unfortunate result in strict audio-linguilism.

There is considerable scope for material which provides students with a repertoire of lexical phrases, opportunities to practise their articulation, and further opportunities to help students feel comfortable using the phrases naturally. Most contemporary linguists agree that the basis of native speaker fluency is control of a vast repertoire of formulaic phrases of this kind; research on first language acquisition suggests that the constant repetition of utterances learned as wholes is an intrinsic part of first language acquisition. However reactionary it may sound, there is a strong case to be made for the lexical phrase drill as an important element in second language learning. Since fluency involves the mastery of a vast repertoire of such phrases, lexical drilling will have a role to play at all levels, and within both general and specifically targetted courses. It differs from the old fashioned grammar drill in that it may be a fully fixed phrase, so that no mastery of the 'underlying structure' is intended. It may be made more interesting than the traditional drill by asking students to say the same phrase aggresively, confidentially, doubtfully, or even while sucking a Polo mint. It would be an extremely retrograde step if the attitude which underlay grammar drilling were to return but as Stevick has pointed out, if properly done with variety, lightness of touch and an awareness that it is acquisition not accuracy-orientated, drills can be fun.

PART 2 — Lexical Exercise Types

Traditionally, language teaching has organised its input and practice around the supposedly central grammatical system. Within a lexical approach greater emphasis is placed on introducing and practising lexis. Practice should be directed towards helping students collocate words, and grammaticalise from word to sentence. Although language teaching has been bedevilled with randomly lexicalised grammar exercises, the danger of random grammaticalisation of lexical exercises is much less, as the following little experiment should convince the reader. Think of a sentence which contains the word *bus*. Do you think I can guess your sentence? Probably not. Now, think of a sentence which contains the words *bus, last*. Do you think I can guess your sentence now? Now think of a sentence which contains *miss, last, bus*. Now, although there are many possible English sentences that you could have constructed — and if you are trying to 'beat' my ability to predict, you will have tried hard to produce a nonce form — there are only two or three probable utterances which contain the three words: *Hurry up or we'll miss the last bus. Sorry, I missed the last bus.* There is nothing wrong with *If we'd missed the last bus we'd have had to walk home* except you don't believe anybody has ever said it — it sounds like the language of the language classroom in a way that the other two examples do not.

Words carry more meaning than grammar so, in general, words determine grammar. Lexical exercises should exploit this, but it is important to remember that they are to help students to acquire the ability to grammaticalise. Wrong or inadequate grammaticalisations are not failures if they contribute to the student's overall acquisition.

EXERCISE 1

Draw two lines down a piece of paper. Write a noun in the third column. You can use any noun you like, a very easy one or a difficult word. Now write an adjective in the second column which often comes in front of your noun. In the first column write a verb that often comes in front of your noun.

Pass your paper to the person on your right. Try to fill in the first and second columns for the paper you get from the person on your left. When you have done that, pass the papers on again. When you have seen all the papers in your group, check the word partnerships you have made with your teacher. Record the most useful partnerships.

EXERCISE 2

Look at these news headlines. What do you think the stories are about?

1. SCHOOL EXAM RESULTS DELAY
2. DEATH WISH WOMAN'S LEAP
3. CONSUMER SPENDING PEAK
4. SPACE EXPLORATION FUND SLASHED
5. AIR TRAVEL FIRM COLLAPSE

EXERCISE 3

Work in pairs.Write a short story. Your story must have **exactly** 100 words — but you must not use any single English word more than once.

It's not as easy as it sounds. It's not impossible either. Remember, you cannot use any word more than once, not even *a, the, is, of.* Every word must be different!

Students may need some help with this, but in my experience they are often better at it than teachers because they quickly discover certain principles, and treat it as a challenging game rather than a difficult exercise. Here are some language tips to help:

1. Do not use the very common words — *a, the, and, is* in the first two or three sentences. You may need them later.
2. Not all sentences need to be full sentences. The story might be more exciting if some sentences finish . . .
3. Remember synonyms.
4. For extra words add adjectives and adverbs.
5. Remind intermediate students of participles: *Waiting for the bus, I* . . .
6. Write a few extra words and then cut a few to get exactly 100.
7. The present simple makes a better story than the past simple.

Groups with whom I have done this usually take about twenty minutes to produce a story but need forty minutes to produce a neat, effective story. Here is an example story.

> Big red motorbikes roared past. Someone had no time to lose. They drew up exactly outside number seventeen. Huge gates meant no-one could enter easily. Two riders, wearing long black coats and dark glasses, climbed off their machines. Glancing around uneasily the men seemed very suspicious. What are these fellows doing? Who knows?
>
> Silence surrounds them. Apparently nobody suspects something sinister might happen at any moment . . .
>
> Inside, too, everything looks peaceful. Danger seems far away. Inspector Crane pours another drink.
>
> Suddenly, noises everywhere. Guns fire; bodies fall. Death can be very noisy.
>
> Both bikers lie dead in pools of blood.

EXERCISE 4

Which of these adverbs can be sentence adverbs, commenting on the whole sentence which follows?

amazingly	indefinitely	incidentally
certainly	finally	regrettably
doubtfully	hopefully	surprisingly
frankly	generally	unusually

Which of them

a. do you use when you speak?
b. do you know/understand but not use?
c. are new to you?

EXERCISE 5

Which of these are used as qualifiers or intensifiers in front of an adjective?

amazingly	particularly	really
fortunately	generally	shockingly
awfully	dangerously	slightly
extremely	surprisingly	unusually

Which of them:

a. do you understand and use?
b. do you understand but not use?
c. are new to you?
d. do you not like, and don't think you will ever use?

EXERCISE 6

How many expressions can you make which use:

a. part of the verb *have* with:
b. part of the verb *give* with:

1. a party
2. lunch
3. a pound
4. a present for . . .
5. a present to . . .

6. a cup of tea
7. time to . . .
8. a hand
9. a cold
10. the opportunity to . . .

EXERCISE 7

Which of the following can come immediately after the verb *play*? Mark each one P = possible or X = not possible.

1. the piano
2. the typewriter
3. a record
4. a car

5. up
6. over
7. football
8. back

9. chess
10. 'Happy Birthday'
11. a cassette
12. for time

EXERCISE 8

We say *on television*. How many other words can you think of which are similar to *television*, and go in the sentence *It's on. . . .* .

McCarthy's work in discourse analysis has suggested that agreement and disagreement are more frequently expressed in speech through lexical, rather than grammatical devices. He has suggested lexical exercises of the following type:

EXERCISE 9

1. Agree with a synonym.
He was very strange.
— Yes, very odd.

2. Agree, with an antonym
Joe didn't stick to the subject.
— He wandered off too much.

3. Agree, with a more general word.
The cat is great company.
— All pets are.

4. Agree, with a more specific word.
Books are badly printed nowadays.
— Especially paperbacks.

EXERCISE 10

Gairns and Redman propose a lexical exercise for 'extreme' adjectives from the following list:

priceless	hilarious	ghastly
invaluable	gorgeous	colossal
unique	outrageous	minute
terrifying	revolting	hideous

1. It must have been unpleasant to see everyone around you on the boat being sick.
— Unpleasant? It was absolutely revolting!
2. Their dog is rather ugly, isn't it?
3. They give very small portions in that restaurant, don't they?
4. Do you think he was funny?
etc.

It is notable that both of the above exercises involve supra-sentential lexical linking. It has been a constant theme of this book that practice based only on the production of correct sentences is severely deficient. It is precisely the suprasentential and co-textual aspects of language which are intrinsic to the nature of language itself.

Dictionaries

Most serious language students start with an L1/L2 dictionary, and later graduate to an L2 dictionary. For many, however, it remains a greatly underused resource which predominantly or exclusively defines the meaning of unknown items, a term which itself is usually restricted to unknown **words**. Sinclair has specifically claimed that the Cobuild dictionary is intended, in his phrase, to 'licence composition'; he intends students to exploit the dictionary for productive as well as receptive language use. Elsewhere a good L2/L2 dictionary has been referred to as 'the native speaker on your desk', a resource which can be consulted to answer the inevitable *Can you say ... ?* questions. Within a lexical approach, an important element in all courses involves teaching students how to use the dictionary to investigate word grammar, collocational range, separability of phrasal verbs, and many other features. Unfortunately, at the moment dictionaries remain largely restricted to vocabulary or fixed collocations. A resource book of lexical phrases, including sentence heads and institutionalised utterances should be an important priority for one of the major publishing houses. If lexis is to assume its rightful role within language teaching, there is an urgent need for a reference book which is truly a lexicon.

References

1. In Carter and MacCarthy, p.111.
2. ELTJ 39/1
3. Proper Words in Proper Places, Vienna 1989.
4. Linguistics in Language Teaching, p.111
5. In Carter and MacCarthy, p.70
6. In Carter and MacCarthy, p.74
7. ibid p.65.
8. Working with Words, p.66.
9. ibid p.67.
10. op cit p.71.
11. In Carter and MacCarthy, p.162.
12. ibid, p.78.

Chapter 8

Grammar Content in the Lexical Approach

PART 1 — Misunderstandings about Grammar

The basis of language is lexis. It has been, and remains, the central misunderstanding of language teaching to assume that grammar is the basis of language and that mastery of the grammatical system is a prerequisite for effective communication.

Although it is possible to communicate quite complex messages through lexis alone it is self-evident that the ability to grammaticalise is important. Any approach to language teaching which emphasises lexis and de-emphasises grammar represents not a revolution, but a change of emphasis. It is important to recognise, however, that, as Swan has observed, it is grammar which tends to be valued on a day to day basis in language teaching. While this is perhaps untrue for many teachers of adult or professional students, it remains central to the teaching of languages in schools, and correspondingly remains a powerful influence on students' expectations for the whole of their learning careers. The pre-eminent role given to grammar is regrettable for a number of reasons:

— Much of the grammar that is taught is inaccurate or plain wrong.

— The rules which are taught are frequently incomprehensible to the students who are taught them.

— Failure to understand abstract meta-language and rules produces unnecessary failure.

— There is no research evidence that explicit knowledge of grammar aids acquisition of the grammatical system.

— Most tellingly, grammar is not the basis of language acquisition, and the balance of linguistic research clearly invalidates any view to the contrary.

There is little doubt that some grammatical information is useful to students. There is also evidence that awareness-raising activity can help students perceive underlying patterns more quickly than they would if unguided. Full, competent use of the language involves mastering its grammatical patterns. These factors clearly suggest that grammar has a role to play, but not the pre-eminent role which it is frequently still accorded.

Many native teachers of English have never made a formal study of the grammar of the language they teach; they have a tendency to equate 'the grammar of English' with the kind of language information found in typical EFL textbooks. This is frequently grossly over-simplified and even wilfully contradicts the evidence of naturally occurring language data. Many non-native teachers made an extensive study of English grammar as part of their university training. Regrettably, depending where and when that training was done, much that they were taught was confused, mis-categorised and, again, often in direct conflict with naturally occurring language data.

To produce a context for any discussion of grammar we must first challenge some received views.

1. Grammar is not static or canonical.

There is no fixed canon of English grammar — reported speech, first, second and third conditionals, the difference between *make* and *do*. These are just narrowly selected examples which once occurred in popular grammar books. In fact all of these points are hopelessly misrepresented in almost all language teaching materials

2. Grammar is not prescriptive.

Old-fashioned grammars, including those intended for native speakers, unashamedly told the reader how the language should be used. Modern grammarians insist on their descriptive role. With the advent of computer technology descriptive grammarians can now be more or less precisely statistical, drawing attention to how things are always, usually or frequently used. Unusual examples need to be considered, not marginalised or dismissed.

3. Grammar is not well-defined.

Almost every descriptive statement we can make about grammar is less than absolute — describing 'normal' i.e. not **all,** uses. Most native speakers do not use the continuous with the verb *need*, but many Scots **only** use *Are you needing* ... Chalker has observed that even the word classes into which grammarians categorise words are fuzzy, with many items lying in grey areas. What is the adverb from *quick? - quickly*? or perhaps *quick* can itself be used as an adverb? No two analysts agree on precisely what constitutes a phrasal verb. None of this is a problem unless teachers are in search of certainty, decisive answers to complex questions. The statements we make about language are essentially statistical. They are nonetheless useful for that, but it does mean that unusual or 'exceptional' uses are only further along the Spectrum of Likelihood, not wrong or inferior.

4. Grammar is not the basis of language or language learning.

It is lexis, not grammar which is the basis of language. Grammaticalisation is a relative sophistication in the nature of language itself. For the learner of a foreign language, grammatical accuracy is invariably late acquired, but does not impede the effective use of the language in the earlier stages of learning.

5. Grammar is not the 'correct sentences' of the language.

Traditional grammar teaching emphasises the structure of the verb, together with comparatively few other grammatical items — countability, quantifiers, prepositions and the like. In almost every case, however, grammar exercises concentrate on the production of 'correct' sentences. The impression given, both to students and teachers, is that mastery of these correct sentence patterns is identical with mastery of the grammar of English. This is untrue. There are many sub-sentential grammatical patterns, in particular those associated with word grammar, and many supra-sentential patterns — features which structure discourse as a whole. Preoccupation with 'correct sentences' has meant many important patterns of the language have been overlooked.

There are serious questions to be raised about the use of de-contextualised sentences for grammatical practice. If sentences are to function as utterances, part of extended discourse, then **all** practice materials which claim to attend to the meaning of sentences must use **only** sentences which occur with co-text. This statement dismisses the value for meaningful grammar practice of many, if not most, of the grammar exercises in textbooks and practice books which are currently available.

6. Grammar is not linearly sequenced or linearly sequenceable.

Meaning is essentially differential, any individual item being defined by a set of **contrasts** with other items. This is as true of grammatical items as it is of individual lexical items. This means an understanding of the use of, for example, the present continuous involves the perception of the way in which it contrasts with, among other things, the past continuous and present simple. The present simple acquires meaning through contrast with a more complex set — the present continuous, the present perfect, the past simple, and even the de-grammaticalised verb form usually called the imperative. Mastery of this system of contrasts is inevitably long-term and holistic. No meaning can be attributed to the idea of mastering any bit, however defined; what is useful to the learner is a developing understanding of the **relationships** between any particular bit and **all** the other bits.

7. Grammar is not a set of 'rules'.

Good modern grammars are inevitably based on observation of naturally occurring grammar data, and the primacy of the data over the description is intrinsic to the nature of grammar. The most recent advances in grammar involve the search for explanatory grammar — **why** can some verbs be followed by the -*ing* form of the verb, some only by the base form of the verb with *to* and some by either? Many of these perceptions, however, involve developments in the way applied linguists look at grammar. Sadly, for many language teachers, the grammar of English remains the set of supposed 'rules' which have traditionally (that means over the last 30 years) been considered to be essential to the learning of English. This is a totally distorted, indeed primitive, view.

Three items within the traditional grammar syllabus are particularly unhelpful — reported speech, conditionals and the passive. Statistical evidence, quoted by Maule[1] and Ur[2] show that many verb constructions are possible within sentences which contain *if*; the first, second and third conditionals of traditional grammar are neither comprehensive, nor even particularly typical of *if*-sentences. Willis has convincingly argued that *would*, like the other modal auxiliaries, should be taught lexically not structurally.

Assessing the evidence of the Cobuild corpus, he decided[3]: *That reported speech was not a valid category in a pedagogic, or indeed in a formal, grammar.* The Cobuild corpus evidence is supported by reflection. We do not, typically, manipulate the speaker's words when 'reporting'; we either report the whole event synoptically, or narrate using the speaker's words. Even in literature no antecedent speech event is reported in a novel, it is simply a particular kind of creative writing.

Many supposed 'passives' are indistinguishable from adjectives: *The road was closed (by the police)*. Most supposed passive sentences do not contain the 'agent', and are best analysed as adjectives. Again, Willis working independently, has come to the same conclusion.

It is notable that these three items — conditionals, reported speech and passives — lend themselves to convoluted transformation exercises. Such exercises have no place in the language classroom for they set out to practise language which has simply been mis-analysed in the first case.

8. Grammar is not a set of transformations.

Two different utterances are never pure synonyms. If they contain the same referential information, the selection of one rather than the other form will be made precisely because the speaker wishes to order the information in different ways, for different purposes. The choice of one item rather than the other is intrinsic to the nature of language itself. Purposeless transformation, of the kind exemplified by traditional practices of reported speech, the passive, and many of the perverse exercises of certain examinations are invalidated precisely because they contradict the nature of language.

9. Grammar is not primarily the tense system.

Traditional textbooks had units named the Present Simple, Present Continuous, Past Simple, etc. Although such names are no longer the defining element of a syllabus, most text-books still use them as the principal element. This is largely because of teacher and student expectations. The verb has a central role to play but a number of powerful objections can be raised:

a. The tense system, being a complex interlocking system, is unconsciously acquired. As such, it is impossible to use it for syllabus definition.

b. A great deal of communication is effective while defective, and it is precisely the accurate use of the full central verbal grammatical system which is last acquired for any learner.

c. English has an extremely simple morphology — even a morphologically difficult verb like *take* has only five forms; *take, takes, taking, took, taken.* The morphology of the verb and the tense system are not in one-to-one correspondence — it is by no means obvious that it is the tense system which is primary, and modern grammatical research suggests that it may be precisely the morphological verb forms which are more 'basic'.

d. Over-emphasising the tense system will necessarily lead to an under-emphasis on all sub-sentential and supra-sentential grammar.

e. Many of the important features of the grammar of spoken English are provably centred on the auxiliary system, rather than the tense system. The proportions of material for both presentation and practice in most current language teaching materials ignores this.

10. Grammar is not logically distinct from 'vocabulary'.

We have already discussed a Spectrum of Generalisability at one end of which lie powerful words which enter into a very limited number of patterns, and at the other end of which lie widely generalisable patterns. It is this spectrum, and our placing of items upon it, which allows us to identify useful grammar.

Individual words, whether lexically powerful (*submarine*) or lexically weak (*take*), have their own grammar. Recognition of these factors suggests a much wider concept of grammar than that traditionally adopted in the teaching of English.

PART 2 — Grammar emphasised in the Lexical Approach

Grammar is the search for powerful patterns. Historically, this has led to what Willis calls 'an inordinate attention' being paid to the verb phrase. But many other items within the more strictly grammatical side of the syllabus deserve increased attention within the Lexical Approach.

1. Basic morphology and word formation

Some bound morphemes are fundamental and powerfully generative features of English grammar. Central examples are:

- s	Most plurals
- ed	Most past tenses
un -	Most general way of making adjectives negative
- er	General transformation from verb to noun: *bake-baker*
- able	General transformation from verb to adjective: *wash-washable*
- ness	Basic transformation adjective to noun: *dark-darkness*

It is also the case that many words can be placed with almost complete certainty in their word class by observation of their endings. Typical noun endings, for example, are: - *tion*, - *ment*, - *ity*, - *ology*.

Since these items are part of pattern generating systems, they are clearly of benefit to students in both encoding and decoding **from the earliest stages of learning.** Recognising the 'bits' of a word, in particular any bound morphemes, is helpful.

2. Auxiliary manipulation

One of the central factors contributing to fluency in spoken English is an ability to recognise and manipulate auxiliaries. They are central to at least six major functions — expressing negatives, questions, tags, making short answers, interested responses, and adding emphasis to what is said. In addition, they play a pivotal role in determining the way words are grouped into small 'packets' when articulated. It is astonishing that a language feature central to spoken English from both a pragmatic and articulatory point of view plays only a minor role in most elementary and intermediate courses. Again, over-concentration on sentence grammar and the supposed tense system is responsible.

Ironically, an approach centred on meaning must give increased attention to these important language items which themselves carry comparatively little meaning. It will be noted that many of the patterns in which the auxiliaries are particularly important are supra-sentential.

3. Oppositions

Consider also the following examples:

The new office is a wonderful change — it's so light and airy.
I'm not really hungry, but I wouldn't mind something light.
Since his accident he can only do light work.
We were lucky, the traffic was very light so it only took an hour.
You'll enjoy The Barber of Seville — it's a very light piece.

As these examples show only too clearly, it is meaningless to identify 'the opposite' of *light*. At the same time, there is some similarity of meaning in those different uses of *light;* there is a core meaning, never fully realised in an individual example, which is crudely expressed in the *light/heavy* and *light/dark* oppositions. Although words do not, in general, have anything which can usefully be described as their 'opposite', certain words can be useful in generating a set of collocations, and then a **set of oppositions.** This would involve a fuller version of a table such as the following:

a light meal	a substantial/big/heavy meal
a light opera	a serious/heavy opera
a light tread	a heavy tread
a light touch	a heavy hand
a very light room	a very dark room

4. Negation

Just as the concept of oppositions extends that of elementary supposed 'opposites', so negation extends the concept of negatives. Negation is usually seen in language teaching — particularly grammar practice — as an essentially structural idea — *I know her/I don't know her. I'll be there tomorrow/I won't be there tomorrow.* We return to the distinction between sentences and utterances and the observations that the structural negative of a sentence may not be the normal pragmatic way of negating the utterance.

How, for example, would one reply in these interchanges if the proto-reply was *No* rather than *Yes*?

Do you think we will be there on time?
   — *Well, I certainly hope so.*

I wouldn't be surprised if it rained.
   — *No, neither would I.*

Negation is a primary feature of any semantic analysis of English. Surprisingly, it has entered language teaching only in the extremely restricted form of structural negatives.

5. Adjuncts

Interestingly, this is another non-sentential element which deserves increased emphasis. Traditionally, grammatical teaching of adverbs has been of the singularly unhelpful *She's a beautiful skater — She skates beautifully* variety. Once again we see the unhelpful nature of all exercises based on transformation. More importantly, this paragraph draws attention to that kind of adverb — sentence adjunct — which indicates the speaker's attitude to the whole following utterance.

Rather artificially, each of the four sentences in the preceding paragraph began with an adjunct: *interestingly, traditionally, once again, more importantly*. Communicative power is increased if a speaker is able to guide the listener towards the macro-meaning of what is being said. Apart from a few obvious discourse markers: *I'd like to begin by ..., secondly, and finally ...* this language, which structures extensive discourse, has been largely ignored. Adjuncts are at least as useful in structuring written discourse such as essays.

6. Grammatical holophrases as lexis

Acceptance of the idea of functions meant teachers felt comfortable with sentences previously thought to be 'advanced' at a much earlier place in the syllabus. Recognising *Would you like a cup of tea?* as 'offering' rather than 'the conditional', allowed it to be taught without structural analysis. In a similar way, acceptance of the integrity of lexical phrases allows these to be taught as self-contained items, without analysis into possible component parts. The following full sentences have more or less institutionalised pragmatic meaning:

Oh hello, I haven't seen you for ages.
What on earth do you think you're doing?
What will you have?
We'll have to do something about it soon.
What are you going to do about it?

In the same way that individual nouns may be seen as naming real world objects or entities, complete sentences of the kind listed may be seen as naming particular situations. As such, on one level they represent wholly non-generative single-item patterns. Clearly they can in the short term increase students' communicative power very efficiently if chosen to coincide with situations in which the students may find themselves. Equally importantly, however, the whole sentences, fully grammaticalised, can provide an additional resource against which other, novel sentences may be judged.

7. Supra-sentential linking

In conventional grammar teaching this is represented by interested responses: *I've just been to London. Oh, have you?* — and little else. In fact it represents a major theoretical and practical change, central to a lexical approach.

Individual sentences — except those which can readily be identified as sentential lexical items — are meaningless when decontextualised. Sentences become utterances only when they occur with co-text. Any text — story, report, lecture or conversation — is very much more than a succession of sentences. Cohesion and coherence are maintained using a wide range of language items, which are themselves more or less rigidly patterned. McCarthy, describing informal conversation says:

> Even apparently loosely structured talk adheres to norms and is regularly patterned. It is this type of patterning that can be as useful to the language teacher as the regular patterns of syntax are in clauses and sentences.

Both cohesion and coherence exhibit both structural and lexical patterning, and both need to be taken into account in devising language practice materials. Sadly, many grammar practice books consist almost exclusively of single, de-contextualised sentences. If this represents students' staple diet of practice, it is hardly surprising that they find it difficult to take part in conversations, or produce coherent and cohesive paragraphs in writing.

Consider for a moment how the word *such* is used. Which of the following examples comes more readily to mind? *He's such a thoughtful chap. Such sentences rarely feature in language courses.* Almost certainly it is the first sentence, with an intra-sentential use of the word which more readily came to mind. The second, supra-sentential item is, however, characteristic of academic written discourse:

> There is as marked difference of style between spoken language and the language of written academic discourse. *Such* language employs a particular variety of grammar, and is characterised by particular sentence types. *Such* sentences rarely feature in language courses.

We have clear and concrete evidence of why much student writing is unsatisfactory. Technically, it lacks cohesion — the employment of precisely those grammatical devices that ensure that we perceive a whole text as more than a sequence of sentences. Grammar of this kind — supra-sentential grammar — forms little or no part of language courses. It must be clear that the kind of 'correction' of written work such as essays which remains widespread, hardly scratches the surface of this problem. What is needed is a radical and total revision of the concept of grammar to include such discoursal features.

If language practice is to reflect the nature of language, **all practices should be supra-sentential.** Notice the difference in these two examples:

PRACTICE 1

Complete the following sentences with the correct form of the verb:

1. I .... late every night last week. (work)
2. I .... a new car last week. (buy)
3. I .... to bring your book, but I'll bring it tomorrow. (forget)
4. I .... my wallet somewhere safe, and then I couldn't find it! (put)

PRACTICE 2

Complete this dialogue with the correct forms of the verb:

Did you remember to call at the supermarket on your way home?

— Oh sorry, I completely .... I .... late, was tired when I .... the office, and I just .... (forget, work, leave)

— Don't worry, it doesn't matter. I .... a couple of pizzas this afternoon and .... them in the deep freeze so we can have one of those. (buy, put)

Neither practice is particularly imaginative, but the second has three major advantages over the first:

a. A holistic event, rather than a disconnected string of random lexicalisations is presented.

b. Both 'bottom up' and 'top down' understandings can be employed, precisely because each part of the language event interrelates with other parts.

c. The practice material contains a great deal of language which is not itself the focus of what the student is required to produce — *Oh sorry; I forgot ... and I just forgot; Don't worry, it doesn't matter.* All of this language is important input for the student, so that the practice material is doubly useful. In addition, of course, this additional language is precisely the language which makes the whole event coherent and cohesive.

Supra-sentential practices practise the atomistic items which are usually the focus of sentential practices, but within the wider, and much more natural framework of something approximating to a whole language event. Willis[4] endorses this view: *only by drawing attention to occurences in text can learners begin to build up a picture of (these forms) in use.*

8. Word grammar

Every word has its own grammar — the set of patterns in which it occurs. Words with a comparatively high meaning-content enter into a comparatively small number of typical patterns. Five useful, and highly generalisable pedagogical strategies are available for exploring the word grammar of a word with relatively high meaning-content:

a. Identifying high frequency **uses,** and distinguishing one from the other. (A dictionary from the Cobuild stable is indispensable here).

b. Identifying and recording in suitable formats high frequency **collocations.**

c. Identifying **cognates** of the key word, and, in turn, **their collocations.**

d. Identifying the other element in the **natural noun phrase — verb phrase equivalence.**

e. Identifying any **lexical phrases** (sentence heads, or fully grammaticalised utterances) in which the key word regularly occurs.

In general, it is lexically vacuous words which enter the widest range of patterns but, as we observed earlier, this is a matter of points on a spectrum. Some words with definite semantic content — for example *light* — are frequently used with more than one meaning, and different meanings exhibit different collocational patterns. Selection may be based either on purely linguistic criteria for general course students or, if students are able to specify some particular area of interest, key words can usually be identified relatively easily.Metaphorical uses of words are often much more frequent than the literal meanings, often supposed to be the basic or core meaning. This has important implications for collocation.

Having identified a key word, and perhaps several senses of it, collocations can be identified. Care must be taken not to over-burden students here. The purpose is to identify **maximally useful** patterns. We have already discussed extensively the fact that syllabus is about both selecting **in and** selecting **out.** That point needs to be reiterated here.

All spontaneous attempts at vocabulary building tend to be noun dominated. There are obvious reasons for this:
— Thought is often visual, and then we 'name' what we can 'see'.
— Nouns, even abstract, seem more 'tangible' than other word categories.
— Most vocabulary items in any language are nouns.

The main study of word grammar is, therefore, likely to produce relatively small, but communicatively powerful sets of **verb + noun, adjective + noun,** and **verb + adjective + noun** combinations. For many words, however, it is also helpful to explore grammatical variants on the same word. Many nouns can also be used as verbs: *a/to deposit, check, house, fax, baby.* Sometimes a slight modification of pronunciation is required (*house*); sometimes the verbal use may be rare or even marginal (*baby*). Often, however, students' communicative power can be increased immediately if they simply recognise that many of the 'words' that they 'know' only as nouns, can also be used as verbs.

Sometimes cognates are derived by relatively generative systems of affixes — *control, uncontrollable; organise, reorganisation.* Sometimes two words in the same word class, but with different meanings and collocational ranges are important: *advisable/advisory, contributor/contribution, variety/variation.*

A particular feature of more formal registers, particularly the written language, is the occurrence of more complex noun phrases as subject of the sentence:

Travel arrangements have not been finalised.
Language learners need extensive exposure to data at the right level.
Massive price reductions have encouraged high street spending.

Many intermediate and advanced students have not developed the ability to make phrases such as *travel arrangements, language learners, price reductions.* They have a tendency to produce much less concise, more fully grammaticalised forms: *Arrangements for the travelling, people who are learning languages, if you reduce the price ...* In many cases their attempts to grammaticalise will be unsuccessful. Their lack of knowledge of word grammar forces them back to sentence grammar, which in turn forces mistakes which, unless the teacher is alert, leads to remedial grammar practice of the wrong kind.

Within the Lexical Approach, teachers need to be constantly aware of the possibilities of exploiting word grammar rather than sentence grammar as a means of extending students' communicative power.

9. De-lexicalised words

The de-lexicalised words may be sub-divided into two categories:

Verbs: *have, make, do, get, put, take.*
Function words: *with, of, by, on, in, out of.*

The first group has been ignored in conventional syllabuses, save for over-emphasis of the *do/make* contrast. The second group has usually appeared in three separate places — prepositions of place, prepositions of time, and prepositions-miscellaneous. This last category has led teachers and students to the conclusion that these small words represent one of the largest problems in mastering English. As the following page shows, however, the de-lexicalised words are among the most powerful pattern generators in the language. Collecting some of their most important patterns and arranging them in an arresting, non-linear format, where words which occur together are recorded together, is more likely to be pedagogically effective. What is clear from the displays is that neither of the words deserves to be treated as a marginal bit of English grammar. On the contrary, both are palpably central to the structure of English, and of much greater frequency than a tense form such as the present perfect continuous.

Delexicalised words as pattern generators

(take someone somewhere)

Who takes the children to school?

I'll take you shopping tomorrow.

They had to take her to the doctor.

·····································

·····································

a picture

a photograph

(a period of time)

I took over an hour on the motorway.

That'll take ages.

It won't take more than ten minutes.

·····································

·····································

take

(travelling)

Shall we take the car?

Don't worry I can take a train.

·····································

·····································

an exam

your driving test

(decisions or choices)

You should take more risks.

We can't take a decision yet.

I'll take the responsibility.

·····································

·····································

(physical feature)

blue eyes

grey hair

a beard

·····································

·····································

(a tool etc.)

with a sponge.

with a long
thin thing.

·················

·················

(+ person or people)

I stayed with her.

We went on holiday with friends.

·····································

·····································

with

(showing a mood)

He was shaking with anger.

She agreed with considerable
reluctance.

·····································

·····································

(illness)

He's in bed with flu.

·····················

·····················

(an institution)

She went on a trip with the Women's Institute.

He was in Germany with the army.

I'm with IBM now.

·····································

·····································

10. Stress patterns and groups

In the early stages of exposure to a new language all that can be distinguished is a stream of sound. No progress at all can be made until the learner can segment this, by observing the 'bits' of which it seems to be composed. Initially, this segmentation tends to break the stream of speech down into what the listener perceives as units of meaning. These may, or may not, coincide with actual sentence, phrase or word boundaries. It is a well known phenomenon of English L1 learning that children often go through a phase when they treat *I wanna* ... , and *I needa* . . . as wholes, only later becoming aware of the morphology. I recall learning Swedish in Sweden, without the aid of textbook or teacher. Quite early on I heard, and even successfully reproduced so that my meaning was understood *Tack ska'ra*. It came as a considerable surprise when I first saw this 'correctly' written down: *Tack, skall du har*.

Over the years, language teaching could hardly have got itself in a bigger mess in dealing with stress and intonation patterns. Some teachers still agonise over whether to present so-called short forms, or whether students must master the 'full form' first. In natural, unemphasised speech it is the unstressed form (which is not 'short' for anything) which predominates and should, unquestionably, be given almost exclusive emphasis in the early stages of learning. The stressed form, which adds emotional content to what is said, is one of the many features of auxiliary manipulation, the importance of which we have already mentioned. Even if spoken English is taken as a model, and unstressed forms predominate it is also important that these be delivered at the natural speed, or something very close to it and, above all, that they are delivered respecting the natural stress and intonation patterns of English. Unfortunately, slowing down almost always distorts these patterns. Since it is precisely the perception of the segments which make up the whole which is the primary aid to understanding the spoken language, any strategy which does not directly contribute to the students' mastering of this process of automatic segmentation of the stream of speech must be counter-productive.

Modern linguistic analysis, in particular Nattinger's chunking, suggests that language is not made up of structure + vocabulary, but of different kinds of lexical phrase. Many such phrases are produced as single units within the stream of speech. In other words, the 'bits' of which speech is constructed are frequently, though not invariably, identical with the bits which are noticeable on a purely phonological level. This serves to emphasise even more the importance of recognising stress and intonation patterns as having an important role to play within the Lexical Approach.

11. Functional patterns

In an early paper Wilkins[5] made the following observation:

> If a notional and functional approach is to be a serious alternative (to a grammatical or situational approach), it must be able to offer generalisations of equal or greater power. Language teachers would be rightly sceptical of abandoning the partly negotiable currency of the grammatical approach for the crock of gold at the end of the functional rainbow.

Notice Wilkins' own warning — generalisations of equal or greater power. As we have already observed, notions have been largely ignored as even possible sources of generalisation. All too often, functions have been similarly reduced to elementary pattern practice of a quasi-structural kind. Functional patterns — the key word is patterns — are often supra-sentential, and often cover much larger areas of discourse than a single initiator-response pair. I know of almost no language teaching materials which make a serious attempt to make students aware of, and practise these larger functional patterns. Not infrequently these larger functional patterns are more lexical than structural and so constitute a natural component of the Lexical Approach.

12. Word order

This topic has always been dealt with in a very piecemeal way — adjective order, the position of adverbs, and not much more. An essential element of effective communication involves the speaker organising the informational content of what is said in particular ways. If we wish to develop communicative power, there are word order patterns of which students can usefully and effectively be made aware.

Summary

The Lexical Approach suggests changes to the content of grammar teaching. Some items could unquestionably be deleted:

Will as 'the future'.
Would as 'the conditional'.
The traditional first, second and third conditionals.
The passive.
Reported speech.

All of these have traditionally been mis-analysed and the way they have been dealt with for the foreign learner has been neither more nor less than nonsense. There is no justification for their retention in **any** language teaching syllabus, whether lexically orientated or not.

Certain items would be treated very differently within a Lexical Approach, most notably, largely reflecting the above list, *will*, *would*, the . . . *ing* form and the traditional 'past participle'.

Patterns not previously recognised will have enhanced status, particularly sub-sentential word-based items, and supra-sentential discoursal features. It would be a disaster, however, if all that happened was a change of content, for the holistic nature of language and learning suggests that much traditional grammar practice was, by its very nature, theoretically unsound, pedagogically inefficient, and ultimately ineffective. The Lexical Approach suggests a change of content for grammar teaching, but equally importantly, a radically different view of methodology and what we mean by the term 'grammar practice'. This forms the subject of the next chapter.

References

1. ELTJ 42/2.
2. ELTJ Correspondence 45/1.
3. The Lexical Syllabus, p.127.
4. ibid, p. 147.
5. In Brumfit and Johnson p.92.

Chapter 9

Explanation and Practice in the Lexical Approach

'Grammar' in the language classroom has usually meant explanation and practice. This has usually been the least popular element of a language course with students, although most still believe it is necessary. In contrast, almost all applied linguists and methodologists writing over the last thirty years have, as a key element of their proposals, tried to dethrone grammar from its central position, and de-emphasise it in the classroom. The Lexical Approach suggests that the particular content to which students' attention can usefully be drawn should be changed, but more importantly, it too suggests that formal grammar explanation and so-called controlled practice are both of very limited value. There are three central theoretical objections:

— Even today, the descriptions we have of the patterns of the language are often partial and tentative. Supposed pedagogic simplifications of these are often inadequate, misleading, or plain nonsense.

— There is no evidence that descriptive knowledge of the system — rules and explanations — is of more than the most marginal value in aiding acquisition of the grammatical system.

— As Willis observes, the essence of language is meaning, and meaning implies choice. 'Controlled practice', which by definition restricts choice, simply conflicts with the nature of language itself. Controlled practice, far from aiding acquisition, may actually impede it.

Teachers must accept that however convenient from a teaching point of view pedagogic explanation and controlled practice may be, the evidence is that neither assists acquisition.

PART 1 — Grammar Explanation

Historically, the description of the grammar of English was strongly influenced by descriptions of Latin. The covert influence of Latin grammar can be found in almost every section of contemporary grammars of English. In addition, the explanations were largely intuitive. Nowadays, corpus linguistics has provided statistical evidence, and it is a matter of simple fact that many traditional explanations are simply not endorsed by the evidence. Contemporary linguistics would expect any explanation to be:

— Descriptive not prescriptive.

— Intrinsically provisional.

— Based on collecting, sorting, classifying and naming data.

— Intrinsically statistical.

— Hierarchic, accurate and accessible.

The method is essentially scientific, based on the Observe-Hypothesise-Experiment procedure. Descriptions not endorsed by evidence must be revised; statistically less frequent or marginal examples cannot be ignored. Most importantly, it is real language data which has priority over any description. Language teachers need a similar attitude; approaching the language with an open mind and a critical attitude. This in turn can usefully be transmitted to students by developing receptive skills, and awareness raising exercises. The recognition of grammar and lexical chunking as a receptive skill is central to the Lexical Approach.

The Lexical Approach proposes a greatly diminished role for what is usually understood by 'grammar teaching'. Equally, there is an enhanced role for grammar work which is radically different. This new style of grammar is primarily receptive, and because it is based on raising student's awareness, is powerfully student- rather than teacher-centred. Teachers will need to show students used to more authoritarian grammar teaching that this new approach is not only valid, but more helpful. The informing principles are an understanding of grammar as a receptive skill, and the symbiotic relationship between explanation and practice. Explanation and practice are inextricably intertwined in a way which has not traditionally been the case.

Explanations in the classroom

The dangers of teacher or textbook imposed explanation have already been extensively discussed. The accuracy and accessibility of any explanation are in permanent tension; truly understanding an imposed explanation entails having already mastered any underlying conceptual difficulty, so that the supposed 'explanation' is really no more than an efficient labelling system for an already understood concept; explanation is knowledge about, but the ability to use grammar is essentially procedural knowledge. These, and other objections already discussed amply demonstrate the inadequacy, even futility, of imposed explanation. If our target is the creation of effective learning conditions, such explanation must be replaced by student-centred exploration, a procedure where students are presented with language data and, usually in small groups to take advantage of the different cognitive styles of different group members, students themselves describe what they 'see'. Put simply, the students 'write their own grammar rules'.

Far from being a soft option for teachers, this imposes considerable demands on them. Their skill lies in perceiving actual or potential confusions in their student's perception of a system of English, and divising a task accompanied by language data focusing on the particular language problem. Teachers must choose when to intervene and provide appropriate tasks, questions and data. That is difficult enough, but then they must resist the temptation to interfere, and allow students the time to discuss, formulate, and if necessary reformulate their perceptions. (In monolingual classes it may be more appropriate and efficient if the students' discussions are conducted in L1). **Whatever** formulation of the rule or description students ultimately offer must be valued as an important contribution to the learning process, even if the particular product — explanation or rule — is inadequate or misguided. The O-H-E paradigm must be respected!

Teachers may help by providing new and differently or better focused questions, or drawing attention to language items which do not fit the students' formulation. Any contributions of this kind, however, must be made in the spirit of partnership, not correction; the emphasis is on formulating a better hypothesis, and respect for the data. In passing, we note that these attitudes are much more fully in tune with the general educational syllabus discussed earlier than any traditional grammar teaching.

All grammar rules used in the classroom should be seen as: **partial**, **provisional**, **personal**. At best, they summarise what we know at the moment. A crucial element in engendering an appropriate atmosphere is the teacher's attitude, and underlying mind-set. Anything resembling the dogmatism of old-fashioned grammar rules must be discarded; the price paid is that certainty must be discarded too and the hesitant, subjective, provisional nature of the knowledge and rules by which we act (in life, as in grammar!) must be truly valued. Certainty can be reassuring, but it can also be inhibiting. Our underlying maxim should not be *I know, therefore I am safe* but rather *I wonder, therefore I see*.

Classroom procedures

If students are to formulate their own rules, grammar materials, and the procedures for using them need major revision. Material which emphasises exploration over explanation should be:

— Essentially receptive — sorting, matching, jigsaws (see below).

— Directed towards awareness raising — *Did you notice . . . ?* and *Can you find . . . ?* will frequently be supplementary questions which follow any other activity for which a piece of material has been used.

— Directed towards effective monitoring of both self and others.

A key element of awareness raising is assisting students in developing the ability to compare their own performance with some norm. Remembering language as skill, we recall that skills are improved by good observation of successful performance.

Finally, we remind ourselves that 'grammar' is not a different phenomenon from language and that, therefore, anything we do which claims to help students master grammar must not violate the nature of language itself. This means the search for grammar explanations through an exploratory process will almost always involve the use of language in context, used where both situation and co-text are part of the data. Traditional grammatical knowledge, endorsed by Chomsky's idea of competence, has concentrated on all the **possible sentences** of English. Language teaching, insofar as it is directed towards mastery of the grammatical system, must take cognisance of possible sentences. More frequently, however, its primary concern must be with sentences which constitute **probable utterances**. Context, and in particular co-text, make many possible sentences improbable. Learning a language is not primarily the pursuit of grammatical competence *per se*. It is astonishing to find Ur[1] in her popular *Grammar Practice Activities*, happily accepting short practices, of single de-contextualised sentences, and even attributing value to students producing sentences such as *I'm going to drink tea from it*. Her Activities concentrate largely on sentences; many of the proposed activities are scarcely **language** activities at all. Within a perspective which values communicative power, you do not 'learn' sentences so that you may at some future time use and contextualise them; you derive your understanding of the possible sentences from a developing awareness of the patterns which underly the actual — and therefore frequent and probable — sentences to which you are exposed. If students are exposed to natural language data (receptive skills), presented with appropriate tasks and questions (awareness raising) and their perception of differences heightened (effective monitoring), the 'explanations' which students will generate will be intensely personal, and fully internalised. The proposed procedure may, indeed, be a step towards a grammar for acquisition, rather than a grammar for learning.

PART 2 — Grammar Practice

The connotations of *We are going to do some language practice* and *We are going to do a grammar practice* are, surprisingly, very different. The latter suggests a tightly controlled, narrowly focused atomistic activity. As we have already seen, language is more adequately represented holistically and organically. However shocking it may seem, it is unquestionably the case that 'grammar practice' which violates the nature of language itself cannot be doing what it claims to do — namely develop the student's language skills. This invalidates much of the grammar practice activity of contemporary language teaching. If such activity benefits the students, the benefit is wholly incidental to the supposed objective of the practice. It would be merely iconoclastic, and indeed absurd to suggest that grammar practice should form no part of language teaching. It is essential, however, to re-evaluate what we mean by this term.

The grammar of the written language and that of the spoken language differ radically. Written practice is clearly uniquely appropriate to practising the skills involved in producing good written English. Equally, it seems uncontroversial to suggest that spoken language is best practised orally. Remarkably, most grammar practice books with which I am familiar largely or wholly ignore this distinction.

Spoken practice is different in one other critical way from any written practice — it is performed in 'real time'. Written practice usually affords the opportunity for reflection and revision. Self-evidently, if students are exposed only or predominantly to written practice, they will be unable to process language successfully under normal operating conditions in conversation.

Despite earlier strictures on behaviourism, I see a role for what some will see as traditional 'grammar drills'. There is no conflict here — they have a small role precisely because they impose a different kind of time constraint and therefore promote a different kind of cognitive response.

Controlled practice required students to produce a particular, usually uniquely defined, grammatical structure; accurate production was the focus of such practice. **Free practice**, always conceived of as the 'last stage' of learning, emphasised fluency over accuracy, and imagined (usually unsuccessfully) that the students would use the new language immediately, in situations where there were no apparent linguistic constraints. In practice, teachers often omitted this phase of the lesson, and if it did occur, students regressed to 'earlier' language over which they felt they had more control. Recognition of language acquisition as more holistic has discredited the controlled practice — free practice sequence.

Willis[2], recognising that the important and difficult thing is the ability to **use**, not knowledge of form, is clear about controlled practice:

> Finally, what about controlled practice? Does it have a place? In order to answer this question we should first consider the aim of controlled practice activities. I think the first thing here is to dispel the notion that practice of this kind **teaches** grammar. It highlights acceptable patterns in English, but it does little more than that.

He sees controlled practice as a particular, rather limited kind of awareness raising activity. Bearing in mind that students will often produce potentially demotivating errors, and that the errors can all too easily stimulate time-wasting correction, it is easy to see that controlled practice can be one of the least efficient or cost-effective classroom strategies.

Discussing language as skill, we have already noted Johnson's distinction between knowledge about and knowledge how to. That part of grammar which we have called grammar as fact can be told to students, and their knowledge of it can be tested — spellings, irregular past tenses, possible and impossible collocations. Knowledge of this kind is part of knowing a language. So practice of this kind of knowledge is part of grammar practice. But a small part. Vastly the most important component of what we think of as 'knowing the grammar' is knowledge of how to, procedural knowledge. It involves the developing ability to express relationships, and to process increasingly complex grammatical forms. Inconvenient as it may be, this kind of procedural knowledge is almost impossible to practise using single sentence, written practice.

The essential characteristic of grammar is that it permits generalisation, with corresponding lowering of the memory load and a developing ability to create novel language. If this is the purpose of grammar practice, then effective practice involves making students aware of, and helping them increase their facility with, useful patterns. Too often, material which claims to be practising a particular pattern is severely defective because:

a. The pattern is inaccurately, or more frequently only partially, identified.
b. Students remain unaware of what pattern is supposedly being practised.
c. The practice material contains examples which exhibit alternative, marginal, or even contradictory sub-patterns.

This stricture applies most strongly to the kind of practices which teachers themselves write. Despite the abundance of published material too many teachers produce practice material hastily, and then muddle their way through its defects in class. Such practice material is unprofessional, and indefensible on any ground. Regrettably, it is common. The following extracts are edited abbreviations of material I have seen recently submitted by teachers as polished and ready for use:

PRACTICE 1

Complete the following examples with prepositions:

1. He really rubs me .... the wrong way.

2. It's .... you, I can't decide.

3. It was pouring, so I got soaked .... .

4. You have to face .... to the fact that there's nothing you can do.

The four examples I have quoted were four of twenty. Not all the examples were defective but here we have a so-called preposition practice where many examples do not even pass the elementary test of being prepositions!

PRACTICE 2

(This practice introduces collocations of *out of*. They are listed at the head of the practice and some are marked with an asterisk. Here is an extract.)

*out of order	out of date
*out of use	*out of doors
out of control	out of stock
*out of place	out of the question

Those collocations marked with an asterisk have a phrase of opposite meaning formed with *in* or *within*.

Is *indoors* really the opposite of *out of doors*? Is *The phone is out of use* meaningfully opposed to *The phone is in use*?

The examples and information are reassuringly clear until you ask whether actual occasions of language use support what is said. Readers may be tempted to suggest that I have merely criticised **bad** grammar practices. Regretttably, as an editor to whom many practices are submitted for publication, I must record that the above are typical. In many cases, even the most cursory linguistic criticism leaves one wondering not about the efficacy of the practice, but of what is actually being practised at all.

Receptive grammar practice

We come now to a much more positive and linguistically sensitive area of grammar practice. Conventionally, students and teachers see grammar practice as the students **producing** language, usually sentences, for evaluation by the teacher. Grammar practice is conceived in product-orientated terms, with the underlying question *Can you do/produce . . . ?* But the holistic, organic nature of language strongly endorses the view that mastery of the grammatical system is acquired not learned, and that the process of acquisition is best aided by making students **aware** of features of the target language, and, in due course, of how their own production of the target language differs from its norms. Central to Rutherford's study of the acquisition of second language grammar is the concept which he names 'consciousness raising'. Krashen has suggested that 'better' language learners are better precisely because they are more acute monitors of their own production, better able to compare their intermediate production with the norms of the spoken language. 'Awareness raising' is a term which has recently acquired currency in language teaching terminology. The unifying feature behind all these commentators is the assertion that it is the students' ability to **observe accurately**, and **perceive similarity and difference** within target language data which is most likely to aid the acquisition of the grammatical system. Within this theoretical framework, **grammar as a receptive skill** has an important role to play.

Here is a major re-emphasis; students should be encouraged to observe language before, or as well as, being required to produce it. The underlying question becomes *Can you see . . . ?* From a methodological point of view particular kinds of exercise automatically suggest themselves as appropriate to this approach. Receptive grammar practice will include:

Recognising   Comparing
Checking   Matching
Sorting

Typical practice rubrics will include:

Underline all the 's in this dialogue where *'s = is*; circle the 's where *'s = has*.

Listen to the tape. Raise your hand each time you hear /əv/ = of

Look at these two texts. What differences can you see? Which text is easier to read? Why?

Sort the following into two groups: *walked = walk +/t/, played = play +/d/*

Choose one sentence from list 1 and one from list 2 so you make six two-line dialogues.

Most of these exercise types are already familiar to teachers. At the moment, however, they usually form a small percentage of grammar practice material, which still emphasises productive rather than receptive use. Linguistic theory and SLA research strongly suggest that practices of this type need to be given a much greater role.

Sub-sentential and supra-sentential practice

Any comprehensive programme of grammar practice cannot be wholly, or even predominantly sentence-based. The assumption that the sentence is the primary unit of language is, quite simply, wrong. It is increasingly obvious that language does not consist of grammatical sentences with 'slots' into which appropriate vocabulary can be inserted; continuous text does not consist only of sequences of sentences. Grammar practice must not violate the nature of language, and language consists of discourse, not sentence strings.

McCarthy has cogently argued that the model for the teaching of spoken language should be spoken language. In spoken language, isolated sentences are rare, and de-contextualised sentences do not occur. The force of Widdowson's perception that a sentential utterance is a great deal more than a sentence deserves to be much more widely respected. (*pace* Swan ELTJ 1985!)

Written language is more self-consciously constructed than spoken language. It is, at a very profound level, not only differently grammaticalised, but more grammatical. I stress that I mean this in the sense outlined by Rutherford[3] — it is strictly **grammatical**, rather than **semantic** relations which dictate many features of the written language. This is in no way to suggest the superiority of written over spoken language; its more profoundly grammatical character merely means that the employment of strictly grammatical elements permits more concise expression, through, among other things, the ability to generate complex noun phrase subjects, and to subordinate or embed clauses. This suggests that effective grammar practice which aims at improving students' ability to produce coherent written text needs specifically to concentrate on the generation of sub-sentential noun phrases, and supra-sentential textual coherence and cohesion. Even native speakers consciously redraft written material. Written language is highly conventionalised and the conventions need to be learned. Here conscious learning **can** aid acquisition.

One of the most widely used forms of grammar practice is the gap-filling exercise. Its easy-to-produce, quick-to-do, easy-to-mark quality suggests a certain scepticism. Its almost inevitable atomistic quality suggests its ubiquitousness is unjustified. In fact, depending which items are represented by the gaps to be filled, it has a valuable role to play in supra-sentential grammar practice, and lexically based exercises.

Cloze procedures are well established. Items are deleted from a whole text – continuous prose or dialogue using selective deletion. Critically, **whole** texts are involved and if selective deletion is used, awareness of cohesive devices and collocation can be increased.

Ironically, the thought which motivates the speaker to speak at all is frequently at the **end** of the sentence — the focus or rheme, the 'new' rather than 'given' information. Consider these examples:

Have you booked your ticket yet?
I'm going to change my job.
Would next Thursday be convenient?
I have no idea where I put my briefcase.

Clearly, the 'lexical centres' of those sentences are, respectively, *ticket, job, convenient, briefcase*. If this lexical centre is expanded — *get a ticket, put my briefcase* — it is clear that the utterances are grammaticalisations of this lexical content. This suggests (correctly) that completion practices which involve students providing the subject and verb phrase of a sentence, will be useful. Here we have sentential practice, derived from essentially lexical content; grammar practice wholly appropriate to a lexical approach.

Many lexical items consist of a sentence head with the possible completions more or less tightly determined:

Have you ever been to . . . ?
If I were you I'd . . .
I can't imagine why they haven't . . .

Recognising the possibility that much language is made of phrases rather than sentence plus vocabulary, it is comparatively easy to identify utterances which consist of sentence-head plus content phrase. This suggests that completions based on sentence heads have a role to play.

The exercise types based on completion which are likely to be effective, and find a natural place in a lexical approach, are radically different from the arbitrary gap-filling kind currently so familiar. Whole text Cloze procedures, and the beginnings and ends of sentences clearly based on a **specific lexical focus** have an important role to play. Other kinds of completion, in particular gap-filling, will serve only a minor role in checking grammar as fact.

Jigsaws

The jigsaw technique, in which the student is required to re-assemble a whole from constituent parts is a natural extension of activities based on matching. It may be applied to language at any level: words, phrases, sentences, turns in a dialogue or fragments of text. Its obvious advantage over pairing and matching is that it relates to larger texts or stretches of discourse.

Transformations

Together with gap-filling, this practice type is perhaps the most familiar. It is therefore regrettable that it is the one practice type which is least theoretically sound, indeed indefensible. It is characterised in grammar practice books by the rubric *Re-write the following sentences using . . .* Almost always it is applied to sentences, and this is no accident. Frequently, the same propositional content can be expressed in more than one way but, contextualised, one variant is obligatory or strongly preferred. The language item most often subject to this treatment in general language courses is the passive. Although all linguists insist that this is a fully independent form, it is almost always taught as a 'transformation'. Only rarely, however, are active and passive alternatives equally suitable **in context**. Any transformation practice based on single decontextualised sentences is fundamentally unsound. Language simply does not work like that. There is value in encouraging students to compare two (or more) ways of expressing the same propositional content but such practices will be based on grammar as a receptive skill and comparison, not on meaningless, decontextualised transformation of individual sentences.

Productive practices

The use of language material for receptive grammar practice is, as we have seen, intimately linked with a developing awareness of language patterns. Student-formulated explanations and receptive practice have unimpeachable theoretical credentials. But few teachers would be happy with the idea that grammar practice should be confined to the development of awareness and understanding; traditionally, indeed, grammar practice is almost exclusively based on productive practices in which the student is required to complete or produce examples of correct English, usually sentences, less frequently whole dialogues, texts or essays. What is the status and role of such practices? If prejudice and tacit assumption are set aside, five possible purposes for productive grammar practice may be identified: **aid to learning, reinforcement, testing, diagnosis, experimentation**. Readers might like to reflect on which of these justifications motivates their own use of productive grammar practice.

Aid to learning

This depends entirely on the construction of the practice and the degree of cognitive involvement of the student while actually doing it. Decontextualised sentential practices are difficult to defend as they violate many aspects of the nature of language. Even well-constructed fully contextualised practices will be effective only to the extent of the internal effect on the student, on the process of **perception**, and ultimately acquisition.

Reinforcement

This is the argument which many teachers would use — written practice provides 'good homework' to follow up what was done in class. If it is truly designed as reinforcement — the hammering home of a presented and partly perceived pattern — the theoretical justification is nil. Behaviourism is discredited; the repetition of correct sentences is not an aid to the further production of correct sentences. Language, or grammar, is not the accumulation of entities in this way, but the dynamic, organic development of a whole set of complex relations.

Testing

Productive exercises naturally form a part of almost all teaching programmes. All too often, in exam-orientated situations it is the ability to do particular kinds of exercise which assumes priority over long-term language acquisition and the development of communicative power. Productive grammar exercises are wholly appropriate to testing grammar as fact and knowledge about. Whether they test acquisition is much more questionable.

Diagnosis

The same productive practices which are questionable if regarded as 'testing', become a valid part of the teaching sequence **providing** the teacher conceptualises them as having a diagnostic, rather than testing function. 'Evaluation' will be directed not towards the students' achievement or failure, but towards the appropriate selection of tasks, materials and data to ensure maximum benefit for the students' long-term acquisition.

Student experiment

Self-evidently, the ultimate purpose of grammar practice is to help students towards the ability to produce effectively — successful communication. Language which is too riddled with error, or deviates too far from the norm, impedes communication. Accuracy, then, has a role to play, but a **subordinate** role, as **final** goal rather than intermediate objective. Students' language should develop as they become familiar with an increasingly wide range of patterns, but also they develop increasing mastery over particular patterns. In order to do this, they need to 'try out' language and see if it 'works'. If it does, their (implicit) hypothesis is supported but, more importantly, if it does not, the hypothesis is challenged. Within this perspective, productive grammar practice is an element of the O-H-E paradigm.

The students' attitude to productive practice will be largely conditioned by the teacher's attitude. Once again it is essential to emphasise the importance of the teacher's mind-set, and to recall Swan's words that this mind-set will influence **what teachers value on a day to day basis** — by what they include and exclude, encourage and discourage, by their overt evaluations, but also by body language, tone of voice, and other more covert ways. If the student is to see productive grammar practice as an experiment, a threefold focus for teachers is emphasis on **reformulation** rather than correction, **successful** language rather than accurate language, and successful **learning** rather than teaching. Any approach to productive grammar practice which focuses exclusively or predominantly on accurate production is failing students.

Although the teacher's primary focus should be on successful language and communication, teachers, particularly in state school systems, are not only sympathetic interlocutors, they are also representatives of 'the system'. This second role can conflict with the first; they may feel the need to insist that students re-do a careless piece of work; they may penalise the student for what they see as a culpable error for that particular student, at that stage of learning. Sometimes, I readily concede, students' learning will genuinely benefit from external demands imposed by the teacher. 'Sometimes', but it should not be the prevailing attitude behind grammar practice.

Oral practice

Language teaching is, perhaps irretrievably, addicted to bandwagons. There has always been a tendency to uncritical acceptance, and in due course equally uncritical rejection, of methodological procedures. Several times I have drawn attention to the deficiencies of a behaviourist view of language teaching. Oral drills were an intrinsic part of a behaviourist approach and, as such, at one time greatly over-valued. This does not mean, however, that they are valueless. A more critical evaluation is required.

Behaviourist drilling was based on the assumption that saying correct sentences made it easier to say those same correct sentences, and others of the same pattern, later. Emphasis lay exclusively on saying and accuracy.

Meaning, rhythm, pleasure and interpretation either formed no part in the procedure, or were seen as incidental features of the practice. Such drills were most popular in the heyday of the language laboratory and, despite Dakin's thought-provoking distinction between meaningless and meaningful drills[4], it was the meaningless variety which predominated. Both in the laboratory and in class, such drills almost invariably consisted of individual, de-contextualised sentences and, although often done rythmically, the most obvious characteristic was that the speech pattern employed for model sentences, and answers, was a neutral citation-like form; the language was delivered with the focus on form, in a way which rendered it **as devoid of meaning as possible!**

Anything remotely resembling this sterile procedure would be an extremely retrograde step. The criticisms, however, involve the uses to which drills were put, and the classroom realisation of the methodology, rather than being intrinsic to drills. Drills concentrate on pattern which, *prima facie* should make them a useful tool. The ability to segment the stream of speech is essential, both to understanding and clearly comprehensible production. This, in turn, is based on rhythmic chunking, a feature which lends itself to strict patterning of spoken language. Rhythmic activity can be anxiety-lowering, and indeed deeply reassuring. 'Feeling' a pattern in the mouth, as well as in the ear and mind is almost certainly helpful, even if we do not know precisely how. Oral drills — even if involving rigorously patterned single sentences — should have a part to play. But only if teachers recognise the purposes behind such drilling, so that the atmosphere, and teacher's manner and technique are appropriate to the real purpose of the activity. Stevick discusses an enormous range of alternative ways of conducting drills (in *Teaching and Learning Languages*, particularly Chapters 6, 9, 10). His analysis, and methodological suggestions are rich in variety and, in stark contrast to behaviourist drills, undogmatic in their theoretical justification. His whole approach emphasises the **probable** value to **some** students of different **alternatives** amongst the many he suggests. The following is typical of his style[5]:

> Your delivery will be some combination of slow versus fast (a two-way choice), loud versus soft (another two-way choice), and playful versus plain versus emphatic in tone. The twelve combinations (2 x 2 x 3) of these choices are options that are available to you. These twelve options are, if anything, even more important here than in the modelling of pronunciation because now you want your students to respond to meaning as well as to sound. You can shift (among these possibilities) during the first step of the drill procedure that I am outlining ... teachers who use such shifts as these (are) able to keep a drill alive long after it would have died in the hands of most other teachers.

In addition to the variety of presentation proposed here, he also suggests that teachers may draw attention to the pattern but may prefer to let students discover the pattern for themselves, explaining in their own words the pattern they perceive. This reflects the shift from explanation to exploration discussed earlier. He points out that drills may be done loud and fast, or at a more leisurely, but steady pace. But again[6]:

> A third possibility is to leave a two or three second pause between your voicing of a sentence and the student's repetition of it. This allows even more opportunity for cognitive processing, while the auditory echo is still there for the students to fall back on if they need it.

And, in sharp contrast to the discredited behaviourist view of drills[7]:

> How should you respond to an incorrect sentence from a student in a drill like this one? There is no one right answer to this question.

This indicates a clear break with behaviourist drilling — the theoretical under-pinning of the activity has changed. The emphasis now falls on varied presentation, relaxing and reassuring, both 'mindless repetition' and opportunities for cognitive reflection. Stevick also suggests that a teaching sequence centred on a drill will usually be quite short, and be followed by:

a. Asking students to recall sentences from the drill, either verbatim, or with more or less experimental variations.

b. Asking students to re-word or re-phrase one or more of the sentences from the drill.

Both of these suggestions emphasise Stevick's idea that the drill contributes a small element to the learning programme, but that **mastery** of pattern is in no sense to be identified with drilling. He opens the procedure up in many ways, all of which reflect total awareness that language is essentially about meaning so that a technique which is essentially mechanistic, and based on de-contextualised language, should be used sparingly, and almost always within a framework which re-directs the focus of attention towards meaning. Many sentences can convey very different meanings dependent entirely on **how** they are said. Consider these examples:

Not at the moment thank you.
What are you doing?
I'm reading the paper.
I'd be very grateful if you could/would/did.

Traditionally, drills were focused precisely and uniquely on a particular feature of sentence grammar. The teacher or tape provided the 'cue', and the student the (usually uniquely determined) 'correct' answer:

Could you pass the salt please?
— My book
Could you pass my book please?
— Those papers.
Could you pass those papers please?

Within the Lexical Approach three alternative strategies suggest themselves:
a. Instead of grammar being lexicalised, lexis can be grammaticalised.
b. The roles of initiator and respondant can be reversed between student and teacher.
c. The same sentence can be said in different ways, using either an oral cue, or a set of cards each of which indicates how the response is to be given (angrily, thoughtfully, hesitantly, in a whisper, twice with **exactly** the same words, the second showing irritation through slow, deliberate, heavy enunciation).

More complex, but even closer to 'real' language use is the combination of taking a 'how' card, simultaneously with an oral content cue. Critically evaluated, even if mindless mechanical drilling is dismissed, semantically orientated, pedagogically sensitive oral grammar practice still has a role to play, but it is meaning and lexis not 'pattern practice' which must be the primary focus.

Written practice

The principal advantage of written productive practice is that it is normally done without severe time constraints. Used in class for quick checking or diagnostic activity, it is usually done as homework or for self-study. This immediately suggests one word of caution — such practice need not be private, individual activity; written practice can be, and probably is, better done in small groups. Doing such practice in groups takes advantage of different cognitive styles, different students' individual knowledge, and the doing of the practice can itself be a communicative activity. Such activities, however, should be constructed to exploit the primary advantage they offer — the opportunity for reflective, cognitive involvement. With this in mind, I have already emphasised the importance of grammar as a receptive skill, but even when the focus of a practice is the student's own language production, the opportunity for reflection and revision should not be ignored. A process view of writing activities (see page 174) is central to the Lexical Approach which values the ability to communicate meaning effectively above all else.

The primary distinction is between students reorganising language and producing language *ab initio*. The former is a natural halfway house between receptive and productive practice, the latter — free writing of sentences, paragraphs, essays, talks etc. — fully orientated towards the student's own original production. Immediately a warning is suggested — few people write competently even in their own language; extensive writing such as essays should be reserved for those for whom it is a necessary specialist skill. Even if carefully prepared, asking most students to write a single paragraph is a very demanding activity. Despite its popularity in schools, this activity is, unless required for higher studies or professional purposes, comparatively useless. The language skills involved in producing a coherent paragraph differ radically from those required to understand or take part in natural conversation. If the primary objective of teaching is that students should speak English, such extensive written activities should have a low priority.

For all of the above reasons, productive written practice will usually be most helpful if it involves:
— Re-organising rather than creating.
— Pattern perception and organisation into non-linear formats.
— Grouping, by reflection on experience.
— The production of data for exploitation in the classroom as part of the Observation - Hypothesis - Experiment cycle.

In short, although by definition product-orientated, written productive practice should be a fully integrated aspect of an approach whose primary focus is the learning process.

Too often written grammar practice has been used primarily as a tool for assessing or grading students. This means that in most teachers' minds it is intrinsically associated with error and correction. This connection needs to be broken so that written practice plays a small but constructive part in the teaching programme rather than the intimidating role it frequently now occupies. This is another aspect of the change of teacher's mind-set proposed earlier and which is intimately bound up with the teacher's attitude to error and correction, discussed in Chapter 11.

Metalinguistic grammar practice

One kind of grammar practice which has nothing to do with the nature of language does find a natural place in language teaching — its purpose is to familiarise students with terminology which their course programme requires. Many students will need or find useful a **limited number** of metalinguistic terms — auxiliary, present perfect, negative etc. For most students, a **very** limited range will be sufficient. Once such terminology is introduced, it is essential to ensure that students are fully conversant with it **before** they are required to use it. Grammar practices which match terms to examples of language covered by the terms are an appropriate way of doing this.

Summary

If grammar practice is to have a role in developing students' language skills, the practice must:

— not violate the nature of language itself.

— pay due respect to grammar as a receptive skill.

— invariably contextualise (not only situationalise, it is situation **and co-text** which are important).

— be process- rather than product-orientated, with intermediate or long-term objectives which recognise clearly the difference between meeting and mastering grammatical features.

— raise grammatical awareness, often by comparing correct and incorrect forms, or alternative 'correct' formulations.

— respect the fact that language consists of grammaticalised lexis, and therefore ensure that practices other than those exclusively concentrated on the form of words (which will be few) involve the expression of real meaning. As befits a lexical approach, they must at all times avoid the present all-pervasive kind of grammar practice which, as Widdowson[8] has pointedly observed, are frequently based on random lexicalisation.

It will be clear from the above that I am dismissive of, and regard as fundamentally theoretically unsound, much that currently passes for grammar practice.

The Lexical Approach recognises meaning as central to language, and choice as the basis of meaning. These insights automatically invalidate many of the standard practices. Within the Lexical Approach grammar practice will be based predominantly on awareness-raising receptive tasks and activities.

References

1.   Grammar Practice Activities, p.94 and passim.
2.   The Lexical Syllabus, p.72.
3.   Second Language Grammar: Learning and Teaching, Chap 4.
4.   The Language Laboratory and Language Learning.
5.   Teaching and Learning Languages, p.92.
6.   ibid p.94.
7.   ibid p.95.
8.   Paper, TESOL, San Fransisco 1991.

Chapter 10

The Nature of Error

A teacher's attitude to mistakes and correction is central to what is done, avoided and valued in the classroom on a day to day basis. A misguided, or more likely unformulated, view of error and correction can undermine everything else. It is also a matter upon which dogmatic positions are rather thoughtlessly taken. This survey of the nature and role of error, and, in the next chapter, attitudes to and techniques of correcting provides an excellent opportunity to summarise and review many of the ideas already discussed. Some theorists use the terms *mistake* and *error* with different meanings; in general, I do not find the distinction convincing and the two words are used in this chapter interchangeably.

Connotations

Add eight words which you associate with the central key word to the following diagram. The words do not need to be connected with language teaching, but may be connections of any kind.

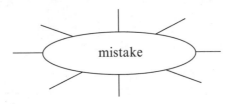

Whenever I have used this in seminars, a wide range of words has been suggested of which the most common are: *error, fault, wrong, sin, stupid, fail, careless.* The most noticeable feature is that all the words have strongly negative connotations. Roget's Thesaurus lists many words under *mistake;* again, all have unreservedly negative connotations.

More importantly still, many of the words to describe *mistake* are the same, whether referring to a language mistake, a social gaffe, or something morally reprehensible. Ellis quotes Brookes, writing in 1960: *Like sin, error is to be avoided and its influence overcome* ... The fact that the language of sin and moral disapproval can also be used to comment on language mistakes should warn us that the role of error and correction is a sensitive, not to say emotive, subject.

In view of its unreservedly negative connotations, it comes as a surprise to realise that all change throughout human history has resulted from the perception of difference, fault, and thus the possibility of improvement. The scientific method is essentially purgative; error is intrinsic to any learning process. This perception clearly suggests that any learning strategy which seeks to avoid error is counter-productive. This applies as much to language learning as to any other subject. Error has a central and valuable role to play; somehow teachers, and in their turn students, must see it in this positive light. In the wider context, many mistakes are associated with blame; it is essential to avoid this connotation in the classroom.

For a long time, language teaching employed a methodology which sought to avoid mistakes. Many teachers remain influenced by this. Many students quite naturally 'feel silly' when they make language mistakes, so they too have a tendency to avoid them; often silence seems better than saying the wrong thing; but it isn't. Teachers must encourage students whose motto is *The student who never said anything never made a mistake* to see the reality: *The student who never made a mistake never learned anything.*

Accuracy

Arrange the following words in two groups, using any criterion you think appropriate:

conformist	creative	exciting
imaginitive	orthodox	reassuring
normative	stable	incoherent

When you have made your two groups, add the word *accurate* to one or other of your lists. However artificial the exercise, I suggest we all recognise a spectrum whose poles are stability/order and creativity/chaos. While *creativity* is positively connoted, *incoherent* is negatively so; but what of the other pole—are all its words positively connoted? Above all, what about *accurate?* Asked if it is better to be accurate or inaccurate, most of us would unhesitatingly choose the former but performing artists and games players whose primary concern is safety and accuracy rarely achieve the highest levels. An **excess** of creativity is incoherence; over-emphasis on accuracy produces inflexible rigidity. Accuracy is unquestionably one important element in successful performance in any field, but accuracy cannot be equated with success.

Very rarely is language used with accuracy as a primary focus; sometimes it is —a mis-spelt application form will lose you a job; certain mistakes in an exam have a significance there which they would have at no other time; language which is **too** full of mistakes can mean people find you tiring to talk to and simply avoid you. Accuracy **may** matter, but it is a special case. Teachers need constantly to bear in mind that if they over-emphasise accuracy, it is at the expense of other aspects of the successful use of language which we have referred to extensively earlier.

Language in the school curriculum

Many students' attitudes to language learning are formed by their experience of language learning in State schools. The vast majority of classroom language learning is still done not in private language schools with small groups, but in State systems with relatively large classes and relatively formal methods. Not all school subjects are the same, and the methods and objectives appropriate to one subject may be wholly inappropriate to another. Within the 'academic' subjects, languages are uniquely and importantly different. The importance of this, particularly in relation to the treatment of error, is not always appreciated.

Most answers in a maths lesson are either right or wrong (except at advanced levels where the analysis of a problem may be correct but a slip in the work produces the wrong answer. Then, the simple right/wrong dichotomy breaks down). Factual knowledge in a subject such as history is right or wrong although, again, the simple right/wrong dichotomy breaks down if the question is about interpretation, not factual knowledge. Grammar as fact— spelling, irregular forms, concord — largely corresponds to this kind of knowledge. But this is only a small part of "knowing' a language; the ability to use a language is essentially procedural knowledge, where simple right/wrong distinctions do not apply.

Most school subjects lend themselves to partial, sequential presentation. Multiplication is dealt with before division; linear equations in a separate lesson from quadratic equations; the French Revolution and the American Revolution at different times. Language cannot be sequenced in this way, however much syllabuses may try. A linguistically simple question may need a linguistically complex answer; students almost inevitably meet English outside the classroom; most textbooks ask students about their own experience so, if they wish to answer honestly, they may try to say something beyond their current linguistic level. The organic, holistic nature of language means that it does not lend itself to linear presentation in the way most school subjects do.

Good methodology suggests students need to be exposed to substantial quantities of good listening material. In most situations the primary source of this will be the teacher talking to the class in English. Inevitably and indeed deliberately, much of this language will be beyond (ideally on the edge of) the student's current productive level. In addition to any language formally 'taught', the intention should be for students to acquire from reading and listening. In due course, students must be encouraged to try out new language, on the periphery of what they have mastered. Their tentative, and probably only partly successful efforts, are signs of progress. If such progress is met by criticism — either overt or 'correction' perceived as criticism by the student, they will be unlikely to experiment further and long-term acquisition will be inhibited.

An elementary student who says in *We don't must to school tomorrow. It is Saturday* has not produced correct English. At the same time, it is nonsense to say *It is wrong;* it **contains** a mistake, but **most** of it is correct. Even the part which is 'wrong' successfully conveys the student's meaning. It is methodologically absurd, and positively anti-educational to see such language as exhibiting failure; it shows partial **mastery** of English, and partial **success.** Ultimately, language is not about right or wrong but about successful or unsuccessful communication. Despite the constraints of the school system, teachers should never lose sight of the intrinsic nature of their subject.

Every language teacher is also a teacher, particularly in State schools. Their obligations, to students and the system, extend far beyond the particular subject they are teaching. Language teachers are never 'just' explaining, or 'just' doing an exercise; every activity contributes, positively or negatively, to the intellectual, emotional and social development of their students in both the short and long term. Within the context of this responsibility, it is of great importance for teachers to have thought out the nature and role of their subject, and their own teaching so that it contributes positively in this wider context. Woolly-mindedness in this matter leads to bad practice which has negative long term effects. The important difference between foreign language learning and other school subjects should constantly be in the teacher's mind.

Factual and procedural knowledge

Part of learning a language is factual knowledge; but by far the greater part of learning is procedural knowledge, ability to perform under real operating conditions. This is language as a skill, so performance is improved by perceptive observation of superior performance. This emphasis on language as skill, and receptive skills in general, means a radical revision of our understanding of the role of error in learning.

Error in learning

A behaviourist approach to language teaching suggested linearly sequenced syllabuses, emphasis on the what-you-meet-you-master principle, and the fundamental Present-Practise-Produce paradigm. Ellis, in his Survey of SLA Research, summarising attitudes at that time puts it precisely: *There was almost total agreement that errors should be avoided.* Nowadays, there is almost a total agreement that the psychological idea of language as habit, and the grammatical idea of grammar as an accumulation of entities were both wholly misguided. The theory which supported a methodology which encouraged the avoidance of error is discredited; sadly, classroom practice sometimes clings to the past. It is now generally agreed that students acquire mastery of elements of the grammatical structure by developing ever more complex relationships based on repeated applications of the Observe-Hypothesise-Experiment paradigm.

Within the traditional paradigm errors represented failure, both on the part of the student and on the part of the teacher. The assumption was that what was taught would be learned, retained, and could be accurately produced in free situations. If not, the assumption was either that it had been badly presented (teacher failure) or inadequately practised (teacher or student failure). Even today many teachers who have never heard of behaviourism or Skinner still wonder why students cannot do successfully today what they could do yesterday. Training courses emphasise careful presentation, but frequently give the impression that good presentation and practice are **sufficient** to ensure long term acquisition. Not infrequently teachers and students believe that 'more practice' will ensure mastery. Perhaps, but how much more? And, more importantly, long-term acquisition seems not to be greatly affected by this step-by-step approach. Perceiving error as failure frequently induces feelings of guilt or inadequacy, either in the student or teacher. While carelessness or laziness may be factors, it is far more likely that the student is simply 'not ready' to integrate the new language fully into his or her repertoire at that stage. The errors may be neither more nor less than symptoms of partial mastery.

Within an Observation-Hypothesis-Experiment paradigm, a radically different attitude to error prevails. Behaviourism values only successful performance; a process view of learning values the confidence-building aspects of successful performance, but recognises the contribution to learning of **unsuccessful** performance, providing it produces well-chosen appropriate feedback from the teacher. As we shall see in the next chapter, only rarely is formal correction the best feedback.

A simple example exemplifies the change of paradigm. A post-beginner student is on a language course in England. The teacher asks *How did you come to England? Did you come by boat?* The student has met the word *fly,* and half suspects it is irregular. However, the student, anxious to avoid a mistake, replies *No, I came by plane.* No error, no feedback, and consequently no learning. Better if the student had said *No, I ... er ... flied.* Then, the wise teacher, familiar with reformulation, could have said: *Oh, you flew, did you? Well I suppose that's much quicker.* Here, the student has the encouragement of successful communication, and immediate feedback of a language item—*flew*—which is:

— just on the edge of present vocabulary
— a word actually needed
— language which is new, but immediately comprehensible

A learner strategy of avoiding mistakes is always counter-productive. Self-evidently, we want students to 'try out' new language. In those circumstances, it is essential that the teacher's mind-set is such that the response—verbal, tone of voice and body language — all value and endorse the student's efforts, even if the language produced contains formal errors. That is as far as possible from the vigorous insistence upon repetition of correct sentences, and the drill-orientated mentality which, based on behaviourist principles, so loathed errors.

Norms

We need to remind ourselves of the Spectrum of Likelihood; language is not a matter of right/wrong but of what Halliday calls 'tendencies'. Even within a school system we recognised earlier the value of a Spectrum of Acceptability — this means teachers should have different expectations of the language students produce at different stages in the students' programme. Acceptability should be related to age, length of study, course orientation and other factors. What is acceptable is **relative** to these criteria, rather than being an absolute concept. Within this framework, 'level', rather than being intrinsic to language, is much more a matter of the teacher's attitude and expectations.

Research work on error gravity involves asking people to identify and evaluate different errors. Typically, the materials offered for evaluation contain a number of sentences drawn from native speaker language, and even dictionaries or grammar books. It is not unusual for some people to mark as defective original native speaker utterances, or even examples from reliable reference works. Even **identifying** error is fraught with difficulty. With that caution, the reader may care to evaluate the following sentences, awarding 0 points for a correct sentence, -1 for a slight error, to -5 for 'a serious mistake'.

1. I think taking the train is the least worst option.

2. All the stupidest people I know smoke too much.

3. We sightsaw every morning, and then worked in the afternoons.

4. Mozart started young. He was playing the piano at three, and performing in concerts at 5.

5. Some of the more traditional handicrafts are not so popular as previously.

6. It is not normally something I am very interested in.

7. How are you spelling that?

8. My brother was injured when he was hit by a golf club.

9. I work in Kuwait but was out of the country at the invasion.

10. The town I live in is undershopped.

How many minus points have you awarded? In fact all of the example sentences were produced by educated native speakers, several of them in writing. We can be fairly sure that if non-native students had produced them in written work, some at least would have been 'corrected'. In Hughes and Lascaratou's research on error gravity, they took the sentence *The boy went off in a faint* from the Oxford Advanced Learner's Dictionary of Current English. Of thirty judges, including twenty native speakers, eighteen judged that sentence to be in some sense 'wrong'! In any consideration of the nature of errors, it is essential to bear in mind that the criteria are much more subjective than we pretend. Language changes, and is used creatively. Sometimes change is ephemeral or words are coined for one-off use. Gifted speakers often bend and break the language into new meanings, creating according to need. There seems no logical reason why this creativity is the prerogative of native speakers, or even advanced learners. Which users of English have the right to use it creatively? Native speakers? Native speakers of British English? American English? Indian English? German English? No one wishes to lapse into Babel, but it is cultural and intellectual imperialism to impose a particular norm on anyone's use of English. Creative use, which communicates meaning, is clever and commendable whenever meaning is successfully communicated. Looking for error — deviation from some non-existent idealised norm — is a perverse way to look at language. For all that, it is and will doubtless remain, characteristic of language teaching.

The gravity of mistakes

As already mentioned, a number of experimenters have asked teachers, both native and non-native, and non-teachers to classify mistakes according to the 'seriousness' of error. Typically, the experimenters use authentic examples, usually taken from student essays. As a control, they frequently include sentences presumed not to contain an error. Davies[1], Hughes and Lascaratou[2], and Sheorey[3] have all done this. Two important generalisations can be made from their research:

1. In all cases, native speakers tend to use only one principal criterion for seriousness — comprehensibility. They grade errors as 'serious' only if they are either unable to understand, or have considerable difficulty in understanding what the students have written. In contrast, the non-native teachers in almost all cases use a totally different criterion in assessing 'serious' error. For them, the principal criterion is the 'basicness' of the rule infringed. This criterion is, in turn, strongly related to the incorrect language's position in relation to a formal syllabus. This leads Davies to a disconcerting conclusion:

> It would be naive to suppose that the average teacher's evaluation of his or her students' errors constitutes an objective assessment of their grammatical skills, their ability to communicate with native speakers or the extent to which their efforts appear 'foreign'; rather it is likely to be a measure of how successful they have been in following a particular course, and the extent to which they satisfied the requirements which the teachers consider appropriate, given their particular background and experience.

Non-native teachers' evaluations tend to judge the success of the teaching, and are based on short term criteria, rather than evaluating the student's long term acquisition or overall ability to communicate.

2. All researchers reported that non-native teachers are much more severe in their marking than native speakers (either teachers or non-teachers). In the Hughes and Lascaratou experiment, for example, Greek teachers deducted 958 points, compared with English teachers 780. The results of other experiments are similar. It is important to note that non-natives approach the evaluation of their student's work in this rather severe, critical way. For the best reasons — helping their students — their attention focuses on the **defects** of the student's production. It may well be that a more relaxed view of error, and greater attention to the successful communication of content, would be more helpful.

Comprehensibility as a criterion

Native speakers usually employ this as the principal criterion in judging students' work; non-natives could usefully accord it a higher priority. It is not, however, a totally straightforward idea. In speech, meaning is negotiated so that incomprehension, or ambiguity often disappears within two or three turns of a conversation. It is not each individual sentence which is evaluated, but short stretches of conversation. This should influence the teacher's methodology for oral work — rather than 'correcting' error, reformulation, and a **natural** response, possibly showing incomprehension, is in every way more appropriate. In writing, a more finished product is created, intended for comprehension outside the particular circumstances of creation. But then we must ask questions about comprehensibility: in or out of context? comprehensible by whom? How easily comprehensible?

Much language is comprehensible in context which would not be so as single isolated sentences. If the teacher knows the students' first language, material may be comprehensible which would not necessarily be so to people unfamiliar with the students' L1. More formal writing may be difficult to understand not because of the surface errors, but because at a much more fundamental, profoundly grammatical level, its informational content is inadequately or inappropriately organised.

In evaluating the comprehensibility of either speech or writing, it is the relation of individual elements over stretches much longer than a single sentence which is important. Teachers have an unfortunate tendency to concentrate on easily identified errors — interference mistakes, and other surface errors. It is not the correction of such errors which most assists the effective communication of meaning.

Sources of error

'Incorrect' language may be produced for many reasons such as tiredness, inattention, or a lapse of memory. It is, however, helpful to think of three possible linguistic sources of error:

— Interference
— Lexical deficiency
— Partial mastery

Students usually try to get language correct. If they produce an interference error this is, presumably, because they did not know how to say the same thing correctly. They had to choose between an unprincipled guess, and a principled guess, using L1 as a resource. However irritating interference errors are to teachers, particularly those who share the students' L1, they are signs of intelligence at work and should be viewed positively.

Many errors result from students trying to say something for which they do not have the linguistic resources. If I do not know the word *sister-in-law*, I could guess: *the wife to my brother*. If the student says that, the temptation is to correct it to *my brother's wife*, treating it as a grammatical error. The real problem was a defect in the student's **vocabulary**. Similarly, a student may say *We made some studies to get informations about what the people want*. Again, the temptation is to see a student with grammatical problems. The student would have little problem with the grammar if (s)he knew the collocation *market research: We made some market research*. There would be **no** problem if the student knew the collocation *do market research*. Too often once the student has produced some language — either writing or speech — the teacher moves in to 'correct' the grammar mistakes. This can be very time-consuming, and very time-wasting. Many grammar mistakes are caused by vocabulary deficiency, and particularly by lack of collocational power. Recognition of the centrality of lexis in language readily suggests that the teacher's response to student error may need to be lexically rather than grammatically orientated.

The successful learner

Many, perhaps most, traditional 'grammar mistakes' result from imperfect mastery of the principal generative patterns of English. That imperfect mastery can be seen as partial mastery, and viewed in a positive light. Within the Present-Practise-Produce paradigm, and a what-you-meet-you-master mind-set error must be seen as failure, and the language and learning as defective. Within the Observe-Hypothesise-Experiment paradigm that same defective language may be viewed positively. There is ample theoretical support for the second view. Willis[4] acknowledges the value of error:

> They make mistakes. But if they make mistakes by manipulating language to achieve the meanings they want to achieve teachers should learn to recognise this as a sign of useful creativity and ingenuity.

The successful language learner will be confident, fluent, accurate and creative. Whatever teaching strategy is employed, accuracy is always achieved last. Over-emphasising accuracy in the early stages of learning is to demand the impossible of the student, and often to inhibit confidence, fluency and creativity. Accuracy has a part to play, but it is characteristic of **terminal** behaviour. Almost all elementary and intermediate language will be highly inaccurate. This defective language is an essential stage on the way to long-term competent language use. Language mistakes are not sins, they are creative experiments. The shift of mind-set required to see this is so great, that it is hardly surprising that the teacher's attitude to mistakes is perhaps the single most important element in determining what (s)he does and values in the classroom.

References

1.   ELTJ 37/4, Oct 1983.
2.   ELTJ 36/3, April 1982.
3.   ELTJ 40/4, Oct 1986.
4.   The Lexical Syllabus, p 65.

Chapter 11

Responding to Error

It is necessary to reiterate — error is intrinsic to learning, and any strategy of error avoidance will be counter-productive. Anyone who learns a foreign language to a reasonable level of proficiency will inevitably make thousands of mistakes on the way. Correcting every one is an impossibility. Fortunately, it is also highly undesirable.

Teachers must recognise that, whatever their normal practice or received opinion in their school or education system, correction of language error needs to be justified. It is **not** self-evident that correction helps. Indeed, I know of no research evidence which suggests that it does. On the other hand, it is self-evidently time-consuming, and often inhibits students. Equally, every teacher knows that it is frequently ineffective. Such evidence as there is suggests that it is either a useless procedure, or at best an inefficient use of teacher and learner time. Curiously, teachers often correct because they and their students see it as the teacher's role, and they wish to give students value for money. In fact, correction is rarely a cost effective use of class time, and what we know of SLA suggests that, even well done, it plays only a marginal role in aiding acquisition.

The suggestion that 'most teachers probably correct too much' invariably provokes a strong reaction, often with strongly emotional and even moral overtones. In my experience, the following reactions are typical:

So there's no difference between right and wrong, then?
So anything goes?
It's my job to set certain standards!
If I don't correct them, they'll never improve.
They ask to be corrected — what do you expect me to do?

As we saw in the previous chapter, the last twenty years have seen a radical shift in the theoretical basis of language teaching, particularly grammar teaching. Increased attention to receptive skills, the role of hypothesis formation, recognition of the organic nature of grammar, the role of comprehensible input, are all principled and well-researched ideas. To suggest teachers correct too much is neither irresponsible nor iconoclastic, merely a reasonable response to the current stage of understanding of the nature of grammar and how it is acquired.

Correcting or responding

Most theories exist in 'hard' and 'soft' forms. The 'hard' form of correcting requires four conditions to be fulfilled:

1. You know what is correct, and are sure that what the student has produced deviates in some way from that correct form.

2. You are sure that the **net** effect of drawing the student's attention to the difference between the student's language and the correct form will be helpful.

3. You are sure you can successfully tell the student, or explain to the student, what is correct.

4. You invite/ask/insist that the student produces the correct form.

We have already noted that it is not always easy to be certain what is correct, or that the psychological effect of being corrected will not have a negative effect which outweighs any possible benefit, or that explanations are available which the student understands. Each of the first three criteria suggest a certain caution is appropriate. The fourth criterion — requiring the student to produce the correct form — is that most influenced by behaviourism, particularly with reference to oral mistakes. In my experience of observing teachers in the classroom this narrow view of correction — the teacher tells the student what is wrong and requires the student to produce what is correct — is precisely what the correction of oral mistakes usually involves. Such a narrow view is counter-productive. Moneyhun, in a paper given to a JALT convention, takes the fairly extreme view that: *Mistakes are so much a part of (the students) that to correct them is a frontal assault on who they are.* I confess some sympathy with this view. I have often expressed the same idea in different language: *You never correct a mistake, you always correct a person.*

At the same time, teachers are part of the education system, with professional pressures on them to behave in certain ways. Ignoring mistakes, even if it were theoretically desirable, would not be acceptable. What is needed, is a way of **responding,** without 'correcting' in the narrow sense defined above. Language teaching research provides two suggestions for broadening teachers' response strategies: **reformulation** and **feedback**.

Reformulation

Most modern theorists, approaching the teaching of writing adopt a process approach. Students gather ideas, form a draft, submit the draft for consideration by others — either a peer group or the teacher or both — and then reformulate the material into a new draft. If necessary this process is repeated several times before the final product is completed. This process approach to the production of text parallels the process of learning **how** to produce text — in other words it is a realistic part of language teaching. At several points in the process, others react by agreement, question, or in other natural ways thus helping the student to produce a text which will ultimately communicate better. This is a substantial step forward from the primitive procedure of student product — teacher evaluation.

The process of production involves correcting surface error, rewriting sentences, and perhaps rearranging the whole text. Input comes in the form of peer group or teacher questions, and possibly comparisons between the student's text and some other reference text. Johnson[1] recommends reformulation, referring particularly to its use in correcting essays:

> Reformulation is different from reconstruction, which is what most of us do to student's essays. In reconstruction, errors and mistakes are simply corrected. The result will be sentences free from gross malformations but ones which may not remotely resemble sentences a native speaker would produce to express the same content. ... What reformulation offers, and reconstruction fails to offer, is information on how an efficient speaker would have said the same thing.

While Johnson sees reformulation as predominantly a strategy for dealing with student writing, Wilberg[2], referring specifically to the problems of one-to-one teaching for oral presentation, says:

> The product and test of one-to-one teaching is a piece of work done by the student and requiring that he or she reformulates his or her own content at a new level of awareness, skill and linguistic competence.

In both cases, students perform the **same** task several times. With the help of linguistic input, they reformulate their own content. Reformulation is also a strategy for the **teacher,** particularly relevant to spoken language:

T   See you all on Thursday.
S   No, we don't are here on Thursday.
T   You won't be here on Thursday? Why not?
S   We don't must be here.
T   You don't have to be here? I don't understand, why not?
S   It is sports day. We are to the stadium. So we don't are in school.
T   Oh I see, it's sports day so you won't be here on Thursday. Well, let's hope the weather is good.

Is this teacher 'correcting'? Not in the hard sense — students are **not required to repeat correct forms.** But the teacher's language use is skilful, reacting primarily to content, but also reformulating in such a way that students hear the correct version for what they were trying to say. Some teachers will feel this kind of reaction is inadequate. While perhaps not wishing formally to correct students, they would at a minimum like to draw attention to the student's mistake, and the difference between what the student has said and the correct expression. This is an improvement on formal correction, but there is no experimental evidence that indicates that this more didactic approach is helpful. Krashen is not alone in believing that simply **exposing** students to the correct forms in situations where they constitute comprehensible input is sufficient. Krashen[3] regards errors not as something to be corrected, but as a stimulus to expose students to further natural language around their own current level:

> The intent of the activity is to create the opportunity for conversational interchange which is as natural as possible, so the instructor will unconsciously and automatically use these sorts of reformulations and expansions, just as in real life situations. It is not clear that this sort of expansion is actually responsible for encouraging the students to speak more accurately and correctly. It is more likely that although some students do use this direct natural feedback for conscious inductive learning, the main contribution of the instructor's expansion is that it provides more comprehensible input.

Murphy[4], while happy to provide something which many teachers would see as closer to correction than Krashen's comprehensible input, takes a similar view:

> Correction is a form of feedback to learners on their use of language. Providing there is a minimum of accuracy, the message may still be comprehensible. Take, for example, *Who he is the woman who came yesterday?* Context would make this clear, and in any case the message can be confirmed: *You want to know who the woman was?* This shows one way in which the hearer may give feedback, checking on the message not the grammar, even though inaccuracy has obscured the message.

In common with most commentators, these emphasise two points — the naturalness of the teacher's response, and emphasis on the content of the communication rather than the language in which it is encoded.

The Lexical Approach endeavours at all times to reflect the nature of language. Teacher reformulation of the kind just illustrated, where the primary focus is on the **content** of the message not the language used to express it, is fully consistent with this emphasis. Four major conceptual points endorse the value of the strategy:

— In real language use, meaning is negotiated.
— The emphasis in language is on process, not product.
— Acquisition is based on receptive skills.
— A positive human response to content is more fundamentally valuable than any formal pedagogic correction.

Marking written work

Many teachers who are happy to take a relatively relaxed view of oral errors face considerable difficulty in marking written work, particularly essays. There is general consensus that:

— Teachers must avoid 'covering student's work with red ink'.
— Approval as well as disapproval should be indicated.
— Any 'correction' should be forward- rather than backward-looking.

These are fine principles, but, without appropriate techniques, are difficult to implement. The tendency must be to correct comparatively trivial surface errors, and ignore considerably more complex questions of how the information content is organised. It remains understandably but regrettably true that many teachers remain loath to leave mistakes **unmarked**, even if uncorrected, as it easily suggests carelessness or even irresponsibility on their part. Writing is a much more reflective, self-conscious process than speech; even competent writing in L1 involves a process of making notes, drafting and editing. It is unreasonable to expect any students to be able to write in L2 without going through such a process, probably much more laboriously than with L1 writing. Once this is accepted, and a process-approach to writing adopted, the question is no longer one of correction but of feedback — input intermediate in the production process which permits and encourages reformulation.

Feedback

If students are used to writing essays, handing them in and having them returned corrected and graded, it is essential to introduce them explicitly to the idea of process writing. Typically, the procedure involves in-class brain storming, students drafting the material then receiving 'editorial' input from either fellow students or the teacher before the material is re-drafted. This procedure may be repeated more than once depending on the students, and the precise orientation of the course. Apart from more linguistic considerations, all researchers in this area report improved student involvement and a more positive and relaxed approach to writing as a result of this change of emphasis in methodology. Keh[5] says:

> Once students have received input for writing, they write their first draft (D1). They are made aware that D1 is only a draft — it is not a sacred process. After D1 is written, students receive their first form of feedback from peers.

Some of the advantages of feedback of this kind are directly attributable to the fact that the creation of the end product is acknowledged as a process, but not 'sacred'.

Bartram and Walton[6] encourage teachers to develop a marking code to indicate particular kinds of surface error — SP for spelling, GR for grammar, etc. Hyland[7] prefers what he calls Minimal Marking, making only a cross in the margin beside each surface error. A line which contains three errors has no other markings than three crosses. The text itself is wholly unmarked, and no indication is given of the kind of error. Students look again at their work with the specific purpose of correcting these errors, possibly with the assistance of peers. As Hyland points out, this procedure is effective for surface error, but has little to contribute on the more complex problems of the overall organisation of the text. Hyland specifically suggests that Minimal Marking permits a preliminary removal of surface error **before** tackling more global, organisational difficulties. For these, he suggests a highly innovative technique, reflecting the negotiated nature of meaning. With a written assignment students are asked to hand in a blank or used audio cassette. As the teacher reads the text the tape is kept handy and **while** reading the text (not **after** reading) the teacher reacts to the text. The reactions may be of different kinds — questions about what the writer means at a particular point, expressing agreement, asking for an example, giving an additional example, indeed, in the broadest sense **interacting** with the text. Unsurprisingly Hyland has had considerable success with this technique. It makes the text less 'sacred', and the writing process more interactive. There is a valuable and important gain for teacher and student — teachers, used to working with a pile of scripts, a red pen and a shortage of time quickly develop a system of coded marking for surface error or brief comments. The problem is that these comments, perceived as brief and precise by the teacher, may be seen as abrupt and unhelpful by the student. Hyland himself says of the tape recording technique:

> It also influences how I say things, being more conversational and discursive in my comments, and seemingly less coldly abrupt than a few lines of demoralising red ink. As a result, some of the threat which students feel about written assignments is removed. In addition, the method provides a useful second language learning experience in itself. It helps

to reinforce the written assignment with an authentic listening exercise which has the extra motivating factor of being directly relevant to the student's progress.

Nothing, perhaps, could more adequately illustrate the positive, interactive and developmental aspects of the teacher responding to the student rather than engaging in time-consuming, but ultimately rather sterile 'correction'.

Charles[8] has developed a quite different way of making the writing process more inter-active and less intimidating. She invites students to write their own questions on their draft texts. This ensures any editorial help she offers is directed to students' concerns. She makes the valuable point that unless you adopt this tactic it is not clear that any editorial comments you make match the students' expectations or needs. There is some experimental evidence that while teachers tend to concentrate on surface error, students may be well aware that the difficulties they are having are with the overall organisation of their text. She makes a further telling point — teachers tend to assume that if the text is 'correct' the writer did not have difficulty in creating that correct text; the assumption is that no surface error implies there were no problems. Charles' experience suggests that students often make the right decisions, while still in doubt and they will not confidently benefit in future from the correct decisions they have made. Allowing them to raise questions about their own work means she is able to reinforce their correct decisions as well as respond to problems. Charles' approach reminds us of the need to be student-centred and of the supra-sentential difficulties students face and the process nature of learning. Emphasising the students' long-term learning needs, rather than conforming to preset norms she says: *If we are concerned to establish a dialogue over the text, then the problems identified by the writer need as much attention as those identified by the editor.*

In providing feedback within the Lexical Approach teachers must constantly bear in mind that many superficially grammatical errors are caused by lexical deficiency. 'Re-writing' a passage from a student's essay, or providing individual linguistic items for input, it will often be more appropriate to re-conceptualise the content, thinking in **lexical** rather than grammatical terms. This is particularly the case for more formal speech events such as presentations, or writing such as professional or academic English. The change of emphasis within the Lexical Approach from grammar to lexis needs constantly be be borne in mind.

The techniques described here are as appropriate for secondary school students as for university students or adult learners. They represent a student-centred and learning-centred approach, so that Charles describes herself as 'editor' of the students' texts, rather than teacher, instructor or marker. Some essays need to be evaluated by teachers as part of the examination process. That in no way implies that essays should **always** involve correction and evaluation.

Correction and autonomy

Sitting at the back of the classroom or talking to teachers, an important difference of attitude quickly emerges. Some teachers, accidently or otherwise, make their students dependent upon them. Students in such classes seldom take risks or try to say what is on the limit of what they can safely say without knowingly making a mistake. Experimentation on the students' part is kept to a minimum. When in doubt they pause, and either wait for the teacher's help or ask for it. Such teachers are often certain that they are doing a good job. They regularly and willingly supply their students with guidance, information and the language that they need. They perceive themselves as competent and helpful. But what will happen to those students outside the class? They may lapse into silence or embarrassment. Short-term expediency, under the positive guise of 'helping the students' may prove inimical to long-term acquisition. Better the teacher who encourages experiment, who interacts linguistically with the students in a way which resembles what would happen outside the classroom — reacting primarily to the content of what is said rather than the linguistic tools which are used to say it. Errors form a natural and intrinsic part of learning. Reformulation and feedback provide the positive ways of using those errors to help long-term acquisition. Within a well-run language classroom formal 'correction' will play a very small part; the emphasis will be on experimental language use which is more likely to be of long-term benefit to the students.

The Lexical Approach values the creation and communication of meaning above all else. Inevitably it emphasises the **content** of communication; this necessarily demotes the importance of error. This is not irresponsible; it is soundly based on the nature of both language and learning.

References

1.   ELTJ 42/4.
2.   One to One, p.5.
3.   The Natural Approach.
4.   ELTJ 40/2.
5.   ELTJ 44/4.
6.   Correction pp.84ff.
7.   ELTJ 44/4
8.   ELTJ 44/4.

Chapter 12
The Role of Materials

In many parts of the world one coursebook per student remains a luxury; other teachers who have access to a Resource Centre are proud of the fact that they do not use coursebooks, but tailor-make every course. Neither situation is ideal; printed material forms a natural part of language teaching. 'Plodding' through a coursebook unit by unit is dispiriting for the learner; a supposedly tailor-made course can easily be disorientating. Elsewhere, I have argued for input-rich classrooms; English language material — printed, video or broadcast — is more widely available than ever before. What kind of materials are most likely to be helpful within the Lexical Approach?

Dictionaries

An English/English dictionary is perhaps the most **under**-used resource in contemporary language teaching. The tendency is to see the dictionary as useful only for looking up the meaning of unknown words. A good dictionary — and for the present that for me means one from the Cobuild range — helps with meaning, stress, collocational range, and archetypical examples. In addition, it conveniently and helpfully blurs the distinction between dictionary and grammar book. All entries contain useful grammatical information about words; because of the alphabetic organisation of dictionaries, this information is easily accessible. Inevitably, it has to be written using some grammatical terminology and codes. But within a lexical approach it is natural, even essential to look at the grammar of individual words — does a new noun have both countable and uncountable uses? Can an adjective be used gradeably? Attributively? Good dictionaries also list polywords, and many of the expressions broadly covered by the term 'idiom'. Collocations are increasingly finding their way into dictionaries (again particularly the Cobuild range), and with increased understanding of lexical phrases we may expect them to be given increased prominence.

The Cobuild dictionary range has changed the nature of dictionary making, making them much more user-friendly and providing much more information in accessible form which would previously have been hidden in corners of the grammar book. As an adjunct to the dictionary range, Fox and Kirby have produced a Workbook, which helps teachers and students access new kinds of information, and makes better use of dictionaries in class as a genuine teaching resource than has ever been done before.

I should perhaps, justify the recommendation today of the Cobuild dictionaries at the expense of all others. The theoretical justification is the nature of their corpus work; in recommending them for classroom use, key points are:

a. Their defining style is to **exemplify** uses of a word in full, natural sentences. This style ensures students see more of the collocational features of a word and means that the dictionary definition is itself useful comprehensible input. It is in sharp contrast to other dictionaries which 'define' in abbreviated form, through supposed synonyms. This synonym approach is unhelpful, encouraging impossible or unlikely collocations, suggesting a rather algebraic view of language. Compare, for example, the following:

> **Empty**[1] *adj* containing nothing
> **Empty**[2] *v* to make EMPTY

> **Empty**
> 1. A place, vehicle or container that is empty has no people or things in it.

> 2. If you empty a container, you remove its contents.

The first pair of definitions involve cross–referencing, difficult use of a de-lexicalised verb (*make*) and are from the *Longman Dictionary of Contemporary English*. The second two are from *Cobuild*. The advantages, particularly for students in class, are readily apparent.

b. The grammatical information about words is extensive, and the printing conventions adopted, in which this information is put in an 'extra column' means that the whole entry is much less intimidating than most dictionaries.

c. Every use is illustrated with one or more archetypical examples from the corpus. These examples offer further useful, and often fully contextualised, comprehensible input.

The innovative nature of the Cobuild project is shown by the fact that their dictionary of collocation will be the first serious attempt to make information on this topic available.

Within a lexical approach every well-balanced course should provide the learners with real training of how to exploit an English English dictionary to best advantage. Taking lexis seriously means ensuring that learners, too, see its value, and are trained to investigate it both for their immediate short–term needs, and as an important learning strategy for use after any formal course.

Grammar Reference and Practice Books

Unsurprisingly, these frequently represent a greatly **over**-used resource. The principal problem of grammar reference books is the nature of their organisation. It is possible to look up what you are in doubt about, but if you are more thoroughly confused, it is not usually even possible to find the information you need. Grammars are useful for checking, but not much else. As for grammar practice, unless it fulfils the criteria discussed earlier — natural co-text, supra-sentential practice, well-chosen archetypical examples — it can do more harm than good. Although fill-in exercises and transformations remain popular with teachers (it is easy to set homework) and even students, (we don't take any real risk) such materials have, at best, very limited value. In passing, we may dismiss most of the tailor-made grammar practices written by teachers for particular classes as a waste of both the teachers' and students' time.

The principal role of a grammar reference book in the classroom should, like the dictionary, be as a source of reliable examples. The perception and acquisition of the structure of the language comes from an ever-developing awareness of similarity and difference. Inevitably, *Can you say ... ?* questions arise. The best solution to such a problem is to refer students to examples which confirm or contradict their hypothesis, rather than to some tendentious, and often over–simplified rule. Many teachers can provide suitable and helpful examples spontaneously, but the grammar book is there as an additional source of data.

Coursebooks

All coursebooks, however out of date or inadequate provide four things: programme, sequence, balance and authority.

Teachers who like to teach without a coursebook sometimes forget that students may need the reassurance of a programme, and the feeling of 'getting somewhere', Working through a coursebook — perhaps omitting bits, and almost certainly supplementing it — is almost always better than working entirely without a coursebook. Advocates of entirely tailor-made courses often forget that most teachers teach twenty or more lessons per week — while it may be possible to prepare twenty individual lessons it is almost impossible to guarantee effective sequencing and balance. Selective use, and supplementing of a coursebook is more likely to be effective than a totally open approach. Finally, the printed word of the coursebook can authenticate and endorse ideas and activities. Awareness-raising, and learner-training activities can direct students' attention to areas which they have previously overlooked, or where they have unhelpful or unrealistic expectations. It remains the case that in our literate society it is the printed word, rather than any suggestion from the teacher which is more likely to be accepted by the student. Books should, and many modern ones do, encourage and endorse helpful attitudes to language and language learning.

A word of warning is necessary — coursebooks are commercial ventures. Lavishly illustrated 4-colour books are very expensive to originate. Inevitably, content and layout are chosen to maximise sales. In recent years this has produced well-designed books, but often influenced by strong commercial pressure towards rather conservative content and methodology. Most mass market textbooks produced in the U.K.:

a. Are designed for a 'typical' school year of 3/4 hours per week for 30 weeks. There is often a more or less obvious division of the material into teaching units of about 45 minutes — individual lessons.

b. Are influenced by what teachers expect from previous experience. In particular, this has 'protected' the grammatical syllabus, and grammatical sequencing long after serious work in linguistics has discredited such a lock-step approach.

c. Almost always exclude material which will appear radically unfamiliar to the non-native teacher. Skills training, common in adult ESP courses, plays only a minor role in basic coursebooks. Questions with non-unique answers remain in a minority. It is reasonable to assume that collocation will be only tentatively introduced to mass market textbooks precisely because it is a new idea for many non-native teachers, and there is at the moment no adequate reference work in which they can easily look up possible and impossible collocations with certainty.

d. Some popular books are available in 'With answers' and 'Without answers' editions. The latter exist because there is a commercial demand for them in countries where teachers wish to protect their position. In such an atmosphere questions with alternative answers, matters of opinion, or students using discovery methods to find their own grammar rules are almost impossible to introduce as they threaten not a detail, but the totality of the classroom ethos.

When evaluating any popular coursebook it is helpful to bear in mind the commercial constraints which will have influenced its content and methodology. If such books need supplementing, the supplementary material is best chosen to compensate for these constraints.

Coursebooks usually involve different kinds of material. At least the following are worthy of comment.

Texts

These should be of different types, and for different purposes. Both intensive and extensive reading should be catered for; material where the student is explicitly not expected to understand every word should be an integral part of all courses. Idiomatic, metaphorical or imaginitive language is intrinsic to the nature of language. If the range of text is confined to factual, literal language, the language is being distorted and the student inhibited. Can you suggest a meaning for *(S)he is very green/red/grey?* Metaphor and imagination are not confined to 'advanced' language!

The range of texts should include dialogue and continuous prose, and be presented in print, on tape, and through both mediums. Some texts should be very short, others very long; some exploited for only a few minutes, others for several lessons. Most importantly, some texts should be exploited on different occasions for different purposes. This remains unusual — most textbooks are still linear in construction and linear in methodology. In natural language we re-read, check for particular information in a text we read earlier in detail etc. The nature of the texts and activities included in a coursebook should make clear to the student that it is not a matter of plodding page by page, always doing the same things.

Examples

While most coursebooks include archetypical examples of grammar or functions, within a lexical approach these lists of examples should be substantially expanded, both in number and range. If receptive grammar practice is to be taken seriously, students need access to a comparatively large number of reliable well-formed examples; this contrasts with the single, archetypical example of 'how the structure is used' common to conventional grammar practices.

Many more examples need to be given which are archetypical and idiomatic in the sense discussed earlier. Examples of lexical phrases and sentence heads, previously given only cursory treatment in textbooks must assume much greater priority, particularly in intermediate courses.

Explanations

Enough has been said earlier about the dubious value of grammar explanations. It remains true, however, that most coursebooks contain them, and will continue to do so for the commercial reasons mentioned above. Such explanations should be treated with some scepticism, and are perhaps best regarded as a resource, against which students may check their own explanations after they have formulated an explanation in their own words, probably in L1.

All of the above categories — texts, examples and explanations — should be regarded as input data. All of it is material to be touched, visited, and re-visited. Although the coursebook provides the advantage of sequencing and balance, it is essential that the teacher's attitude is flexible; re-visiting should be common, and what-you-meet-you-master avoided at all costs.

Activities and exercises

A small element in mastering a language involves factual knowledge; formal exercises are useful in focusing the attention, and checking this kind of knowledge. Exercises should form a **small** part of any coursebook. The emphasis, however, should be on activities or tasks. Ideally, many of the tasks should have as their primary focus a non-linguistic outcome — the solution of a problem, winning of a game; completion of a table, creation of a poster etc. In the real world language is always instrumental; this intrinsic nature of language should be reflected by classroom activities.

This suggestion is in clear conflict with the constraints of the mass market coursebooks already outlined. Tasks or activities do not have fully predictable outcomes, or unique 'correct answers'. If theory changes, methodology should change too; if methodology changes, coursebooks should change; if coursebooks change, teachers' attitudes and expectations must change and if they do not any theoretical advance will be thwarted. But coursebooks remain conservative because teachers remain conservative — my colleague Jimmie Hill has remarked many times that teachers over-value explanation, correction, accuracy and artificial contextualisation. It is these key elements in the teacher's mind-set which provide the most potent impediment to change.

Regrettably, many teachers' methodology is derived almost exclusively from coursebooks, rather than from a coherent theoretical over-view of the nature of language and learning. For commercial reasons, coursebooks are understandably cautious or conservative. Coursebooks and teachers reinforce each others' conservatism long after demonstrably better materials and methods are available. Ask yourself when was the last time you found a sample of English in a basic coursebook which surprised you — it seemed a novel or unusual language item? If you have **never** been surprised by the language in the coursebooks you use, it is obvious that this language has been pre-digested in order to conform to language teachers' expectations.

Think of your recent teaching. How many of the classroom activities from your basic coursebook have had a language outcome which was fairly clearly specified in advance? How many were so truly open that they could not have even 'suggested right answers' at the back of the book? Are you happy with the balance?

Learner training

The printed word can lend authority to what the teacher says. This is particularly the case in encouraging a helpful attitude in the learners' approach to language and learning. A coursebook should provide explicit opportunities for teacher and student to discuss classroom methods and activities, and learning strategies and expectations. Although every learner is different, some predictions can be made of how learner training can help redress the imbalances which many students bring to the language classroom.

Firstly, Learner Training must give students a metalanguage to articulate their experience — if they do not recognise successful language as successful, and experience it only as inaccurate, they will inevitably over-value accuracy, increase their anxiety and lower their perception of their own achievements. Students need to be taught that where they perceive defective language, they may be producing effective language. Many students are poor judges of their own performance, and even of their own needs. Doing particular activities — most notably explaining grammar, doing grammar practice, and correcting — 'because my students ask me to' is frequently a cop-out. Teacher and material must redirect the students' expectations towards strategies and attitudes which will be more helpful for long-term acquisition.

In general, Learner Training will decrease:

— Students' concern with accuracy
— The tendency to believe L1 word = L2 word
— The demand that they understand every word in a text
— Perception of failure
— Anxiety

Learner Training should produce corresponding increases in:

— General language awareness
— Monitoring skills — both of their own performance and of the ability to 'chunk' material to which they are exposed
— Perception of the value of reflection and silence
— A willingness to hypothesise or guess
— A willingness to take risks, to try out new language
— Self-awareness, both linguistic and personal

The ability to be an effective communicator involves much more than mastering vocabulary and grammar. Tone of voice, eye contact, and cultural sensitivity are more than merely peripheral aspects of language teaching. Such matters are often extensively dealt with in materials for adult business students. They could be usefully foregrounded for all levels in general course materials.

Awareness-Raising

Many key ideas in this book suggest looking at language in new ways. Most notably, chunks other than words and sentences are seen as central to language. The chunks include polywords, collocations, more or less transparent/opaque idioms, institutionalised sentences with recognisable pragmatic meaning. Few of these will be familiar to students. Their natural approach to language is to concentrate on message not medium; their previous language learning will almost certainly have taught them to recognise and value vocabulary (words) and sentences ('grammar'). As part of Learner Training, their attention needs to be redirected to these other chunks, the recognition of which is an important aid to speeding the process of language acquisition.

Real materials

Dictionaries, grammar books and coursebooks are explicitly prepared for language teaching purposes. Nowadays, however, most students have access to real English material — printed texts, songs, videos, and T.V. While many coursebooks include 'real' texts — i.e. texts originally written for native speakers for non-language teaching purposes — these are, perhaps inevitably, often dated, neutral or bland in general content, and lose some of their 'reality' simply by being included in coursebooks. Most teachers recognise this and like to take in 'real' supplementary material. Many non-native teachers remain inhibited, however, because they think students will be overwhelmed. Two essential points must remain — long term acquisition is facilitated by material which is only partially understood. Providing the task is chosen so that students can understand **something,** it is absolutely not essential that they understand **everything.** Teachers must make students explicitly aware of this if they are to avoid any possible demotivating effects. A short piece of real material, listened to several times is much more likely to be effective than a longer piece listened to once. A second, and most important point is that students' attention must be carefully focused. This will usually mean that teachers should prepare questions, or formatted pages which guide the students both **before** and **while** watching/listening. Simply taking in 'interesting' real material would be pedagogically most inefficient. The real material needs to be selected, and supplementary material prepared around it. In the world of easily available and cheap videos and satellite TV, it should be second nature to teachers to be looking for short bits of language, relevant to their students (and therefore 'authentic' in the sense discussed on page 28.) which can provide students with an experience of top-down rather than bottom-up understanding, and which show that, even with limited linguistic resources, they are able to cope with naturally occurring language. Careful selection, authenticity, brevity, and above all adequate printed support material, should ensure that real materials, with their natural emphasis on content and communication form an effective part of a lexical approach.

Recording Formats

One book which almost every language student owns is a 'vocabulary notebook'. I have already criticised linear L1 = L2 lists as inaccessible and inefficient. Collocation, the patterning of de-lexical words, and important institutionalised sentences and sentence heads all suggest that one of the most important pieces of material the language student should have is a large well-formatted 'file' in which new language can be recorded, organised and if necessary reorganised. All the other materials we have discussed — dictionaries, grammar books, coursebooks, or real materials — are merely **sources** of language for the student. In other aspects of life when we use sources of information, we characteristically record that information in conveniently accessible, and often personalised forms — diaries or address books. It should be self-evident that a natural part of Awareness Raising, and Learner Training is to show the student the value of creating individually designed and personalised formats to help the process of personal language acquisition.

Chapter 13

Teaching, Teacher Training and Methodological Implications

PART 1 — Teaching and Teacher Training

As already extensively discussed, any changes in the content or methodology of language teaching are dependent on teachers. They need to be both competent — with a theoretical over-view and a range of techniques at their disposal — and confident that they are indeed helping their students. It is worth recalling a few key points and examining some implications for teacher training, particularly for pre-service courses.

Teachers have only been really successful when they have made themselves redundant.

A principal task is to encourage learner autonomy, not teacher dependence.

The teacher's primary responsibility is response–ability.

The art of successful teaching is to intervene, without interfering.

These ideas are central to successful teaching. All value the integrity of the learner, and emphasise the teacher as facilitator, editor, consultant and adviser rather than instructor or, above all else, performer. There is no good teaching which does not result in effective learning. Inevitably teacher training courses guide participants in what they, the teachers, should do; less experienced teachers not unnaturally worry about giving 'good lessons'. One central point must never be overlooked — teaching is not the end, it is the means; all teaching is subordinate to learning.

Successful teaching is measured in terms of successful learning, but successful language learning is much more complex than anything which can be evaluated by a simple test. The ability to use language effectively is potentially a life-long skill. State schoolteachers must never lose sight of this — long-term affection for, or antagonism towards, using the foreign language is an important element in the success or otherwise of the teaching. Teachers, particularly those working in State schools, can usefully ask themselves what percentage of class time is spent promoting accuracy, fluency, confidence? Unless an appropriate balance is maintained the student's long-term attitude to the subject is likely to be affected negatively.

Again, when you are teaching, do you have in mind next week's test, or your students using English on holiday in Japan fifteen years from now?

Many of the most unproductive language teaching attitudes attacked in this book — over-correction, over-eagerness to pressurise students into speaking too early, too fast a pace, the urge to 'finish' something before the end of the lesson or term, emphasis on what students do **not** know or **cannot** do — are all based on too narrow a view of a 'successful lesson'. It is very important to remember that most students of English as a foreign language will never do better than cope in the language — but that itself is an immense achievement and if coupled with confidence to use what you know, a valuable and profoundly personal resource for the rest of your life.

I do not believe that there is **a** method, or set of methods which guarantees successful learning and is appropriate in all circumstances. Language and learning are complex phenomena, and the simple answer of 'the best method' will always be an unhelpful over-simplification. But eclecticism is sometimes an excuse for confusion. There are principles, and research evidence. Language teachers need to have a theoretical over-view so that they may select from a range of strategies and techniques but in a principled way. Widdowson has observed:

> Teachers need to be given techniques, but they must also be educated to see those techniques as examples of certain theoretical principles and therefore subject to continual reappraisal and change. This is necessary in the interests of the learner. If teachers are not educated in this sense, they cannot derive expertise from experience, they cannot act as mediators of ideas, either of their own or those of other people. Also, if they are required only to follow a set of routines, they are unlikely to get much satisfaction from their efforts.

In order to derive expertise from experience, teachers need a theoretical basis so that their selections may be based on explicit principles. Regrettably, such teacher training remains the exception rather than the rule. Many non natives have spent many years studying the language but their theoretical studies — philology, phonetics, linguistics and the like — are frequently not related to pedagogy and the classroom. Extensive theoretical knowledge which **precedes** classroom experience often remains too abstract for teachers to see its relevance. University and college courses for non-natives could usefully increase the emphasis they place on methodology and technique. Their language studies would often be more helpful for teachers if they related to contemporary English, and de-emphasised etymology, the history of English and other supposedly academically respectable elements of their courses.

The training for native speakers is very different, often pitifully inadequate, and frequently counter-productive. Many native speakers claim to be 'qualified' after a course lasting only a few weeks. This is absurd, and those who employ such teachers calling them 'qualified' need to look critically at their professional standards. Being a native speaker can be a help in teaching the language, but much more is required. Many native speakers are linguistically insensitive, and not reliable informants on what is or is not possible within the language. More importantly, it is an extensive knowledge of language as a phenomenon and learning theory, together with the personality to use this knowledge effectively in the classroom, which makes for a good teacher. The short courses provided in Britain claim that those who successfully complete them are 'EFL initiated', and that further study is required before the person is 'EFL qualified'. Sadly, it remains the initiation course which is often treated as a sufficient qualification to teach in many private language schools, both in Britain and abroad. Specific criticism of these initiation courses can be identified:

1. Method is valued above knowledge.

Typically, native speakers are invited to take practice classes on the second or third day of their training. With little or no knowledge of English as a subject they are thrust into classrooms. Unsurprisingly, the emphasis then falls on surviving, and knowing what to do. This frequently degenerates into keeping students happy by relying on personality, and certain activities done with no knowledge of their theoretical standing, objectives, or over-view of the role they play in a balanced programme.

2. Lesson 'recipes' are valued above theory.

Teachers look for lessons or ideas that 'work'. Little or no analysis is offered of why they work, and whether other things might work better.

3. A single method dominates.

Trainees are frequently left with the impression that there is a way of teaching; alternatives are not mentioned. The training assumes the universal acceptability of what is presented — whether classes are large or small, monolingual or polylingual, in the U.K. or abroad, to adults or children, with general or ESP needs. The particular method which is presented is usually profoundly ethnocentric and therefore wholly inappropriate to some situations abroad. This is rarely discussed. Worst of all, the method is almost always irretrievably jolly, as if languages could only be learned, or are best learned in the atmosphere of a party or Club Med holiday.

4. An outdated model often prevails.

Most 4–week trainees implicitly assume at the end of their training that the basic teaching paradigm is based on Present-Practise-Produce. This is a convenience for the trainers, allowing them to break the language and teaching sequence down into steps for individual trainees. Unfortunately, the model is discredited and reflects neither the nature of language nor the nature of learning.

5. Too much emphasis is placed on 'getting the students to talk'.

The 'jolly' methodology, and Present–Practise–Produce paradigm endorse the belief that you learn to speak by speaking. The teachers who are introduced to this simplistic methodology as part of their EFL initiation often remain unhelpfully wedded to it in circumstances where it is hopelessly inappropriate, and when many better and more effective alternatives are available. As such, the initial training has a long-term negative, indeed pernicious, effect.

6. It is assumed students are not active if they are not speaking.

Silence, and reflective cognitive involvement are positively discouraged. The emphasis is on activity at all costs, and as such the implied methodology is almost explicitly anti-intellectual.

7. 'Reduce Teacher Talking Time' is assumed to be a self-evident maxim.

Every trainee I have ever met is convinced that student talking time (STT) should be increased and teacher talking time (TTT) decreased. Since well-directed listening is the best, perhaps unique, way of acquiring the spoken language it is clear that this absurd methodological over-simplification is the precise opposite of the truth in many circumstances. What matters is the **kind** of TTT, and its purpose, and the strategies and techniques through which it is employed. It is a matter of critical awareness, knowing what you are doing. Regrettably, the simple slogan of initiation courses ignores this and simplifies to the point of absurdity.

8. Language sensitivity is largely ignored.

To be an effective teacher of your own language you need to be knowledgeable about it, observant of it, and able to control your own use very precisely. Without these skills, no technique will make you effective. Many people do not have these skills, and they certainly cannot be developed in four weeks. Such courses solve this dilemma by ignoring it.

9. 'The pink card syndrome'.

Despite the many thousands of language teaching books in print, and the enormous range of real material readily available, initiation courses frequently encourage teachers to make their own material — write exercises, make flash cards and the like. Gimmicks are exalted above theory and knowledge. Instead of playing with scissors and pink cardboard, trainees could more usefully study the principles which underlie the selection and organisation of materials of some of the many excellent coursebooks which are readily available.

10. Survival is equated with competence.

This complaint underlines and summarises all the others. Teachers who survive 45 or 90 minute classes are thought to have achieved something. Survival is based on recipes and gimmicks, and 'success' supported by the claim *It works*. We may usefully distort Chomsky's competence/performance distinction — many trainees at the end of their initiation course are merely incompetent performers. Such courses should lay considerably more emphasis on teacher competence — understanding of language and learning — and much less on the teacher as performer.

University qualifications, whether MA's in Applied Linguistics in the U.K. which are usually undertaken after a number of years of teaching, or pre-service MA's in the U.S. are accused by those who have taken them as being too theoretical. It is probably truer to say that they contain too little which is directly practical — techniques, activities, tasks which the teacher can take directly into the classroom. Ironically, while deploring recipes on short teacher initiation courses, they seem an indispensible element for more academically-orientated university courses. Recipes are no use — even if they work — unless we can evaluate why, so that they can be adapted and incorporated into a balanced programme. Mere theory, however abstractly ideal and pure, is no use if teachers and students will not accept it in the classroom. Any theoretical view will be **realised** through games, texts, activities, exercises, tasks and all the day to day paraphernalia of language teaching. Good training would give **both** of these elements equal importance, recognising the symbiotic relationship between them. The practical matters are not subordinate to the theory; each informs the other. Teaching, like language itself, involves knowledge about, but is predominantly procedural knowledge. Many applied linguistics courses could be usefully re-balanced to recognise this.

Methodological absurdity

This book has been partly theoretical — the search for a lexical approach — but also, I hope, largely practical; suggesting how the theoretical principles can be embodied in the classroom. The question of the teacher's mind-set has been raised continually — unhelpful attitudes, tone of voice and body language can undermine so much of what the teacher is trying to achieve. Here is a final summary of a number of sentences which I, and I suspect every teacher in the world, has used. Each is unhelpful, and expresses a methodological absurdity. I would encourage teachers to remove **these** lexical items — learned utterances — from their classroom repertoire:

1. *It's quicker if I explain.*
What is — teaching or learning? Quicker for whom?

2. *They haven't done … yet.*
How do you know? The syllabus may not have — but some of them may have.

3. *Can you say that in a full sentence please.*
'I understood exactly what you meant, but would now like you to use a totally unnecessary grammaticalisation.' If meaning was communicated, what is the purpose of the full sentence?

4. *Can you repeat that, please.*
Say something more natural, directing the student to what you didn't understand, a comment of your own or whatever. Teach, don't interrogate.

5. *Are there any words you don't understand?*
Why **words**? Why concentrate on/worry about the **unknown** rather than the known? Why implicitly suggest that if you don't understand everything, then you understand nothing?

6. *What's the word for … ?*
If you ask this, you encourage the *L1 word = L2 word* idea which you almost certainly complain about on other occasions.

7. *I insist on English all the time in the classroom.*
Why? Talking about English in L1 can be quicker and more efficient — why make life difficult?

8. *I wish they'd say more.*
Why? Are they involved? Listening? Learning? Do you want them to speak because you believe it helps, or because it reassures **you**? Relax — cognitive involvement and acquisition are not less effective for being quiet, even silent.

9. *Do you need help?*
You won't be there outside the classroom. Your whole purpose is your learners' autonomy and your own redundancy. Encourage strategies which help learners to help themselves, including the fact that they ask you for help **without** you needing to make an explicit offer.

PART 2 — Methodological Principles of the Lexical Approach

No one methodology represents the way forward but some principles can be suggested.

1. Students learn best in language-rich classrooms and with language-rich materials. Teachers must be unafraid of exposing their students to real English, at all stages.

2. Listening, listening and more listening. In most classrooms abroad, the teacher is the best source of listening for students. With caution, increase teacher talking time!

3. Language lessons are a combination of input, awareness-raising, learner training, and language practice. Each of these elements is important.

4. Receptive skills are important — learn to value reformulation and feedback as the most effective response to student mistakes.

5. Receptive grammar practice values awareness-raising and exploration above any teacher explanation.

6. Communicative competence is a much wider concept than accuracy. Learn to value fluency, confidence, and imagination as well as accuracy. Recognise that accuracy will, whatever methodology is employed, always be the **last** element of competence to be acquired.

7. Encourage physical recording which mirrors psychological recording. Avoid lists, and encourage non-linear formats where new language is stored with the co-text with which it most frequently occurs.

8. Many 'grammar mistakes' are caused by lexical deficiency. Take lexis seriously — develop the idea for yourself and for your students. Lexis is not another word for vocabulary — it is a much richer concept which we have not exploited in the past. The Lexical Approach is not a revolution, but it is, I hope, a radical and helpful change of emphasis.

9. Develop your own skill in chunking text — identifying different lexical items in it. Help students to develop the same skill. Different kinds of lexical item are the basis of language, and an important component of language learning.

PART 3 — Methodological Implications of the Lexical Approach

We return to the implications listed briefly on page 35. The central consideration is that methodology should ensure maximum communicative power, and be essentially learner-centred.

1. Early emphasis on receptive skills, especially listening, is essential

Every piece of language which we ultimately produce comes from outside us and, as such, is initially based on receptive rather than productive skills. The early stages of a learning programme — in state schools in Europe the first two years perhaps — should unashamedly pursue a methodology based on receptive skills.

2. De-contextualised vocabulary learning is a fully legitimate strategy

Any truly meaning-centred approach must maximise the student's ability to communicate as much as possible as early as possible, sacrificing strict grammatical accuracy as a price well worth paying. In those circumstances, 'increasing vocabulary' in the straightforward naive sense of that term, has an important role to play.

3. The role of grammar as a receptive skill must be recognised

Perception of the difference of meaning, and contextualised possibilities of, for example, *I'll take it* and *I'm going to take it* or *What time will/shall I arrive?* are an important part of the ability to understand English precisely. To require more precision in productive language than the student has available in receptive skills is a highly questionable procedure.

Most teachers recognise that many, if not most of the 'rules' provided by textbooks or teachers for their students are no more than partial and temporary hints. In those circumstances it should be self-evident that student-generated rules, recognised as provisional, must be a greater contribution to the learning process.

4. The importance of contrast in language awareness must be recognised

The existential reality we call 'English' exists independently of other languages, and independent of language learners. Those who use it as a native language make meaning by employing a complex system of contrasts internal to English itself. Occasionally, it may be valuable for students to have the contrast between English and their own language pointed out. Much more frequently, acquisition of the systems of English will be helped by comparing English with English, and offering students the opportunity to form their own provisional rules.

5. Teachers should employ extensive, deitic language for receptive purposes

The methodological imperative of reducing teaching talking time was mis-directed; well-chosen comprehensible language is of immense value to the learner. Such language should not, however, be predominantly reading, telling stories etc. The most important language of this type, is language produced with reference to the Here-and-Now framework. Native speakers begin to acquire the complex system of inter-relationships which is English through extensive exposure to the spoken language. We have no reason to suppose that L2 learning is so different that this does not also play an important role in that process.

6. Extensive writing should be delayed as long as possible

Spoken language is a naturally acquired human activity. Writing, and the ability to write extensively and well, in highly developed societies, remains the prerogative of an educated minority. It is correspondingly bizarre that extensive writing in a foreign language should play anything other than a specialist role in foreign language learning. The artificial exclusion of writing from courses would be absurd, and as most learners can write their own language, it is natural to allow, or even encourage them to label pictures, create notes to aid their memory, word lists, memorable phrases or sentences and the like.

7. Non-linear recording formats are intrinsic to the Lexical Approach

Recording formats regarded by some people as fringe methodology — collocation tables, mind-maps, word trees etc. — are central to an approach which starts from the assumption that language is grammaticalised lexis and places the way words combine at the centre of its theoretical perspective.

8. Reformulation should be the natural response to student error

For students to benefit from input it should be comprehensible; for students to feel that their oral contributions are valued, the teacher should respond to content rather than language. In those circumstances, teacher re-formulation must be preferable to formal correction.

9. Teachers should always react primarily to the content of student language

It is ironic that many teachers who claim to teach 'communicatively' remain so attached to structural accuracy and correction. It is almost impossible to produce language **in context** which will be misunderstood as a result of error, if that error is predominantly structural. In contrast, if a student uses the wrong word — a lexical error — misunderstanding is much more likely. In arguing for a Lexical Approach I do not argue that grammar and error do not matter; such an argument would be irresponsible. I am, however, arguing that emphasis must always lie upon content, and that this should under-pin every methodological decision made by the teacher.

10. Pedagogical chunking should be a frequent classroom activity

Students need to develop awareness of language to which they are exposed and gradually develop ways, not of assembling parts into wholes, but of identifying constituent bits within the whole. Many of these are lexical items and form the most important single key to the Lexical Approach.

Afterword

Any new approach necessarily involves two elements — a mass of detailed suggestions for content and methodology, and a few theoretical principles or insights.

The last chapter has been methodological detail, some intrinsic to the Lexical Approach, some relating more generally to good practice. It is worth re-stating however, that everything in this book is directly based on a small number of superficially rather unimportant perceptions. Basically, the grammar/vocabulary dichotomy is dismissed and lexical items are recognised as having a central role to play. Initially, it seems implausible that increased emphasis on collocations and the different kinds of institutionalised expressions can be of more than marginal interest to language teaching. Gradually it becomes clear that these two categories, and the concept of chunking, challenge all our previously held perceptions of the very nature of language, and consequently of both the content and methodology appropriate to language teaching.

Paradoxically, within an essentially organic, holistic perception of language, it becomes increasingly clear that when language is viewed analytically, our earlier analyses were mistaken. Language is not words and grammar; it is essentially lexical.

Recognising the lexical nature of language overturns many previously-held ideas. It also provides the way forward.

Michael Lewis   Hove, March 1993

Background reading and bibliography

Inevitably, many talks, articles and books have influenced this book. A few have been particularly significant in the development of my thinking. These are listed, with very brief comments here. Because of the inter-textual nature of writing, it is probably impossible to understand my position without familiarity with the half dozen or so works listed here. I dislike intensely the academic pretension of a 'cumulative bibliography' — a list of everything the author has ever written or referred to. The bibliography below includes only material directly referred to in the body of the text.

The following approximately contemporaneous titles provide the best overview of the ideas usually labelled 'the Communicative Approach':

Notional Syllabuses, D.A. Wilkins, Oxford University Press, 1976.

The Communicative Approach to Language Teaching, C.J. Brumfit and K. Johnson, Editors, Oxford University Press, 1979.

Explorations in Applied Linguistics, H.G. Widdowson, Oxford University Press, 1979.

A challenge to many received ideas, and touchstone against which both theory and methodology may be tested, is:

The Natural Approach, Stephen D. Krashen and Tracy D. Terrell, Pergamon Press and Alemany Press, 1983.

My thinking on grammar was most powerfully influenced by:

A Teacher's Grammar, R.A. Close, LTP 1992, previously published as English as a Foreign Language, George Allen and Unwin, 1976.

Current English Grammar, S. Chalker, MacMillan 1984.

Both of these attempt an over-view of the problems of English grammar, rather than an atomistic, point-by-point approach.

In the field of lexicography I can think of nothing which compares with the work of Sinclair and his team on the Cobuild project. Their work has, quite simply, changed the nature of dictionaries. The project continues to produce titles regularly, both general and concentrating on such areas as phrasal verbs and the forthcoming work on collocation. The prototype is:

The Cobuild English Dictionary, Collins/Cobuild, 1987.

Two other books which have exercised an enormous influence over me are much less likely to be familiar to readers. These are:

Metaphors We Live By, George Lakoff and Mark Johnson, University of Chicago Press, 1980.

One to One, a Teacher's Handbook, Peter Wilberg, LTP 1987.

The first of these is essentially a work of philosophy, but may ultimately have as much influence on language teaching as did J.L. Austin's philosophical work *How To Do Things With Words* a generation ago. Wilberg's book, although apparently confined to a highly specialised area, reminds us that in every class each student is, in some sense, in a one-to-one situation. He has literally hundreds of methodological suggestions as to how the student can contribute to what happens in class.

The two most powerfully influential articles, informing much of my thinking on lexis, are Pawley and Syder (1983) and Nattinger (1988).

Bibliography

Abbott, G. The English Explosion: Fission? Fusion? or what? English—A World Language 1/1 Jan 91

Austin, J. L. How to do things with Words. OUP 1962

Bahns, J. Lexical Collocations: a contrastive view. ELTJ 47/1, January 1993

Bartram, M. and **Walton, R.** Correction. LTP 1991

Brumfit, C. and **Johnson, K.** The Communicative Approach to Language Teaching. OUP 1979

Brumfit, C. Communicative Language Teaching: an educational perspective, in Brumfit and Johnson

Carter, R. and **McCarthy, M.** Vocabulary and Language Teaching, Longman 1988

Carter, R. Vocabulary, Cloze, and Discourse, in Carter and McCarthy

Chalker, S. Current English Grammar, Macmillan 1984

Charles, M. Responding to problems in written English using a student self-monitoring technique, in ELTJ 44/4, October 1990

Close, R. A. A Teachers' Grammar, LTP 1992 (Originally published as English as a Foreign Language, George Allen and Unwin 1962)

Collins Cobuild, Collins Cobuild English Grammar, 1990

Cowie, A. Static and Creative Aspects of Vocabulary Use, in Carter and McCarthy

Crystal, D. and **Davy, D**. Advanced Conversational English, Longman 1975

Culler, J. Saussure, Fontana 1976

Dakin, J. The Language Laboratory and Language Learning, Longman 1973

Davies, E. Error Evaluation: the importance of viewpoint, ELTJ 37/4, October 1983

Ellis, R. Understanding Second Language Acquisition, OUP 1985

Foster, S. The Communicative Competence of Young Children, Longman 1990

Fox, G. and **Kirby, D.** Collins Cobuild English Language Dictionary Workbook, Collins Cobuild 1987

Gairns, R. and **Redman, S.** Working with Words, CUP 1986

Halliday, M. Spoken and Written Language, OUP 1989

Heisenberg, W. Physics and Philosophy, Harper and Row 1962

Hill, J. et al. Grammar and Practice, LTP 1989

Hughes, A. and **Lascaratou, C.** Competing Criteria for Error Gravity, ELTJ 44/4, October 1990

Hymes, D. On Communicative Competence, in Brumfit and Johnson

Johnson, K. Mistake Correction, ELTJ 42/4 April 1988

Keh, C. L. Feedback in the writing process: a model and methods for implementation. ELTJ 44/4 October 1990

Keller, E. and **Warner, S.** Conversation Gambits, LTP 1988

Krashen, S. and **Terrell, T.** The Natural Approach, Alemany Press and Pergamon Press 1983

Lakoff, G. and **Johnson, M.** Metaphors We Live By, Univ. of Chicago Press, 1980

Lewis, M. The English Verb, LTP 1986

Lewis, M. and **Hill, J.** Practical Techniques for Language Teaching, LTP, 1985

MacAndrew, R. English Observed. LTP 1991

McCarthy, M. Discourse Analysis for Language Teachers, CUP 1991

Maule, D. 'Sorry, but if he comes, I go: teaching conditionals.' ELTJ 42/2 April 1988

Morgan, J. and **Rinvolucri, M.** Vocabulary OUP 1986

Murphy, D. Communication and Correction in the Classroom, ELTJ 40/2, April 1986

Nation, P. and **Coady, J.** Vocabulary and Reading, in Carter and McCarthy

Nattinger, J. and **DeCarrico, J.** Lexical Phrases and Language Teaching, OUP 1992

Nattinger, J. Some Current Trends in Vocabulary Studies, in Carter and McCarthy

Newmark, L. How not to interfere in language learning, in Brumfit and Johnson

Nunan, D. Syllabus Design, OUP 1988

Nunan, D. Designing Tasks for the Communicative Classroom, CUP 1989

O'Neill, R. In Praise of Intellectual Obscenity or The Confessions of an Embarrassed Eclectic, Cross Currents Vol XV, No 2, Spring 1989

Pawley, A. and **Syder, F.** Two Puzzles for linguistic theory: nativelike selection and nativelike fluency, in Richards and Schmidt

Prabhu, N. S. Second Language Pedagogy, OUP 1987

Richards, J. and **Schmidt, R.** Language and Communication, Longman 1983

Rinvolucri, M. Grammar Games, CUP 1984

Rutherford, W. Second Language Grammar: Learning and Teaching, Longman 1987

Shaw, K. English Grammar Exercises, Collins Cobuild, 1991

Sheorey, R. Error Perceptions of Native Speakers and Non-native speaking teachers of ESL, ELTJ 40/4 October 1986

Sinclair, J. ed, Looking Up, Collins Cobuild 1987

Sinclair, J. and **Renouf, A.** A Lexical Syllabus for Language Teaching, from Carter and McCarthy

Stevick, E. Teaching and Learning Languages, CUP 1982

Stevick, E. Images and Options in the Language Classroom, CUP 1986

Stewart, I. Does God Play Dice? Penguin 1989

Summers, D. The Role of Dictionaries in Language Learning, in Carter and McCarthy

Swan, M. Practical English Usage, OUP 1980

Swan, M. A Critical Look at the Communicative Approach (1) ELTJ 39/1 January 1985 and (2) ELTJ 39/2 April 1985

Ur, P. Grammar Practice Activities, CUP 1988

Ur, P. Correspondence in ELTJ 43/1, January 1989

Widdowson, H. Explorations in Applied Linguistics, OUP 1979

Widdowson, H. Against Dogma: a reply to Michael Swan, ELTJ 39/3 July 1985

Widdowson, H. Proper Words in Proper Places, ELT News No 8, British Council, Vienna, July 1989

Wilberg, P. One to One, LTP 1987

Willberg, P. and **Lewis, M.** Business English, LTP 1990

Wilkins, D. Linguistics in Language Teaching, Edward Arnold 1972

Wilkins, D. Notional Syllabuses, OUP 1976

Wilkins, D. Notional Syllabuses and the concept of a minimum adequate grammar, in Brumfit and Johnson

Willis, D. The Lexical Syllabus. Collins Cobuild, 1990

Yule, G., Mathis, T. and **Hopkins, M.** On reporting what was said, ELTJ 46/3 July 1992

Yule, G. Highly confident wrong answering—and how to detect it. ELTJ 42/2, April 1988